Practice and Learn

Ages 5-7

W9-CGK-726

Editor
Barbara M. Wally, M.S.

Editorial Project Manager
Ina Massler Levin, M.A.

Editor-in-Chief
Sharon Coan, M.S. Ed.

Illustrators
Blanca Apodaca
Howard Chaney
Wendy Chang
Ana Castanares
Agi Palinay

Cover Artist
Denise Bauer

Art Coordinator
Denice Adorno

Imaging
Alfred Lau
Ralph Olmedo, Jr.

Product Manager
Phil Garcia

Publishers
Rachelle Cracchiolo, M.S. Ed.
Mary Dupuy Smith, M.S. Ed.

Written and Compiled by

J. L. Smith

Table of Contents
Part 1

Introduction 3

Language Arts 5

    Letters 5

        Letter Recognition

        Printing

        The Alphabet

    Sounds 48

    Rhyming Words 79

    Words and Writing 87

        Pictures and Words

        Word Recognition

        Printing Words

        Journals

Reading 108

    Nursery Rhymes (*common rhymes with follow-up activities*) 108

    Fairy Tales 134

    Colors 146

        Colors Words

        Colors Recognition

Math 164

    Shapes 164

        Shapes Recognition

        Shape Words

    Numbers 174

    Other Math Concepts 220

    Basic Skills 251

Answer Key 299

Introduction

Practice and Learn, Ages 5-7, reinforces skills appropriate for kindergarten and first grade students. Both parents and teachers benefit from the variety of pages provided in this book. Parents can use the book to work with their children to introduce new material or practice and reinforce familiar material. Similarly, a teacher can select pages from this book to provide additional practice in class or at home for concepts taught in the classroom.

Language Arts

Here you will find activities for working with letters, sounds, words, phonics, spelling, grammar, usage, and reading and writing skills. Activities for both written and oral practice are provided.

Mathematics

This section invites students to explore and practice mathematical concepts by providing practice in developing number sense, counting, grouping objects, and one-to-one correspondence. Other mathematical concepts covered include shapes, patterns, measurement, telling time, addition, subtraction, and geometry. Throughout, students are provided with opportunities to apply mathematical concepts to problem- solving activities.

Basic Skills

This section is devoted to helping children practice and develop skills such as tracking, matching and classifying objects, identifying opposites, visual discrimination, sequencing, and a variety of other skills that provide a foundation for future curriculum studies.

Social Studies and Science

The social studies and science sections of the book are designed to provide students with specific practice identifying concepts related to these areas of curriculum.

Art

A small arts section is included to provide students with an introduction to color theory and experience in drawing by breaking things down into shapes.

Critical Thinking

This section provides students with the opportunity to practice comparing and contrasting, categorizing, and deduction at a level appropriate to first grade.

Practice and Learn

Part 1

Alphabet-asaurus

Trace the letters on Alphabet-asaurus. Use your best handwriting.

Lots of Letter Legs!

Trace the letters on Ollie Octopus. Use your best handwriting.

Copy the Uppercase Letters

A _____ B _____ C _____ D _____

E _____ F _____ G _____ H _____

I _____ J _____ K _____ L _____

M _____ N _____ O _____ P _____

Q _____ R _____ S _____ T _____

U _____ V _____ W _____ X _____

Y _____ Z _____

Now I know my ABC's.

Next time won't you sing with me?

Copy the Lowercase Letters

a _____   b _____   c _____   d _____

e _____   f _____   g _____   h _____

i _____   j _____   k _____   l _____

m _____   n _____   o _____   p _____

q _____   r _____   s _____   t _____

u _____   v _____   w _____   x _____

y _____   z _____

Now I know my ABC's.

Tell me, aren't you proud of me?

Alphabet Snake

Fill in the missing uppercase letters on the snake.

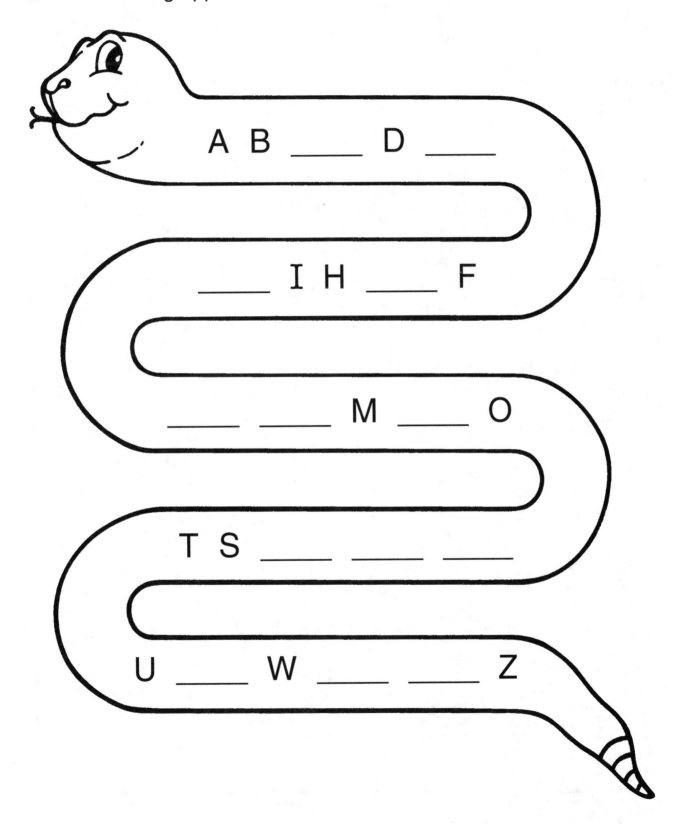

Alpha-Bug

Fill in the missing lowercase letters of the alphabet.

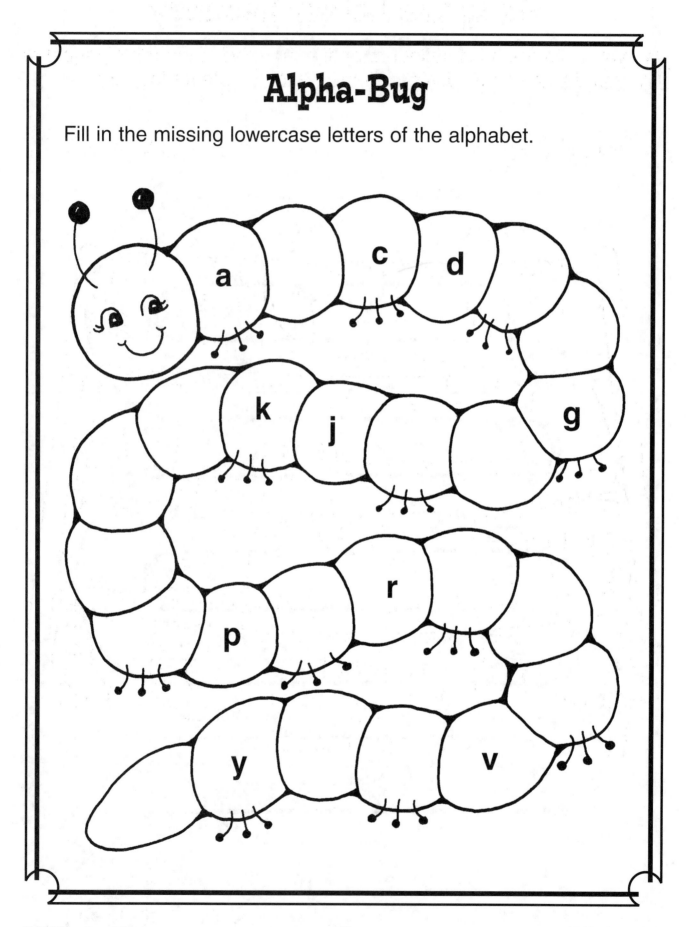

Hang the Letter Laundry

Can you write the missing letters on the laundry? Sing the alphabet to help you discover the missing letters. Color your letter laundry.

A B C D E F G H I J K L M N O P Q R S T U V W X Y Z

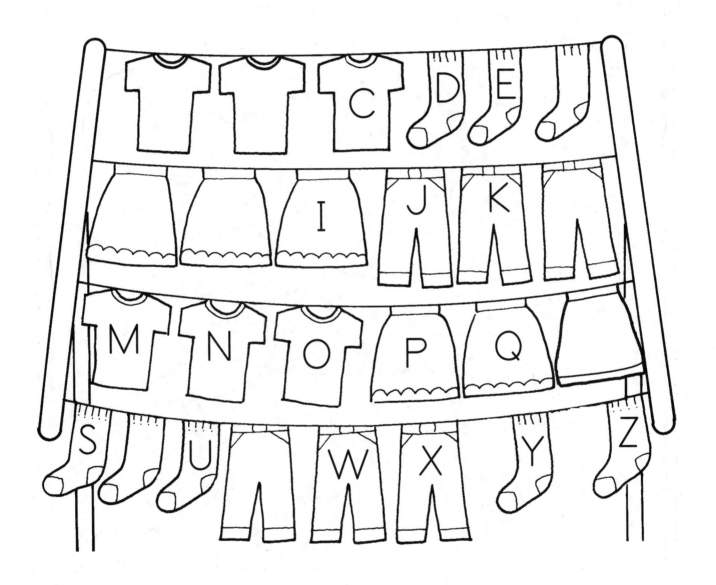

Cow

Draw a line connecting the A-B-C dots. Color the picture.

The Letter "M"

Mm

"M" is for Mommy, my very best friend!

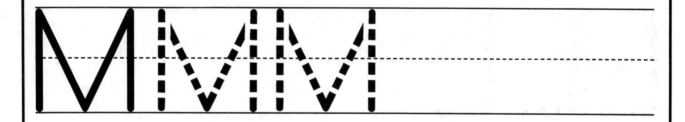

The Letter "N"

"N" is for numbers. Which ones do you know?

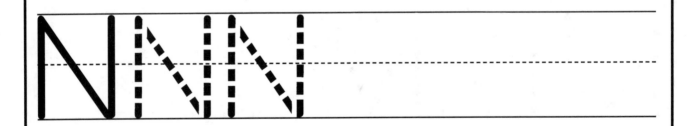

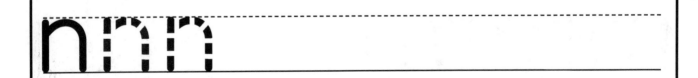

The Letter "O"

"O" is for octopus, my buddy from the sea.

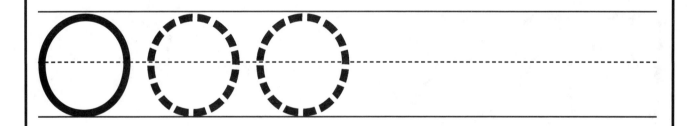

The Letter "P"

"P" is for pie, so tasty, it's true!

The Letter "Q"

"Q" is for queen in her castle so far!

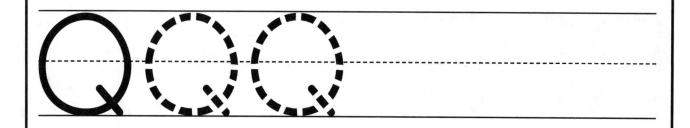

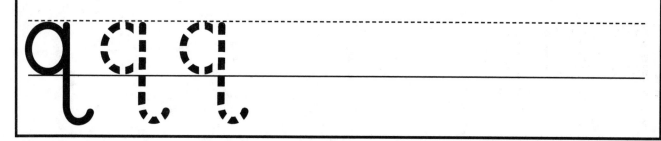

The Letter "R"

"R" is for rabbit. In which hat, can you guess?

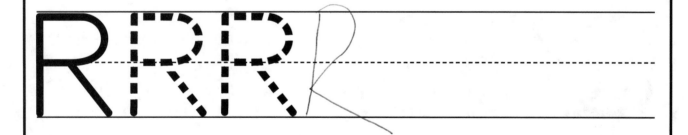

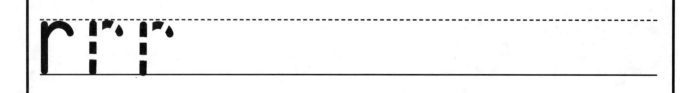

The Letter "S"

Ss

"S" is for snake as harmless as can be!

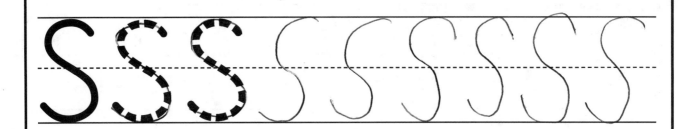

The Letter "T"

"T" is for tail. I have one, do you?

The Letter "U"

Uu

"U" is for umbrella. I'm dry as can be!

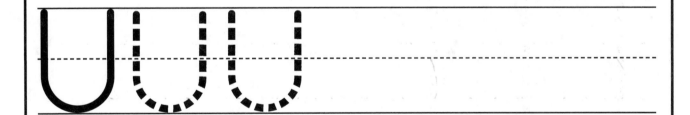

The Letter "V"

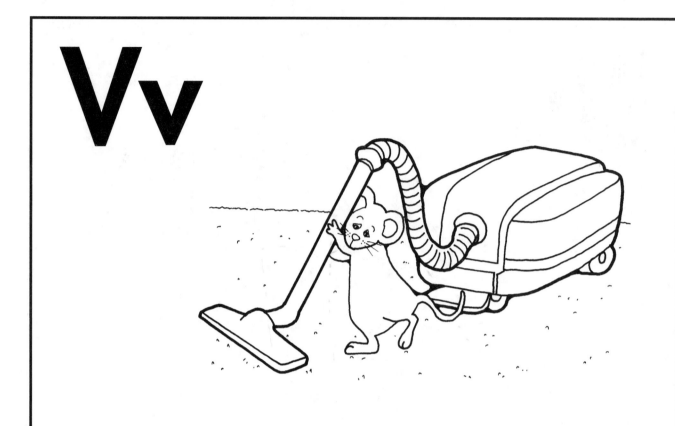

V v

"V" is for vacuum. When I clean, I have lots to do!

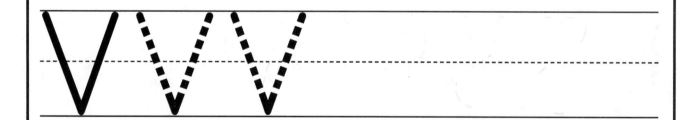

The Letter "W"

"W" is for wagon. Tell me what's next.

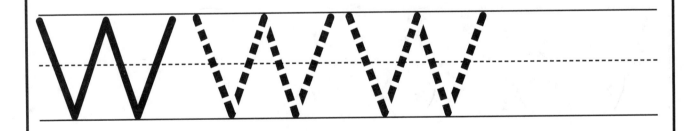

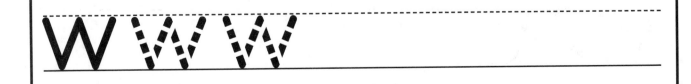

The Letter "X"

Xx

"X" is for X-ray. The doctor sees what's inside!

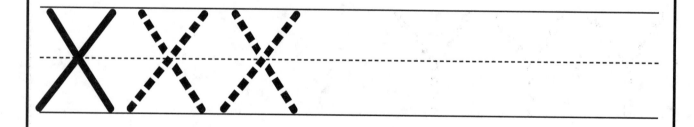

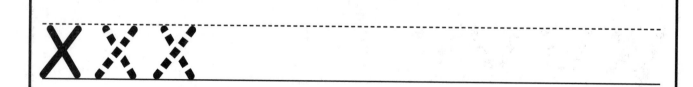

The Letter "Y"

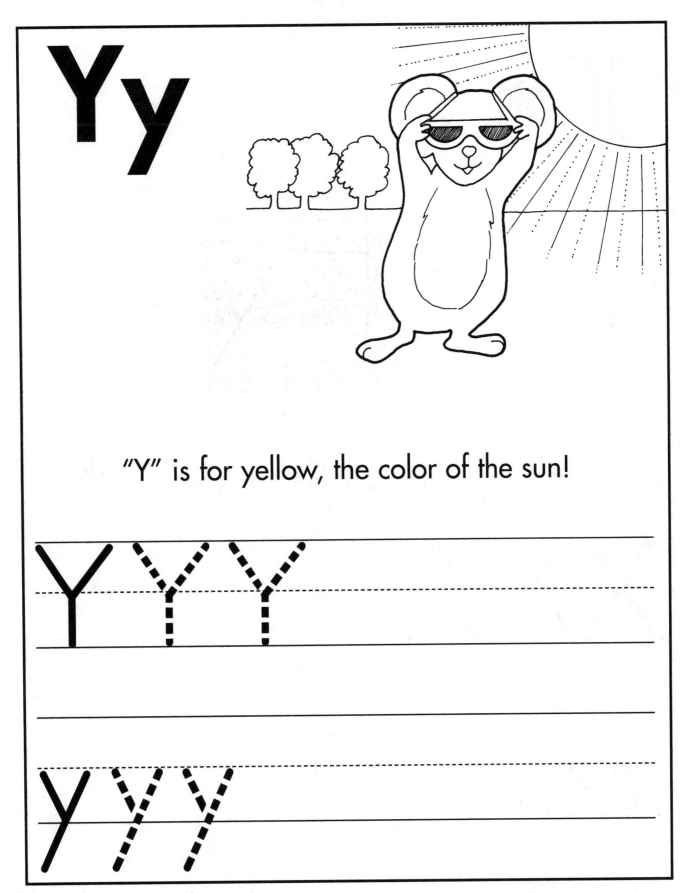

"Y" is for yellow, the color of the sun!

The Letter "Z"

Zz

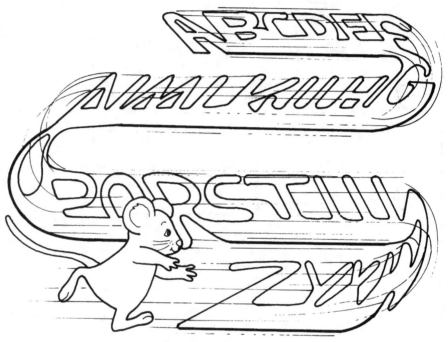

"Z" is for zoom. See the letters whiz by!

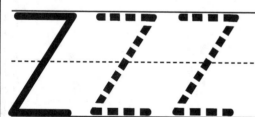

Uppercase

Write the uppercase letter for each lowercase letter.

a _____ b _____ c _____ d _____

e _____ f _____ g _____ h _____

i _____ j _____ k _____ l _____

m _____ n _____ o _____ p _____

q _____ r _____ s _____ t _____

u _____ v _____ w _____ x _____

y _____ z _____

Lowercase

Write the lowercase letter for each uppercase letter.

A_____ B_____ C_____ D_____

E_____ F_____ G _____ H_____

I _____ J _____ K_____ L_____

M_____ N_____ O_____ P_____

Q_____ R_____ S_____ T_____

U_____ V_____ W_____ X_____

Y_____ Z_____

Hidden Reptiles

Color the spaces with dots brown. Color spaces with vowels blue.
Color spaces with consonants green. What reptiles did you find?

Celebrate the Way "A" Sounds

Play this game by finding things that begin with the sounds the letter "A" makes.

1. Say the short "A" sound (as in *ant*) five times. Say the long "A" sound (as in *ape*) five times.

2. Repeat the rhyme:

   The ant and the alligator fishing for an "A"

   Were scared by an ape who chased them both away.

3. Color each thing in the picture that begins with short "A."

48

Celebrate the Way "B" Sounds

1. Make the letter "B" sound (as in *bear*) five times.

2. Repeat the rhyme:

   The bouncy brown bear, singing a tune,

   Was buzzed by a bee who popped his balloon.

3. How many things that begin with the sound of the letter "B" can you find hidden in the picture? Name everything in the picture. If it begins with the "B" sound, color or circle it.

Celebrate the Way "C" Sounds

Play this game by finding things that begin with the two sounds the letter "C" makes.

1. Say the hard "C" sound (as in *cat*) five times. Say the soft "C" sound (as in *centipede*) five times, too.

2. Repeat the rhyme:

   The cool camel and the fat cat sat

   Watching the centipede swinging his bat!

3. Circle things that start with the same hard "C" sound as camel and cat. Draw a box around the things that start with the same soft "C" sound as in centipede.

Celebrate the Way "D" Sounds

1. Say the "D" sound (as in *duck*) five times.

2. Repeat the rhyme:

    The dolphin, the duck, and the deer

    Draw dinosaur shapes in the mirror.

3. Cut pictures out of old magazines of objects that begin with the "D" sound. Paste them in the box below.

Celebrate the Way "E" Sounds

Be a fisherman! Play this game by fishing for things that begin with the two sounds the letter "E" makes.

1. Make the long "E" sound (as in *eagle*) five times. Make the short "E" sound (as in *elephant*) five times, too.

2. Repeat the rhyme:

   The elephant sat on an eagle

   Eating eggs with his best friend, the beagle!

3. Draw a line from the pictures that begin with long "E" or short "E" to the net. Draw an X through the other pictures.

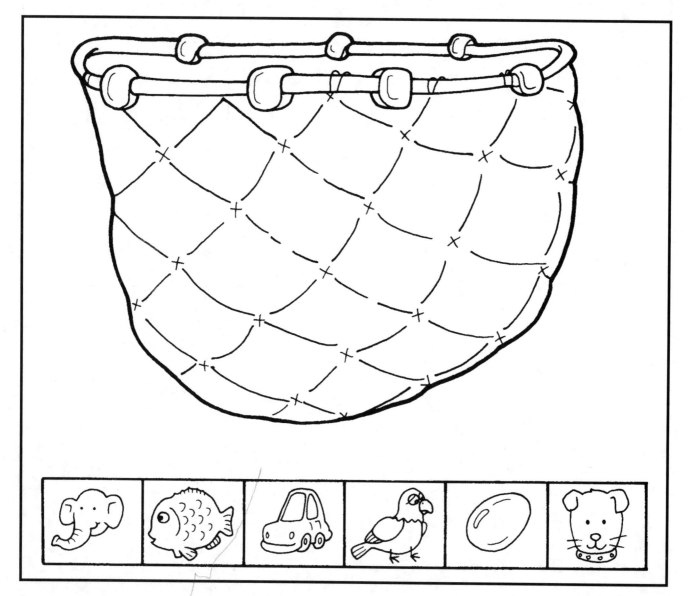

Celebrate the Way "F" Sounds

Play this game by fishing for fish that look alike.

1. Say the "F" sound (as in *fish*) five times.

2. Repeat the rhyme:

   The fox sings happily

   At the flamingo jamboree!

3. Find the matching fish, and color them the same color.

Celebrate the Way "G" Sounds

Play this game by finding things that begin with the two sounds the letter "G" makes.

1. Say the hard "G" sound (as in *gorilla*) five times. Say the soft "G" sound (as in *giraffe*) five times, too.

2. Repeat the rhyme:

   Mr. Gorilla and Mr. Giraffe

   Ate some green grapes and had a good laugh!

3. Color each grape with an uppercase "G" green.

4. Color each grape with a lowercase "g" gray.

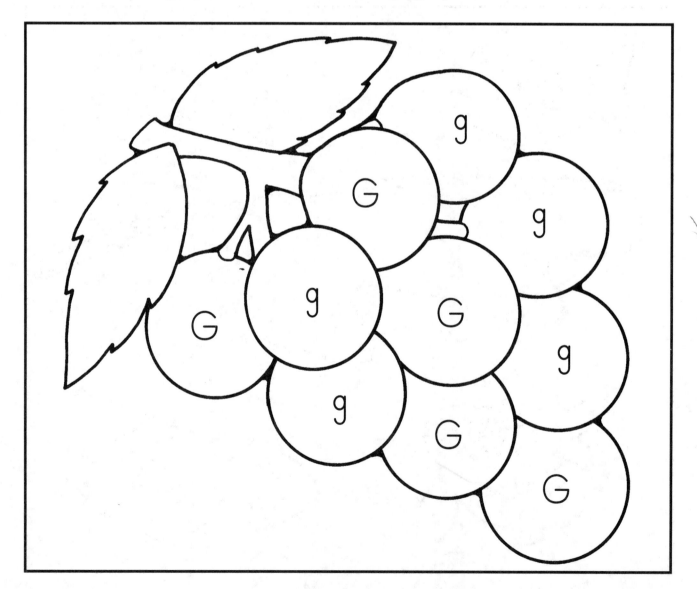

Celebrate the Way "H" Sounds

Play this game by hooking things that begin with the sound the letter "H" makes.

1. Say the "H" sound (as in *house*) five times.

2. Repeat the rhyme:

   The horse and the hippopotamus

   Have a huge happy house that they bought from us.

3. Start fishing for things that start with the "H" sound. Draw a line from fish with "H" pictures to the fish hook. Draw an X through the other fish.

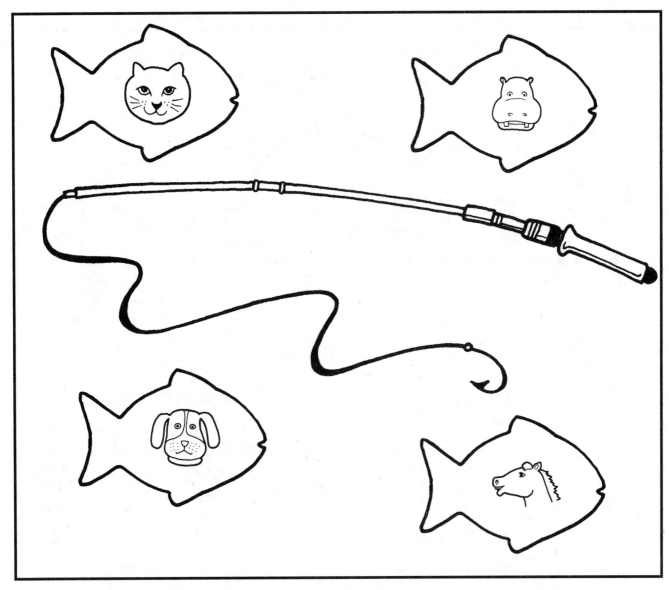

Celebrate the Way "I" Sounds

Make an ice cream sundae.

1. Say the long "I" sound (as in *ice*) five times. Say the short "I" sound (as in *iguana*) five times, too.

2. Repeat the rhyme:

   The iguana licked his ice cream cone

   And talked to insects on the phone!

3. Draw a picture of a word that begins with the "I" sound in each scoop of ice cream.

Celebrate the Way "J" Sounds

Play this game by sorting uppercase and lowercase "J's."

1. Say the "J" sound (as in *jaguar*) five times. Repeat the rhyme:

    The jaguar jumped out of his jacket and boots

    And put on a new jumbo-size jogging suit!

2. Color the jellybeans with uppercase "J" red.

3. Color the jellybeans with lowercase "j" yellow.

4. Color all the other jellybeans different colors.

5. Make the "J" sound each time you color a jellybean.

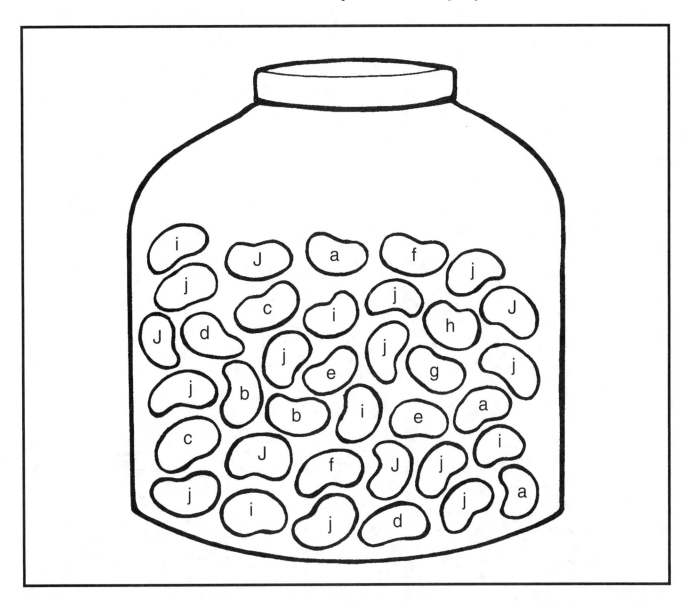

Celebrate the Way "K" Sounds

Play this game by putting things in the kangaroo's pocket that begin with the sound the letter "K" makes.

1. Say the "K" sound (as in *kitten*) five times.

2. Repeat the rhyme:

    The kangaroo king and the kitten queen

    Kissed the koala who acted so mean.

3. If the picture begins with a "K", draw a line to the kangaroo's pouch.

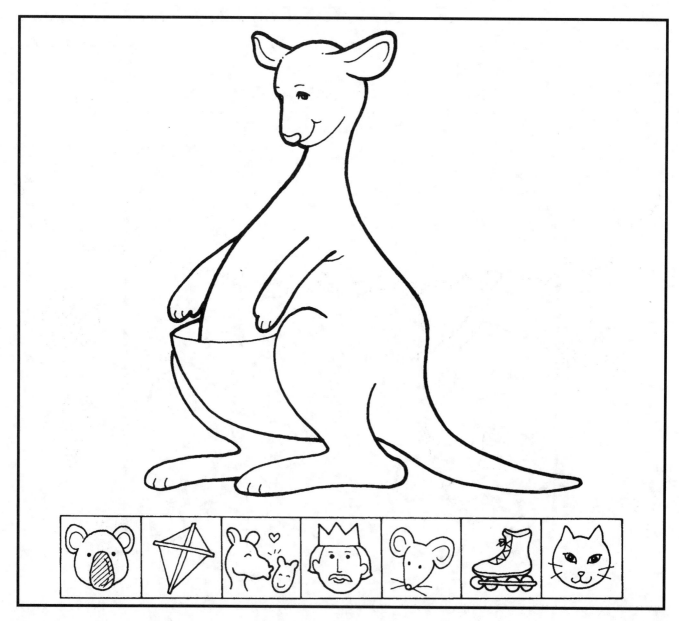

Celebrate the Way "L" Sounds

Play this game by finding things that begin with the sound the letter "L" makes.

1. Say the "L" sound (as in *lion*) five times.

2. Repeat the rhyme:

    The lion, the leopard, and llama were free

    To sit all day long beneath the lollipop tree.

3. Draw a line from the pictures that begin with the sound of "L" to the tree.

Celebrate the Way "M" Sounds

Play this game by finding things that begin with the sound the letter "M" makes.

1. Say the "M" sound (as in *moon*) five times.

2. Repeat the rhyme:

   The monkey, the moose, and the mouse

   Ate macaroni in front of my house!

3. Find pictures of things that start with the same sound as monkey, moose, mouse, and macaroni. Cut and paste them in the moon below.

Celebrate the Way "N" Sounds

Play this game by sorting uppercase and lowercase "N's."

1. Say the "N" sound (as in *nut*) five times.

2. Repeat the rhyme:

   The narwall hid nuts in the nest

   While the newt did his best as a pest!

3. Color purple the nuts with an uppercase "N." Color green the nuts with a lowercase "n." Color the other nuts different colors.

Celebrate the Way "O" Sounds

Play this game by finding things that begin with the sound the letter "O" makes.

1. Say the long "O" sound (as in *oboe*) five times. Say the short "O" sound (as in *octopus*) five times, too.

2. Repeat the rhyme:

   Octopus played his oboe for Owl

   While Orangutan covered his ears with a scowl!

3. Put a circle around things that start with the same sound as octopus, orangutan, and oboe (two different sounds).

Celebrate the Way "P" Sounds

Play this game by finding things that begin with the sound the letter "P" makes.

1. Say the "P" sound (as in *pig*) five times.

2. Repeat the rhyme:

    Mr. Penguin and Mr. Pig

    Sat on a panda and felt so big!

3. Circle all the uppercase and lowercase "P's." Color the picture.

Celebrate the Way "Q" and "R" Sound

Play this game by sorting the uppercase and lowercase "q's" and "r's."

1. Say the "Q" sound (as in *queen*) and the "R" sound (as in *ran*) five times each.

2. Repeat the rhyme:

    The quail quickly ran to the court of the queen.

    The raven and rabbit flew past her unseen.

3. Color the quilt sections with uppercase "Q" red.

    Color the quilt sections with uppercase "R" yellow.

    Color the quilt sections with lowercase "q" purple.

    Color the quilt sections with lowercase "r" pink.

Celebrate the Way "S" Sounds

Play this game by finding things that begin with the sound the letter "S" makes.

1. Say the "S" sound (as in *silly*) five times.

2. Repeat the rhyme:

   The silly squirrel slid down the snake

   Watching seals swim around the lake.

3. Color or circle the things in the picture that begin with the sound the letter "S" makes.

Celebrate the Way "T" Sounds

Play this game by finding the things that begin with the sound the letter "T" makes.

1. Say the "T" sound (as in *turkey*) five times.

2. Repeat the rhyme:

> **The turkey sat on the turtle's back.**
>
> **The tiger chased them around the track!**

3. Cut out things that start with the same sound as turkey and paste them on the train.

Celebrate the Way "U" and "V" Sound

Play this game by sorting "U's" and "V's."

1. Say the long "U" sound (as in *unicorn*) five times. Say the short "U" sound (as in *umbrella*) five times. Next, say the "V" sound (as in *violin*) five times, too.

2. Repeat the rhyme:

   The unicorn's umbrella gave everyone some shade

   While on his violin the vulture played and played.

3. Sort the letters by coloring the "U" sections of the umbrella with purple. Color the sections with "V's" yellow. As you are coloring each section, say the appropriate sound.

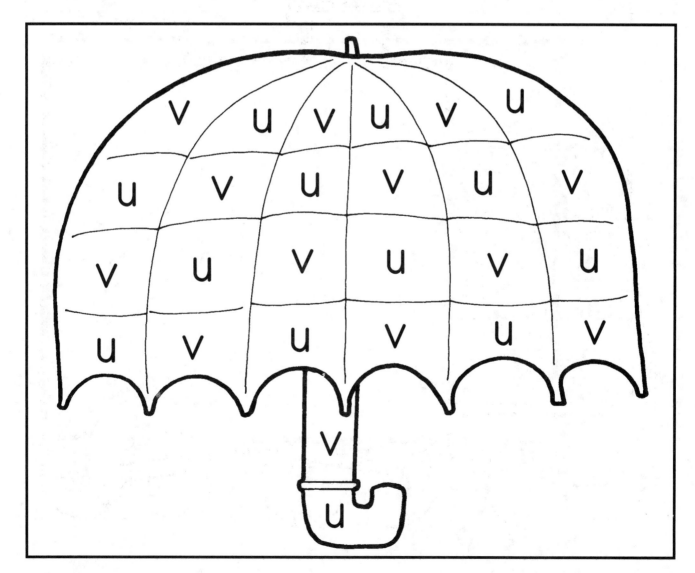

Celebrate the Way "W" Sounds

Play this game by finding things that begin with the sound the letter "W" makes.

1. Say the "W" sound five times.

2. Repeat the rhyme:

   The weasel and the walrus went walking one day

   When a wacky, weird wolf scared them away!

3. Cut out pictures of things that begin with the "w" sound from magazines. Paste them in the wagon below. How full can you get your wagon? After your wagon is full of "W" things, name each thing.

Celebrate the Way "X" and "Y" Sound

Play this game by finding things that begin with the sounds the letters "X" and "Y" make.

1. Say the "X" sound (the two letters "K" and "S" blended together) five times. Say the "Y" sound (as in *yak*) five times, too.

2. Repeat the rhyme:

     The x-ray fish was floating on this back.

     Close by in a yacht, yelled a very loud yak!

3. Put a box around each thing that begins with "Y."

Celebrate the Way "Z" Sounds

Play this game by finding things that begin with the sound the letter "Z" makes.

1. Say the "Z" sound (as in *zig-zag*) five times.

2. Repeat the rhyme:

> **The zebra zig-zagged through the zoo**
>
> **Looking for me, looking for you!**

3. How many things that begin with "Z" can you find? Circle them.

Missing Letters

- Say each word.
- Listen for the beginning sound.
- Write the missing letter.

1.

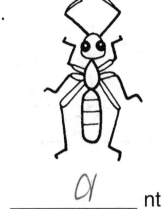

_____a____ nt

2.

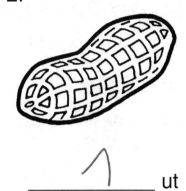

_____n____ ut

3.

_____p____ ig

4.

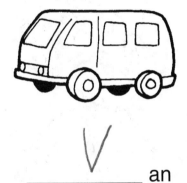

_____v____ an

5.

_____k____ ing

6.

_____c____ ow

7.

_____f____ ish

8.

_____g____ um

9.

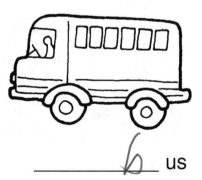

_____b____ us

More Missing Letters

- Say each word.
- Listen for the beginning sound.
- Write the missing letter.

1.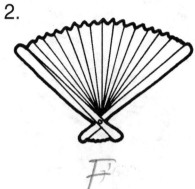

_____ at

2.

_____ an

3.

_____ ing

4.

_____ tar

5.

_____ og

6.

_____ rog

7.

_____ amp

8.

_____ est

9.

_____ up

Ending Sounds

- Say each word.
- Listen for the ending sound.
- Write the missing letter.

1.

ja_____

2.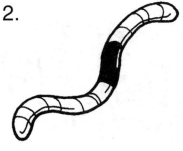

wor _____

3.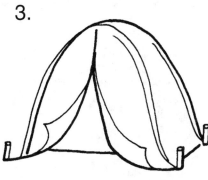

ten _____

4.

han _____

5.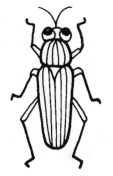

bu _____

6.

le_____

7.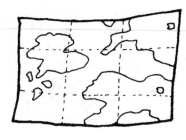

ma _____

8.

su _____

9.

ca _____

73

More Ending Sounds

- Say each word.
- Listen for the ending sound.
- Write the missing letter.

1.

li _____

2.

jee_____

3.

ca _____

4.

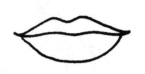

in_____

5.

pe _____

6.

a _____

7.

ne _____

8.

ove _____

9.

we_____

Missing Vowels

- Say each word.
- Listen for the middle sound.
- Write the missing vowel.

1.

p ___ g

2.

d ___ g

3.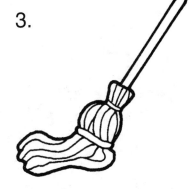

m ___ p

4.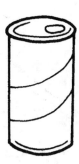

c ___ n

5.

j ___ t

6.

s ___ n

7.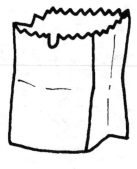

b ___ g

8.

w ___ g

9.

r ___ t

More Missing Vowels

- Say each word.
- Listen for the middle sound.
- Write the missing vowel.

1.

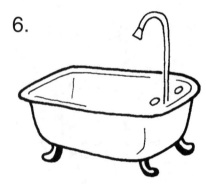

h ____ m

2.

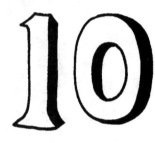

b ____ d

3.

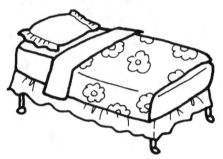

t ____ n

4.

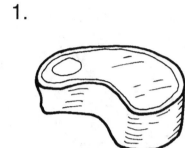

d ____ g

5.

s ____ t

6.

t ____ b

7.

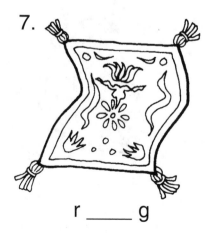

r ____ g

8.

b ____ s

9.

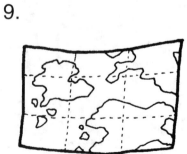

m ____ p

Sound It Out

- Look at each picture.
- Say the word.
- Write the sounds you hear.

1.

＿＿ ＿＿ ＿＿ ＿＿

2.

＿＿ ＿＿ ＿＿

3.

＿＿ ＿＿ ＿＿

4.
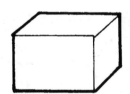

＿＿ ＿＿ ＿＿

5.
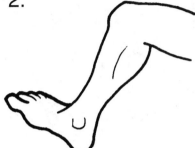

＿＿ ＿＿ ＿＿

6.

＿＿ ＿＿ ＿＿

7.

＿＿ ＿＿ ＿＿ ＿＿

8.

＿＿ ＿＿ ＿＿ ＿＿

9.

＿＿ ＿＿ ＿＿ ＿＿

More Sound It Out

- Look at each picture.
- Say the word.
- Write the sounds you hear.

1.

_ _ _

2.

_ _ _

3.

_ _ _

4.

_ _ _

5.

_ _ _

6.

_ _ _

7.

_ _ _ _

8.

_ _ _

9.

_ _ _

Match and Rhyme

1. Draw a line to the rhyming picture.

2. Color the pictures.

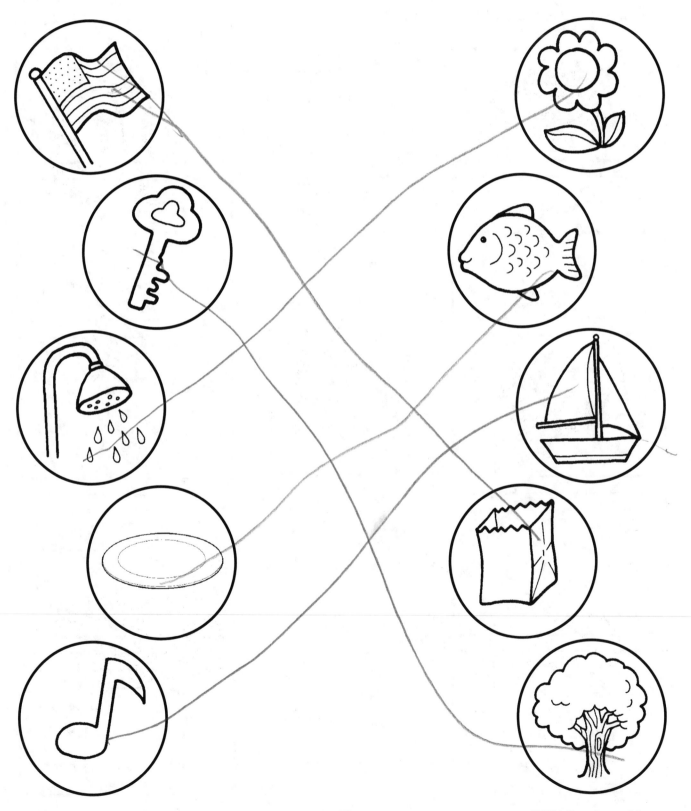

Rhyme the Pictures

1. Draw a line to the rhyming picture.

2. Color the pictures.

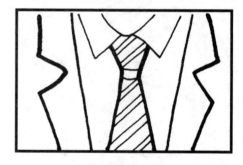

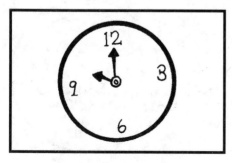

Find My Rhyming Pair.

1. Find the two things that rhyme.

2. Color each pair the same color.

What Am I?

1. Guess what I am.

2. Color the rhyming words. The box below will help you.

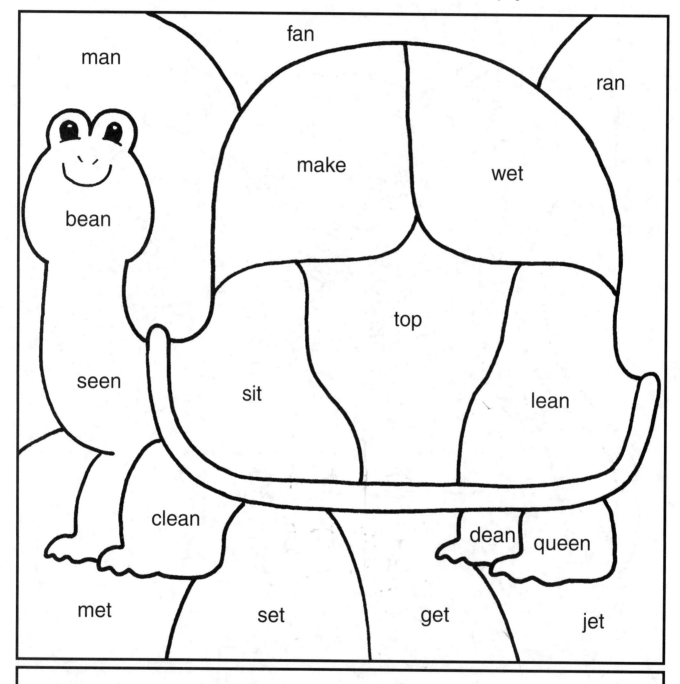

can = blue	hit = purple
let = green	mean = yellow
take = red	mop = orange

My Fat Cat

1. Circle the words that rhyme with cat.
2. Each hidden word begins with a letter from the list.
3. Color the picture around the puzzle.

- **S**
- **M**
- **B**
- **R**
- **H**
- **F**

S	N	F		
L	B	A	D	M
S	A	T	V	A
F	T	R	A	T
H	A	T	J	B

My Pet, Jet

1. Circle the words that rhyme with pet.

2. The beginning letters will help you.

3. Color the picture around the puzzle.

- **M**
- **S**
- **J**
- **L**
- **G**
- **W**

L	E	T	S	Y	U
G	B	W	E	T	V
S	G	E	T	J	K
F	T	R	A	E	T
H	A	M	E	T	F

Making Rhyming Words

Add the first letter to the words below to make words that rhyme with the first word. Look at the pictures for clues.

1. cat

___ at

___ at

2. hog

___ og

___ og

3. man

___ an

___ an

4. pop

___ op

___ op

5. dig

___ ig

___ ig

6. ten

___ en

___ en

#3644 Practice and Learn

Rhyme Time

- Think of a word that rhymes with each picture.
- Write the word.
- Draw the picture.

1.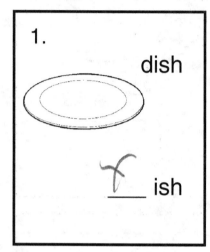

dish

__f__ ish

2.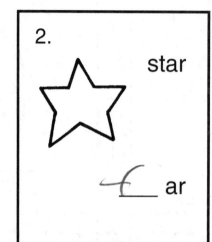

star

__f__ ar

3.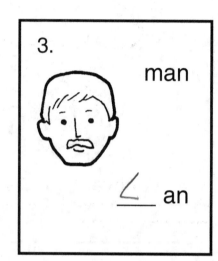

man

__∠__ an

4.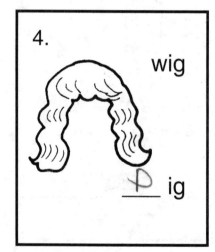

wig

__p__ ig

5.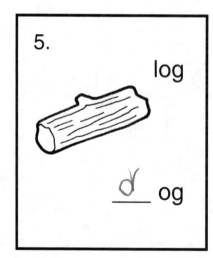

log

__d__ og

6.

lake

__l__ ake

7.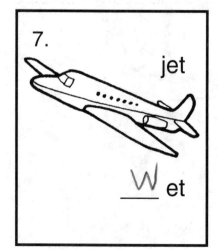

jet

__W__ et

8.

ten

__h__ en

9.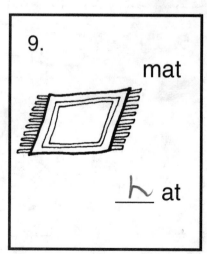

mat

__h__ at

Above or Below

Decide whether the bird is above or below. Circle your answer.

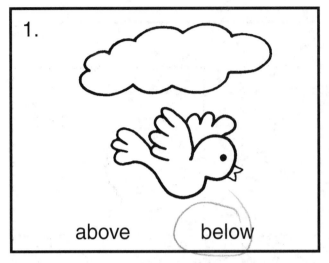

1. above   (below)

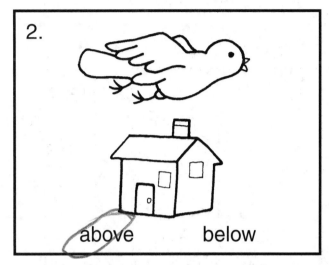

2. (above)   below

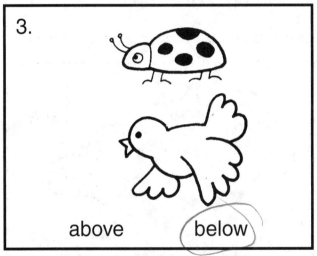

3. above   (below)

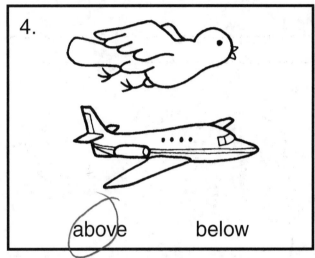

4. (above)   below

Draw a star above the box.

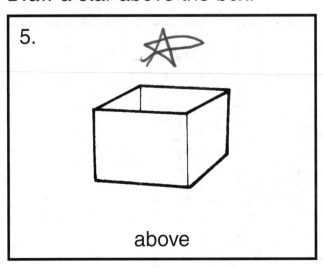

5. above

Draw a star below the box.

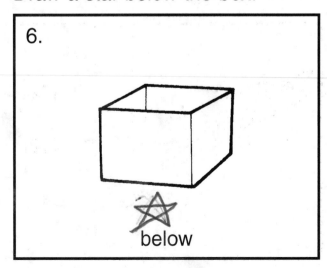

6. below

Left or Right

Decide whether the bear is on the left or on the right of the box. Circle your answer.

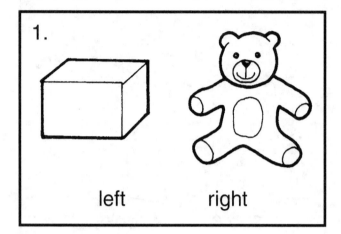

1.

left   right

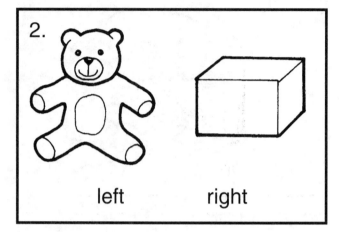

2.

left   right

Decide whether the fork is on the left or the right of the plate. Circle your answer.

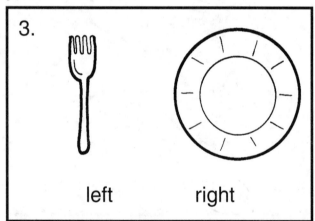

3.

left   right

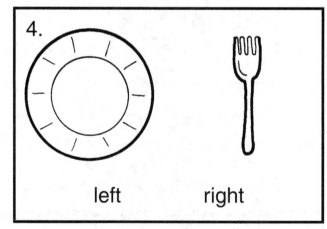

4.

left   right

5. Draw a tree on the left side of the house.

6. Draw a tree on the right side of the house.

In or Out

Decide whether each object is in or out. Circle the correct word.

1.

in   out

1.

in   out

1.
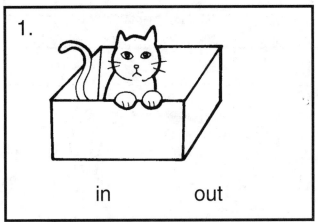
in   out

1.
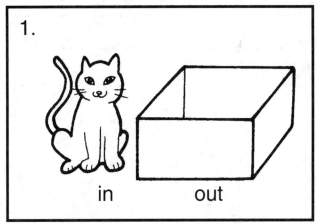
in   out

5. Draw a star in the box.

6. Draw a star out of the box.

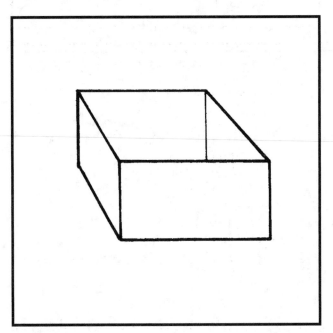

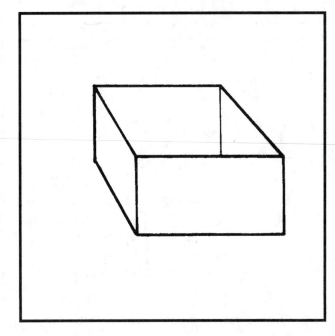

Following Directions

Follow the direction in each box by drawing a worm.

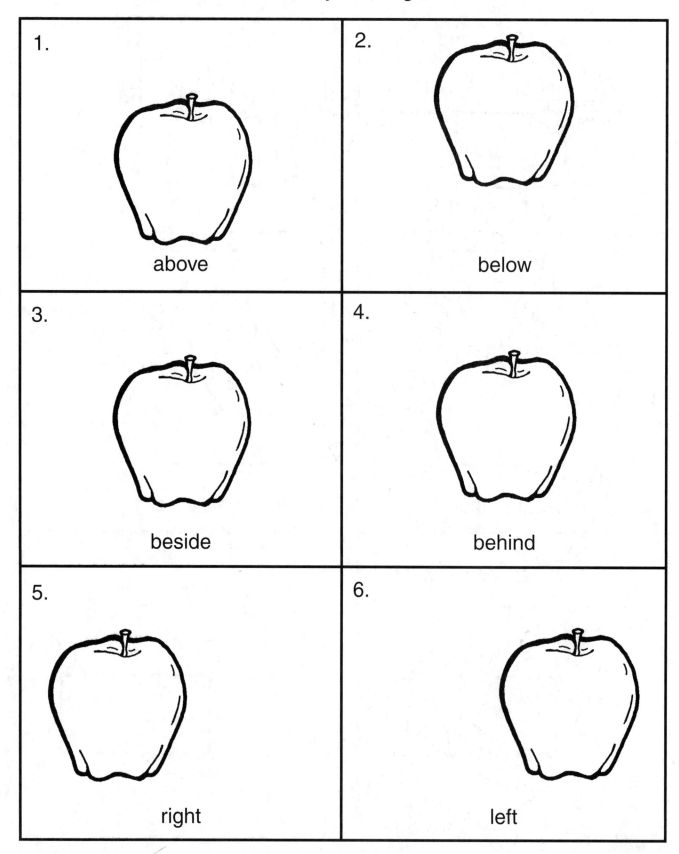

1.

above

2.

below

3.

beside

4.

behind

5.

right

6.

left

Picture-Word Connections

Draw a line to connect each picture to the matching word.

duck

top

man

car

Connecting Pictures to Words

Draw a line to connect each picture to the matching word.

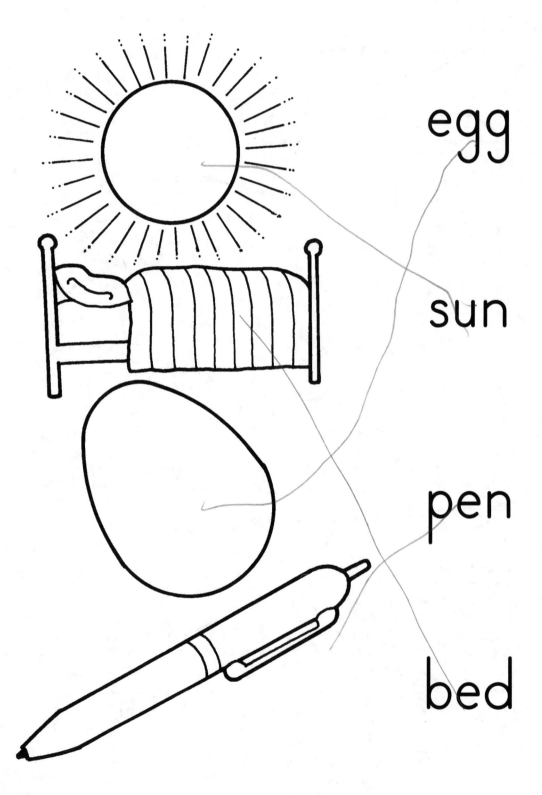

egg

sun

pen

bed

Picture-Word Connections

Draw a line to connect each picture to the matching word.

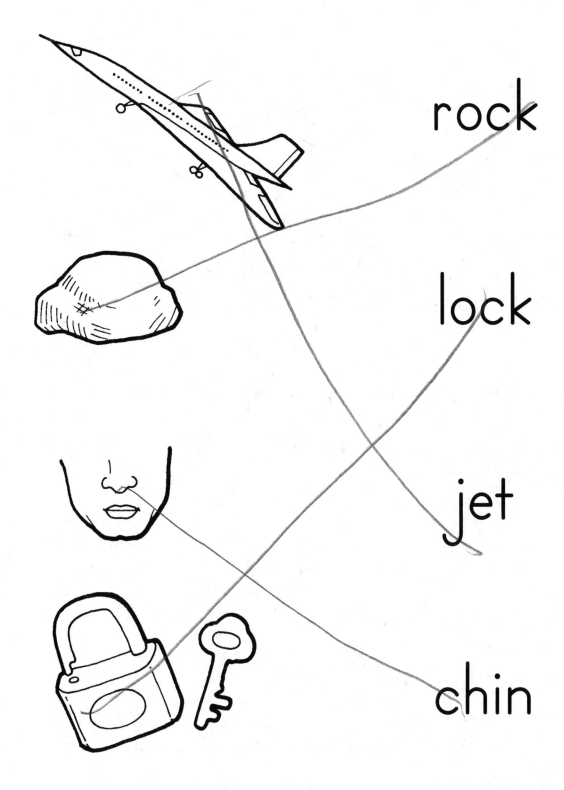

rock

lock

jet

chin

Toy Chest

Use your best printing to write the words.

Color the pictures.

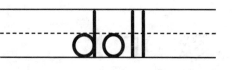

doll

truck

book

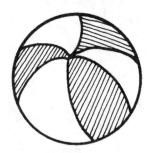

ball

bear

The Zoo

- Use your best printing to write the words.
- Color the pictures.

zebra

giraffe

ape

elephant

monkey

Fruit Basket

- Use your best printing to write the words.
- Color the pictures.

Animal Names

Print the correct name on each line. Color the pictures.

Word Bank

horse	sheep	pig	goat	cow	hen

　　　　　　　97

My Favorite Food

Write some words that finish the sentence below.

Draw a picture about your words.

My favorite food is Macaroni

and cheese.

When I Grow Up

Write some words that finish the sentence below.

Draw a picture about your words.

When I grow up

Playtime

Write some words that finish the sentence below.

Draw a picture about your words.

I like to play with *My dad*

outside.

The Zoo

Write a story about the picture.

_____
- -
_____
- -
_____
- -
_____
- -
_____
- -
_____

Weather

Write a story about the picture.

_____

- -

_____

- -

_____

- -

_____

- -

_____

- -

_____

Pirates

Write a story about the picture.

_____

- -

_____

- -

_____

- -

_____

- -

_____

- -

"Little Miss Muffet"

Little Miss Muffet

Sat on a tuffet,

Eating her curds and whey;

Along came a spider

Who sat down beside her

And frightened Miss Muffet away.

Answer the following questions. Circle the correct answer. Color the picture.

1. Miss Muffet was eating:

2. What sat beside her?

3. Did the spider stand?   YES   NO

4. Miss Muffet was _____ by the spider.

5. Miss Muffet:

Guess the Small Animal

Connect the dots. Color.

- I have eight eyes in my head.
- I have eight legs.
- I spin a silk web.
- I eat insects.

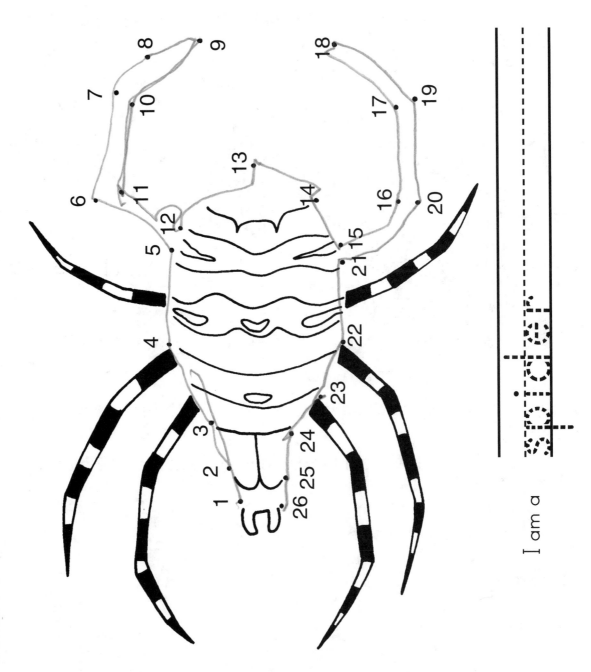

I am a s̲p̲i̲d̲e̲r̲

"Mary, Mary, Quite Contrary"

Mary, Mary, quite contrary,

How does your garden grow?

With silver bells and cockle shells

And pretty maids all in a row.

Circle the things that could grow in Mary's garden. Color the picture.

Mary's Garden

Color things in Mary's garden using the color code.

red   blue   yellow

"Little Bo-Peep"

Little Bo-Peep has lost her sheep,

And doesn't know where to find them;

Leave them alone and they'll come home,

Wagging their tails behind them.

Where Are Little Bo-Peep's Sheep?

Find the sheep.

Circle and color them.

Little Bo-Peep's Sheep

Color by numbers.

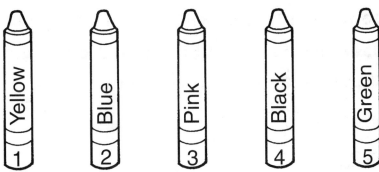

"Jack and Jill"

Jack and Jill ran up a hill,

To fetch a pail of water;

Jack fell down, and broke his crown,

And Jill came tumbling after.

Read the sentence. Draw a blue O around the well.

Draw a green X on Jack.

Draw a red square around the pail.

Fetch a Pail of Water

Help Jack and Jill get up the hill.

"Peter, Peter, Pumpkin Eater"

Peter, Peter, pumpkin eater,

Had a wife and couldn't keep her;

He put her in a pumpkin shell,

And there he kept her very well.

Write the numbers 1, 2, and 3 in the circles to show the order of the poem.

Had a wife and couldn't keep her;

Peter, Peter, pumpkin eater,

He put her in a pumpkin shell and there he kept her very well.

Peter's Pumpkin Shell

1. Read the words.

2. Color.

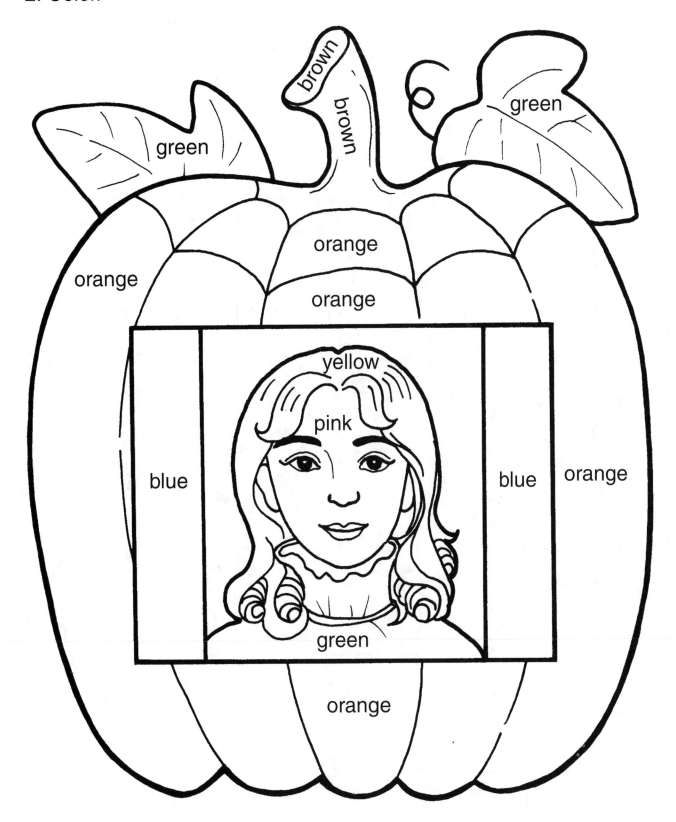

" Old Mother Hubbard"

Old Mother Hubbard went to the cupboard,

To fetch her poor dog a bone;

But when she got there the cupboard was bare,

And so the poor dog had none.

Color by shape.

Old Mother Hubbard's Dog

Color and cut out the dog picture pieces.

Glue the pieces in order, into a stand-up dog figure.

"Little Jack Horner"

Little Jack Horner sat in the corner,

Eating a Christmas pie;

He put in his thumb, and pulled out a plum,

And said, "What a good boy am I!"

Connect the dots.

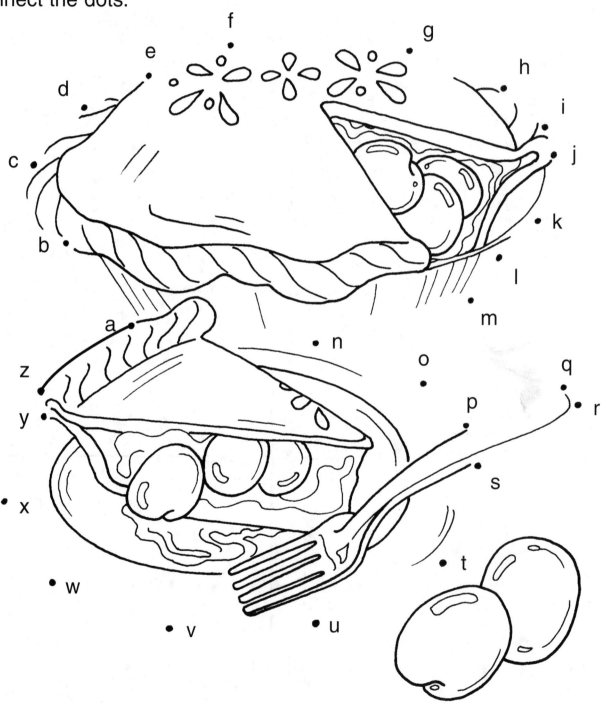

He Stuck in His Thumb...

Find the plum message. Color the picture.

a	n	d		p	u	l	l	e	d
1	6	2		8	10	4	4	3	2

o	u	t		a		p	l	u	m
7	10	9		1		8	4	10	5

"Humpty Dumpty"

Humpty Dumpty sat on a wall,

Humpty Dumpty had a great fall.

All the king's horses and all the king's men,

Couldn't put Humpty together again.

Color the Humpty Dumpty.

Color by shape.

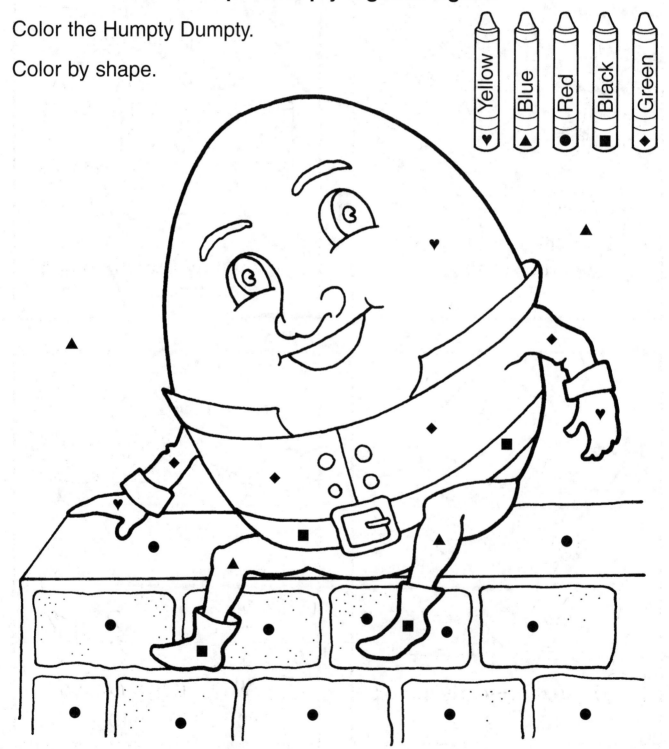

Humpty Dumpty's Fall

Write the numbers 1, 2, 3, and 4 to show the order of the poem.

4 **Couldn't put Humpty together again.**

2 **Humpty Dumpty had a great fall.**

1 **Humpty Dumpty sat on a wall,**

3 **All the king's horses and all the king's men,**

"Little Boy Blue"

Little Boy Blue, come blow your horn,

The sheep's in the meadow, the cow's in the corn;

But where is the boy who looks after the sheep?

He's under the haystack fast asleep.

1. Read and color.

2. Then color the rest of the picture.

Color the ⬚ yellow.   Color the ⬚ black.

Color the ⬚ brown.   Color the ⬚ orange.

"Little Boy Blue"

Circle the things that happen in the rhyme. Color.

"One, Two, Buckle My Shoe"

Trace the numbers.

Buckle my shoe.

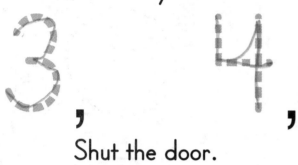

Shut the door.

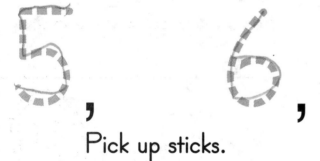

Pick up sticks.

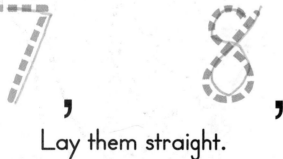

Lay them straight.

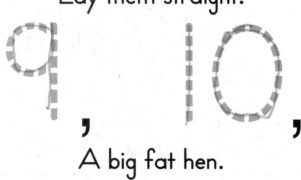

A big fat hen.

"Hey Diddle, Diddle"

Read the poem. Color the pictures.

Hey Diddle, Diddle
The cat and the fiddle,

The cow jumped over the moon.

The little dog laughed to
see such sport,

And the dish ran away
with the spoon.

"Jack Be Nimble"

Jack be nimble,

Jack be quick,

Jack jump over the candlestick.

Color Jack and the pictures that begin with "J".

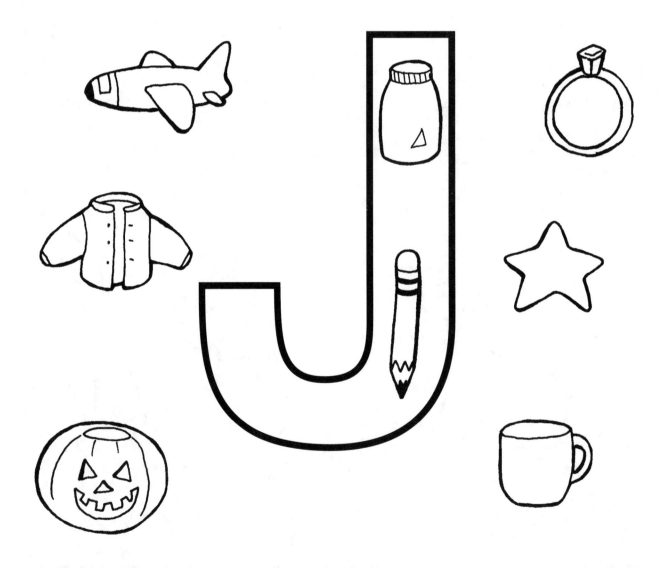

"Pease Porridge"

Pease porridge hot,

Pease porridge cold,

Pease porridge in the pot, nine days old.

Some like it hot,

Some like it cold,

Some like it in the pot, nine days old.

◆　　　◆　　　◆

Color cold pictures blue. Color hot pictures red.

ice cube

soup

ice-cream cone

sun

candle

snowman

"Baa, Baa, Black Sheep"

Baa, Baa, black sheep,

Have you any wool?

Yes, sir, yes, sir,

Three bags full;

One for my master,

One for my dame,

And one for the little boy

Who lives down the lane.

• Count.   • Print numbers.   • Color.

"The Mouse Ran Up the Clock"

Hickory, Dickory, Dock!
The mouse ran up the clock;
The clock struck one,
The mouse ran down,
Hickory, Dickory, Dock!

Connect the dots.

"The Three Little Kittens"

The three little kittens,

They lost their mittens,

And they began to cry.

"Oh, mother dear, we sadly fear,

Our mittens we have lost."

"What! Lost your mittens, you naughty kittens!

Then you shall have no pie."

- Match the mittens.
- Color each pair alike.

"Rain, Rain"

Rain, rain, go away,

Come again another day,

Little Johnny wants to play.

Color all the things you can do in the rain.

Fairy Tales

Kindergarten students should be familiar with a variety of folk and fairy tales. This section of the book presents activities for several fairy tales. Additional activities and sources are listed below.

"The Little Red Hen"

The Little Red Hen retold by Lucinda McQueen (Scholastic, Inc., 1993).

The Little Red Hen by Paul Galdone (Houghton Mifflin, 1985).

The Little Red Hen by Margot Zemach (Farrar, Strauss & Giroux, 1983).

What to Talk About

- Have your child think of times when he or she has helped. Discuss the benefits of helping.
- Ask whether your child thinks the duck, cat, and dog should be able to eat some bread.

Activities

- Have your child help you make a loaf of bread.
- Read the chant on page 136. Your child can help read the repetitive portions of the text.
- After your child has colored and cut out the pictures on page 137, help him or her arrange the pictures in the correct sequence.

"The Three Little Pigs"

The Three Little Pigs by Paul Galdone (Houghton Miffin, 1984).

The Three Little Pigs by Margot Zemach (Sunburst, 1991).

The Three Little Pigs by James Marshall (Puffin, 1996).

What to Talk About

- Discuss the different types of materials the pigs used to build their houses. Of what kind of material is your house made?
- Ask how your child felt when the wolf fell in the boiling water. Be sure to distinguish between fantasy and reality.

Activities

- Read a variation of the story like *The True Story of the Three Little Pigs written by A. Wolf*, as told to Jon Scieszka (Viking Children's Books, 1992) or *The Three Little Wolves and the Big Bad Pig* by Eugene Triviza (Heinemann Young Books, 1993). Compare and contrast the various stories.
- Read the chant on page 138. Ask your child to read the repetitive parts of the text.
- Help your child complete the story map on page 139.

"The Gingerbread Man"

The Gingerbread Man by Eric A. Kimmel (Holiday House, 1994).

The Gingerbread Man by Richard Scarry (Golden Book Publishing Co. Inc., 1997).

The Gingerbread Man by Karen Schmidt (Scholastic, 1986).

The Gingerbread Boy by David Cutts (Troll Associates, 1989).

What to Talk About

- Your child may be upset that the Gingerbread Man gets eaten. If so, talk about why that might be upsetting.

Fairy Tales (cont.)

What to Talk About *(cont.)*

- Ask how your child felt when the Gingerbread Man jumped up, talked, and ran away. Could this really happen?
- Talk about the fox. How did he manage to outsmart everyone else who wanted to eat the Gingerbread Man?
- What lesson does the story teach about being boastful?

Activities

- Read the chant on page 140. Ask your child to read the repetitive part.
- Play the board game on page 141 with your child. You will need a die and some things to use as a space markers.

"The Hare and the Tortoise"

The Tortoise and the Hare by Betty Miles *(Aladdin Paperbacks, 1998)*.

The Tortoise and the Hare adapted by Janet Stevens (Holiday House, 1985).

The Tortoise and the Hare by Carla Dijs (Little Simon, 1997).

What to Talk About

- Who were the main characters in the story? Where did the story take place? Who won the race? How was the tortoise able to win?
- Look at the illustrations carefully to identify the many types of animals in the book. Discuss whether they look real or make-believe. Ask your child to tell you how he or she knows.

Activities

- Read the Hare Versus the Tortoise Cheer on page 142. Ask your child to read the repetitive lines.
- Have your child do research on an animal. Help him or her fill out the Animal Research Report on page 143.

"The Three Billy Goats Gruff"

The Three Billy Goats Gruff by Janet Stevens (Harcourt Brace Jovanovich, 1990).

The Three Billy Goats Gruff by Glen Rounds (Holiday House, 1994).

The Three Billy-Goats Gruff by Ellen Appleby (Scholastic, 1993).

What to Talk About

- What was the problem in this story? How was the problem solved?
- Talk about trolls and name some other imaginary creatures found in folktales and fairy tales (fairies, witches, elves, etc.).
- Talk about how goats will eat almost anything. Ask what the goats in this story wanted to eat.

Activities

- Build a bridge with your child. You can use any materials available such as blocks, milk cartons, or Legos.
- Read the chant on page 144. Ask your child to participate by reading the repetitive part.
- Have your child color and cut out the character pieces on page 145. Attach a wooden stick to the back of each character. Help your child retell the story, using the characters.

The Little Red Hen

Little Red Hen has found some wheat.

"Who will help me plant the wheat, so we may have bread to eat?"
"Not I!" said the duck. "Not I!" said the cat. "Not I!" said the dog.
"Then I shall do it myself," said the Little Red Hen.

"Who will help me water the wheat, so we may have bread to eat?"
"Not I!" said the duck. "Not I!" said the cat. "Not I!" said the dog.
"Then I shall do it myself," said the Little Red Hen.

"Who will help me hoe the wheat, so we may have bread to eat?"
"Not I!" said the duck. "Not I!" said the cat. "Not I!" said the dog.
"Then I shall do it myself," said the Little Red Hen.

"Who will help me cut the wheat, so we may have bread to eat?"
"Not I!" said the duck. "Not I!" said the cat. "Not I!" said the dog.
"Then I shall do it myself," said the Little Red Hen.

"Who will help me grind the wheat, so we may have bread to eat?'
"Not I!" said the duck. "Not I!" said the cat. "Not I!" said the dog.
"Then I shall do it myself," said the Little Red Hen.

"Who will help me make the bread?"
"Not I!" said the duck. "Not I!" said the cat. "Not I!" said the dog.
"Then I shall do it myself," said the Little Red Hen.

When the bread was done, her friends all wanted to eat.
But the Little Red Hen ate the whole treat!

The Little Red Hen Story Sequencing

Directions: Color and cut the pictures along the dotted lines. Then arrange the pictures in the correct sequence.

The Little Red Hen watered the wheat.

The Little Red Hen ate the bread.

The Little Red Hen made the bread.

The Little Red Hen found some wheat.

The Little Red Hen planted the wheat.

The Little Red Hen cut the wheat.

The Three Little Pigs

One pig built his house of straw.
Oh, no! Oh, no!

One pig built his house of sticks.
Oh, no! Oh, no!

One pig built his house of bricks.
Smart pig! Smart pig!

Then the wolf came to blow them down.
Huff, puff! Huff, puff!

Down went the houses of straw and sticks.
Huff, puff! Huff, puff!

But he couldn't blow down that house of bricks.
Huff, puff! Huff, puff!

Who's afraid of the big bad wolf?
Not us! Not us!

The Three Little Pigs Story Map

Directions: Color the pictures below. Cut along the dotted lines. Glue the pictures in the correct boxes on the map to retell the story.

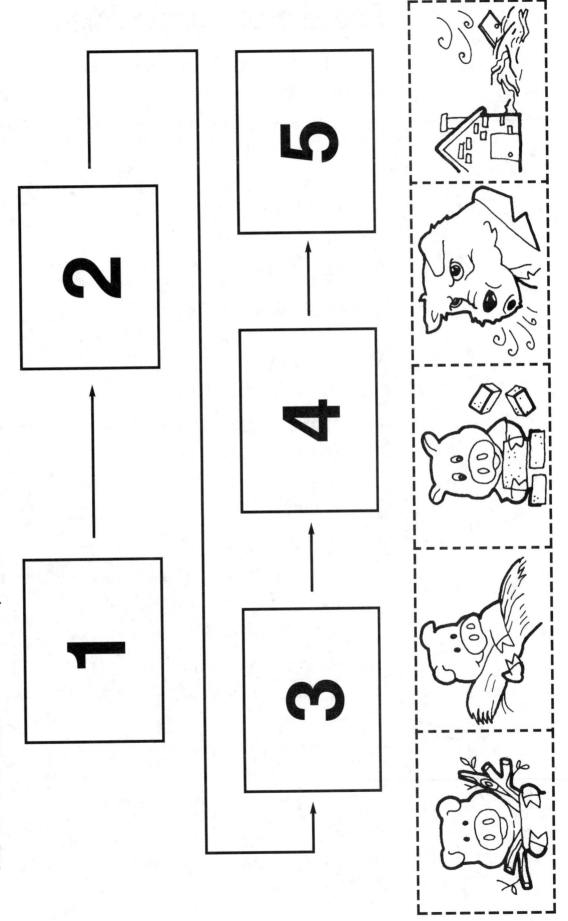

The Gingerbread Man

Run, run,
As fast as you can.
You can't catch me,
I'm the Gingerbread Man!

Here come the old woman
And the old man.
Run, run,
As fast as you can.

Here comes a pig,
Mr. Gingerbread Man.
Run, run,
As fast as you can.

Here comes a dog,
Mr. Gingerbread Man.
Run, run,
As fast as you can.

Here comes a horse,
Mr. Gingerbread Man.
Run, run,
As fast as you can.

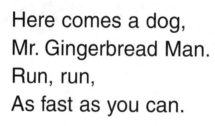

Here comes a cow,
Mr. Gingerbread Man.
Run, run,
As fast as you can.

Run, run,
As fast as you can.
But the fox caught you,
Mr. Gingerbread Man!

The Gingerbread Man Game Board

Materials: a die and space markers

Directions:

Roll a die to find out how many spaces to move. The winner is the person who reaches the gingerbread house first.

Start

Run, run, as fast as you can! Take another turn.

You are getting tired. Go back one space.

Look out for the Fox! Lose a turn.

You are almost there. Take another turn.

Finish

The Hare and the Tortoise Cheer

Hare and Tortoise had a race.
Go! Go!
Slow and steady wins the race.

Hare was fast. Tortoise was slow.
Go! Go!
Slow and steady wins the race.

Hare was running. Tortoise was walking.
Go! Go!
Slow and steady wins the race.

Hare was winning. Tortoise kept walking.
Go! Go!
Slow and steady wins the race.

Hare was sleeping. Tortoise kept walking.
Go! Go!
Slow and steady wins the race.

Hare woke up. Tortoise kept walking.
Go! Go!
Slow and steady wins the race.

Tortoise kept walking and won the race.
Hooray! Hooray!
Slow and steady won the race!

Animal Research Report

Researched by _____

This is a real animal.

It is a _____.

```




```

It lives _____.

It has _____ legs.

It eats _____.

Its babies are called _____.

I also found out that it _____.

The Three Billy Goats Gruff

The three goats are hungry
For something to eat.
Trip, trap,
Trip, trap.

But under the bridge
Watch out for the troll!
Trip, trap,
Trip, trap.

Over the bridge
The little goat crosses.
Trip, trap,
Trip, trap.

Over the bridge
The second goat crosses.
Trip, trap,
Trip, trap.

Over the bridge
The biggest goat crosses.
Trip, trap,
Trip, trap.

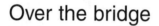

Off the bridge goes the troll
And the goats have their lunch.
Trip, trap,
Trip, trap.

The three goats' story
Has come to an end.
Snip, snap, snout.
This tale's told out.

Character Patterns

Directions: Color and cut out these characters. Staple them to wooden sticks. Use for retelling the story.

Colors

Color each balloon a different color. Name the color you used for each balloon.

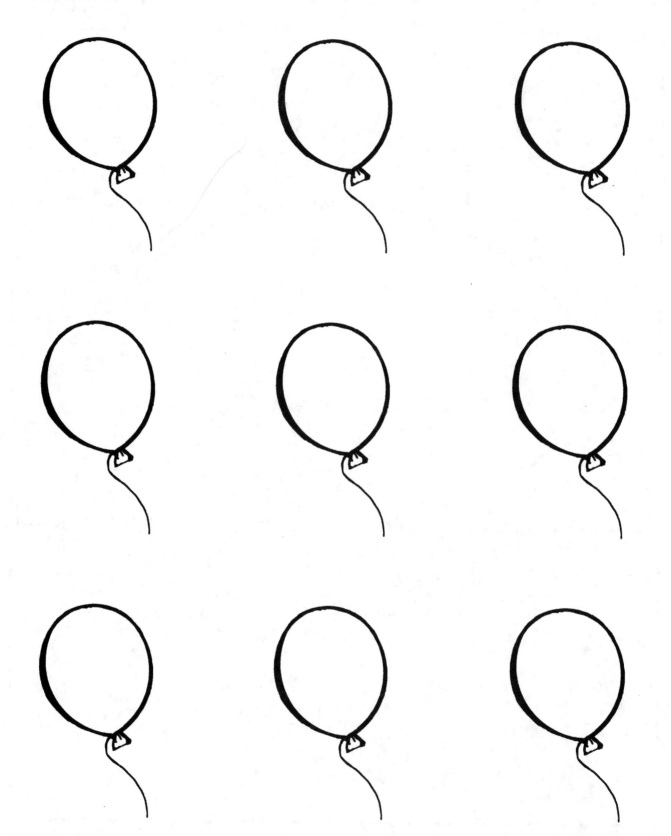

Rainbow Colors

Read the names and color the rainbow.

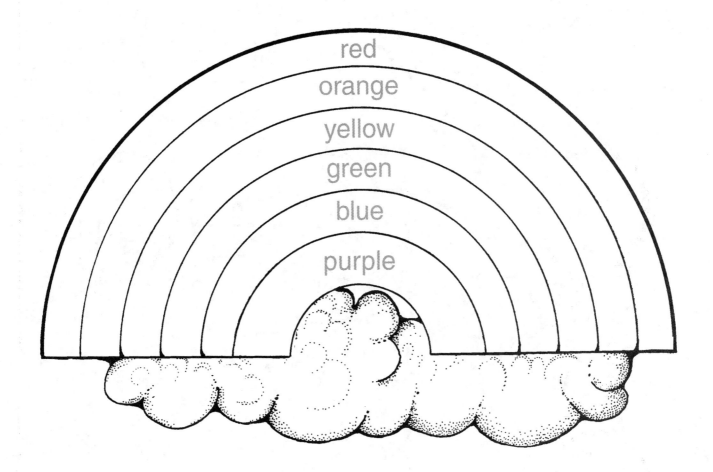

The Color Red

Trace the words below. Color the pictures red.

Red

red

The Color Orange

Trace the words below. Color the pictures orange.

Orange

orange

The Color Yellow

Trace the words below. Color the pictures yellow.

Yellow

yellow

The Color Green

Trace the words below. Color the pictures green.

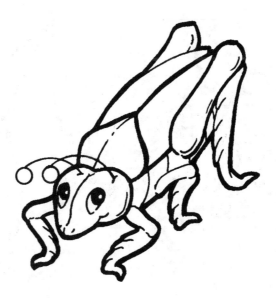

Green

green

The Color Blue

Trace the words below. Color the pictures blue.

The Color Purple

Trace the words below. Color the pictures purple.

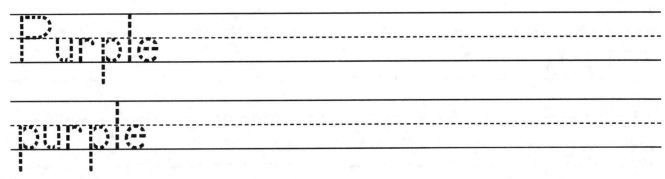

Purple

purple

The Color Brown

Trace the words below. Color the pictures brown.

Brown

brown

The Color Black

Trace the words below. Color the pictures black.

Black

black

Color Match

 Draw lines to match the color words to the pictures.

 Color the pictures.

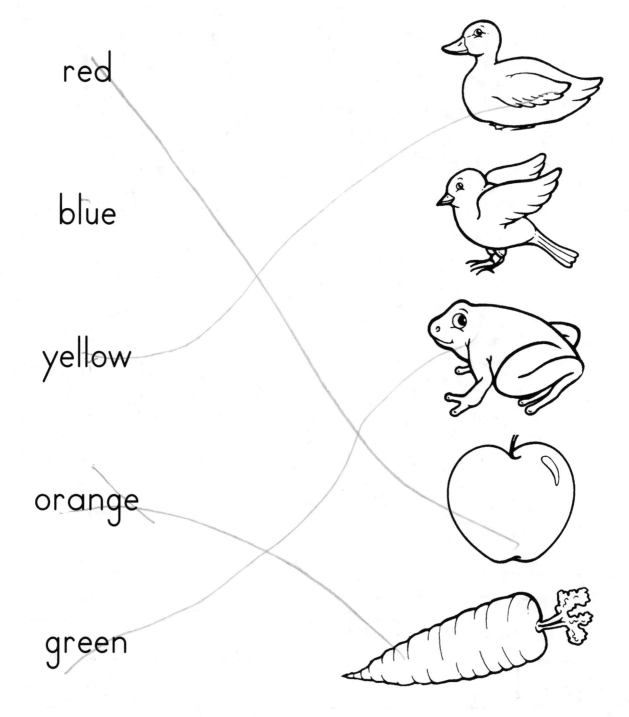

red

blue

yellow

orange

green

More Color Match

 Draw lines to match the color words to the pictures.

 Color the pictures.

purple

brown

pink

black

white

Color a Boat

Trace the boat. Draw a flag. Color.

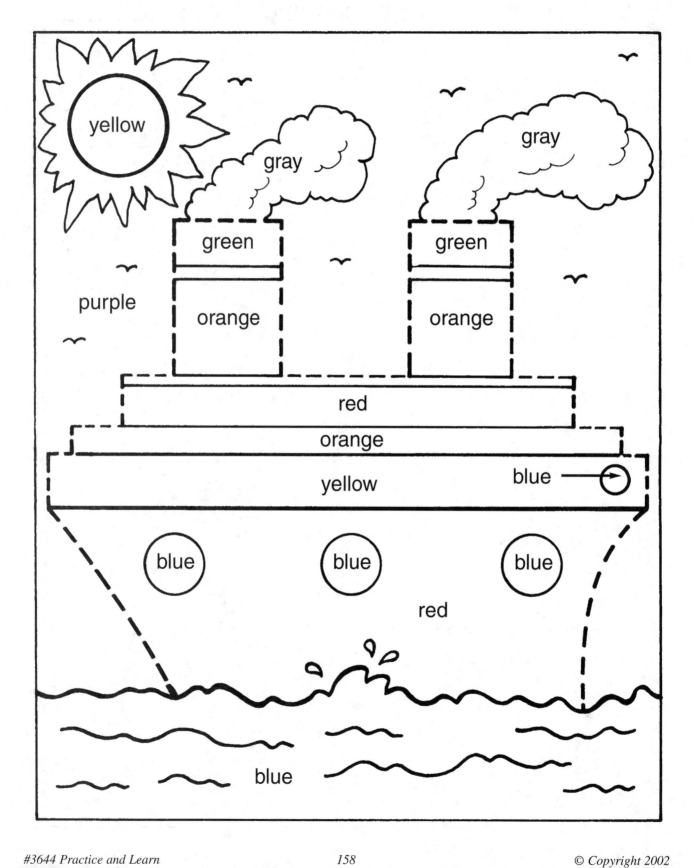

Somersaults

Color the picture.

The Fruit Tree

Color the fruit using the color code.

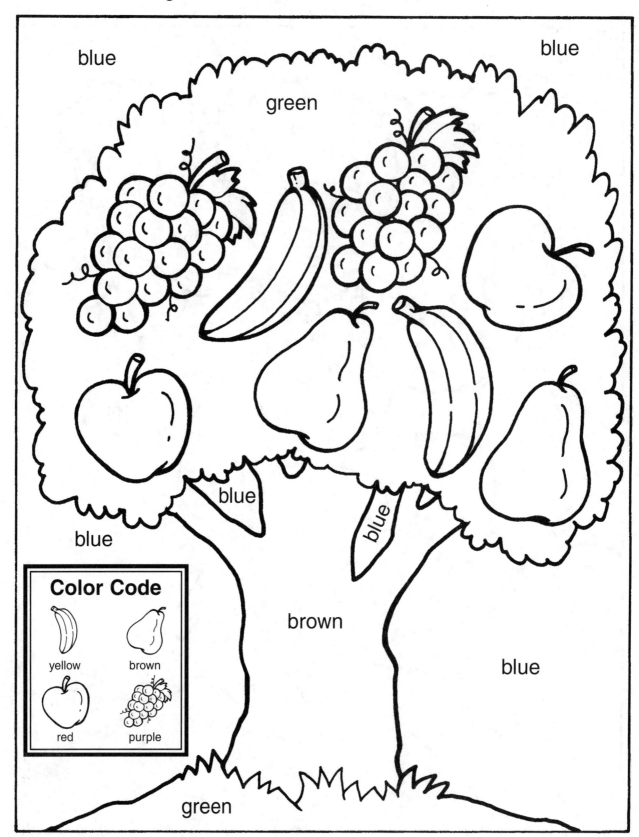

Cat and Mouse

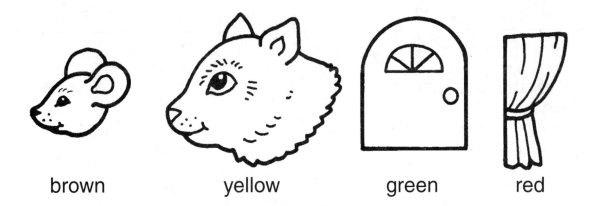

brown   yellow   green   red

1. Color the objects above.

2. Color the objects in the picture below the same as above.

Hang Up Your Clothes

1. Color the dress pink.

2. Color the pants blue.

3. Color the shirt green.

4. Color the shoe brown.

5. Color the hat purple.

6. Color the sock red.

7. Color the blouse yellow.

8. Color the vest orange.

shirt

pants

sock

vest

shoe

dress

hat

blouse

Let's Make a Hamburger

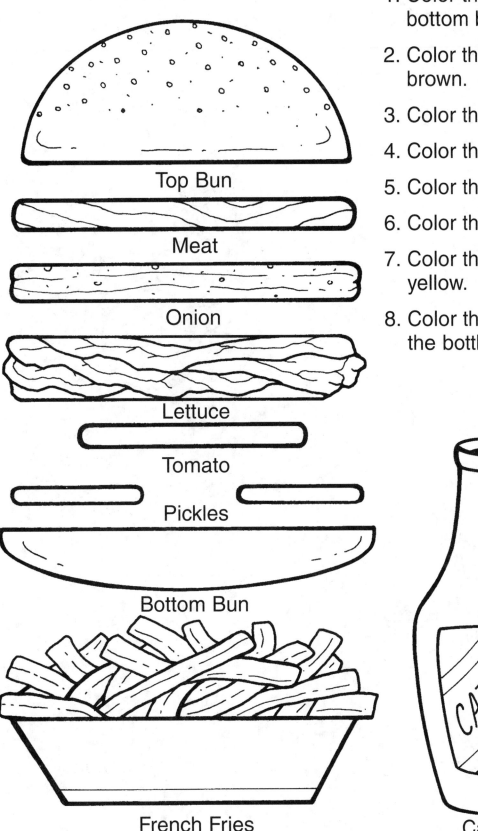

Top Bun

Meat

Onion

Lettuce

Tomato

Pickles

Bottom Bun

French Fries

Catsup

1. Color the top bun and bottom bun light brown.

2. Color the meat dark brown.

3. Color the onion purple.

4. Color the pickles green.

5. Color the tomato red.

6. Color the lettuce green.

7. Color the french fries yellow.

8. Color the catsup, inside the bottle, red.

Strike Up the Band

Trace each outlined shape with a finger, then trace it with a crayon.
Name each shape and the instrument. Color the picture.

Shape Tracing

First, use your finger to trace the shapes. Then use a crayon.

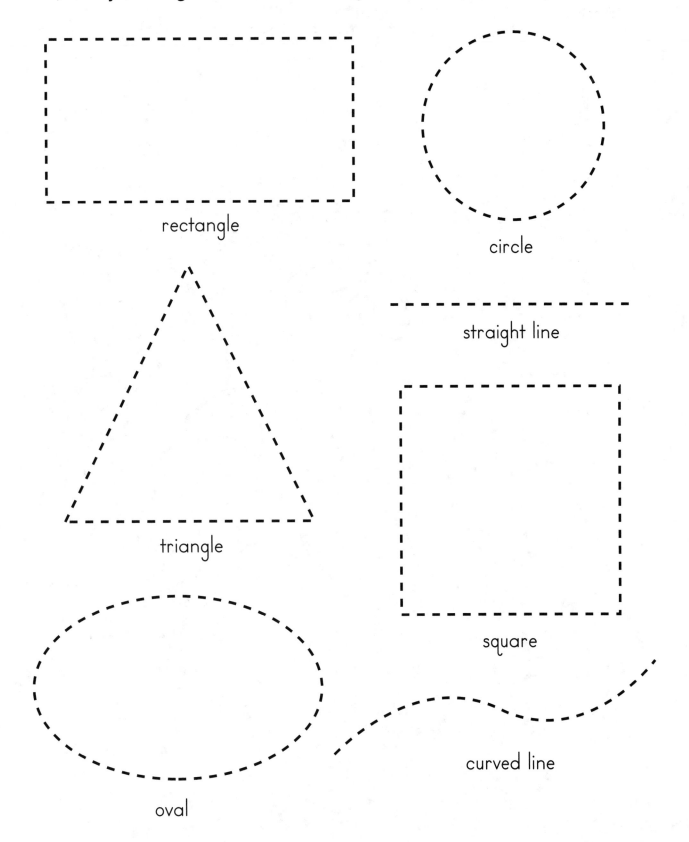

rectangle

circle

straight line

triangle

square

oval

curved line

Shape Master—Clown

Find the hidden shapes in the picture of the clown.

Color all the circles red. Color all the squares green. Color all the triangles yellow.

Shapes and Colors

Color the ☐ 's yellow.

Color the ⬭ 's purple.

Color the ◇ 's orange

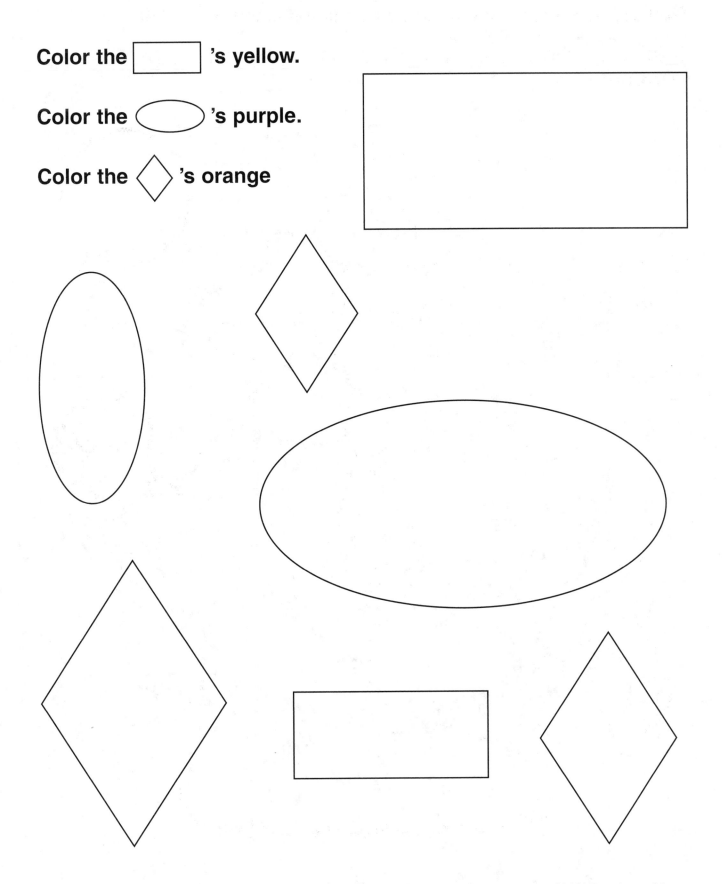

Shapes Clown

Color each shape at the top the correct color. Then color each shape on the picture to match.

Color all the: △ red   ▭ green

◯ yellow   ◇ blue

Find the Shape

Color the matching shape. Name each shape.

Color by Shapes

 Follow the shapes to color the picture.

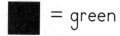 = green   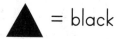 = black    = blue   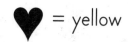 = yellow

More Color by Shapes

 Follow the shapes to color the picture.

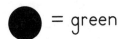 = green   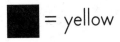 = yellow   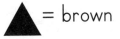 = brown   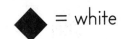 = white

         #3644 Practice and Learn

Shape Names

 Draw a line to match each shape to its name. Color the shapes green.

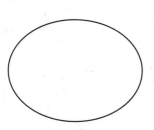

rectangle

heart

diamond

oval

star

square

triangle

circle

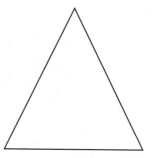

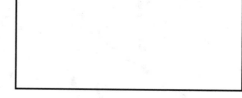

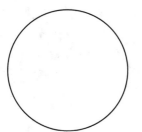

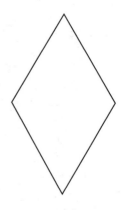

Naming Shapes

 Trace the name under each shape.

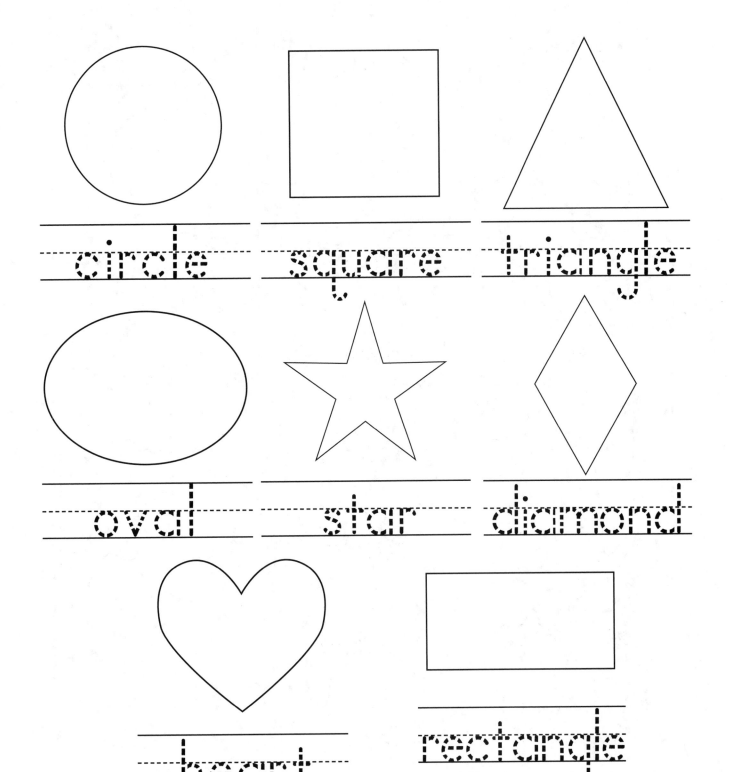

circle

square

triangle

oval

star

diamond

heart

rectangle

Bears on Parade

The bears are on parade today. Some of them have lost their numbers.
Help them get in order by writing the correct number under each one.

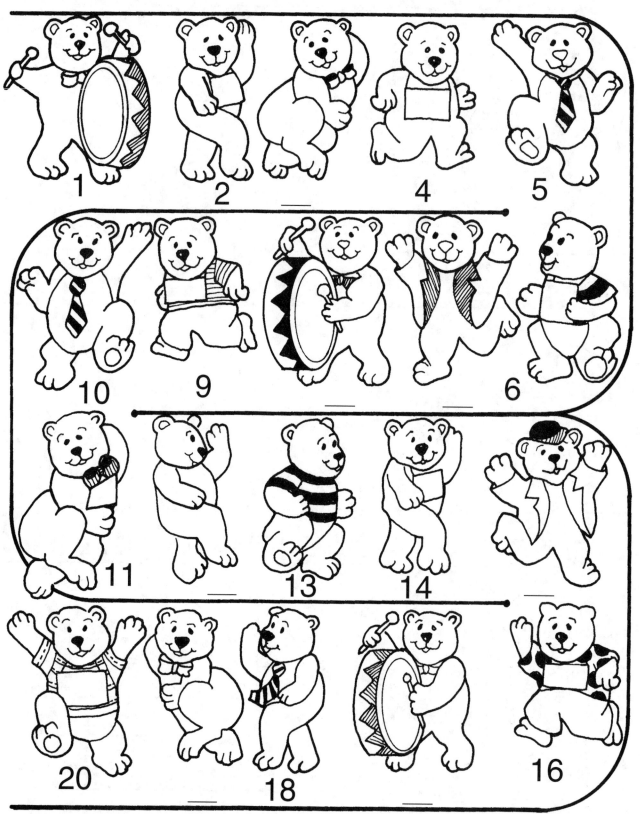

1 2 ___ 4 5

10 9 ___ ___ 6

11 ___ 13 14 ___

20 ___ 18 ___ 16

174

Slow and Easy Wins

To find out who won the race, connect the dots from 1-12. Color the picture.

Dot-to-Dot Number Bear

Follow the dots fo finish the picture.

Another Dot-to-Dot Number Bear

Follow the numbers to finish the picture.

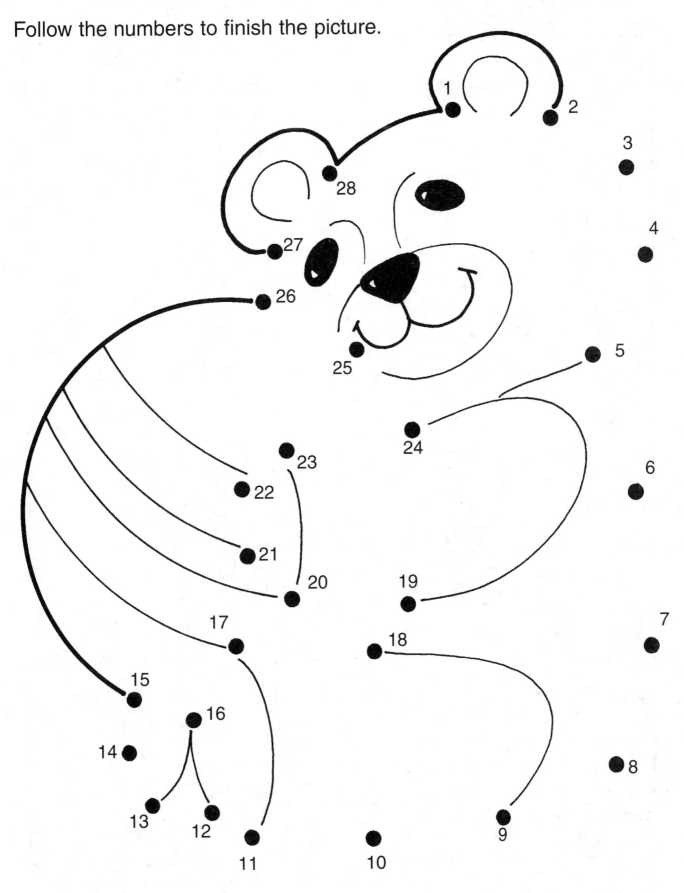

Color by Number

1 blue

2 green

3 red

4 yellow

5 orange

6 gray

Priscilla Peacock

Color key:

1 = red

2 = blue

3 = yellow

4 = green

5 = purple

6 = orange

7 = brown

8 = black

By the Number

Color this picture by using the numbers and colors in the chart.

Color by Number

number	color to use
1	green
2	blue

number	color to use
3	gray
4	brown

Painting the Clubhouse

Color by numbers.

Color key
1 = red
2 = green
3 = blue
4 = yellow
5 = black
6 = brown

Balloon Match

Draw a line from each balloon to its matching number.

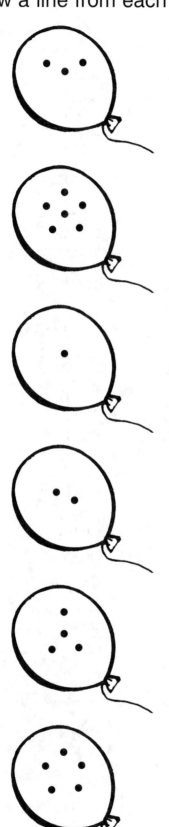

5

| 2 |

| 3 |

| 6 |

| 1 |

| 4 |

Counting 1-5

Count the number of things on each shelf of the food cart. Draw a line to the numeral that matches. Color the picture.

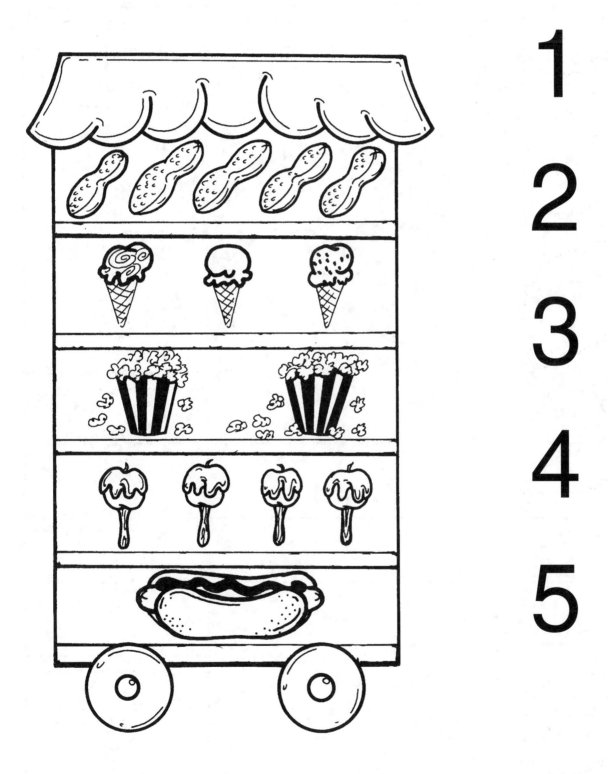

1

2

3

4

5

Team Numbers

The cats play ball with the dogs.

Draw "X's" to show how many.

🐱 _____

🐶 _____

⚽ _____

🥅 _____

🌼 _____

0—Zero

O

O

zero

zero

1–One

one

one

2–Two

2

2

two

two

3-Three

3

3

three

three

4–Four

4

4

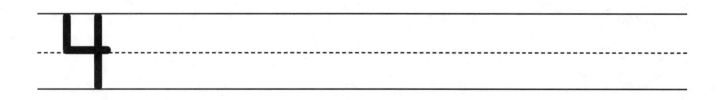

four

four

5–Five

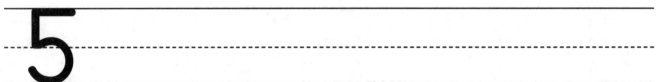

5

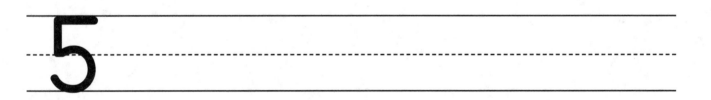

5

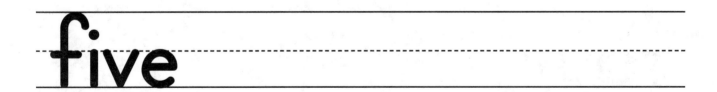

five

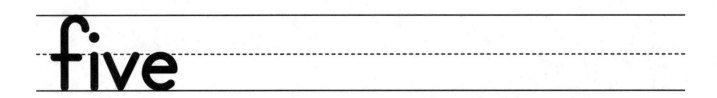

five

6—Six

6

6

six

six

7–Seven

7

7

seven

seven

8-Eight

8

8

eight

eight

9—Nine

q

q

nine

nine

10–Ten

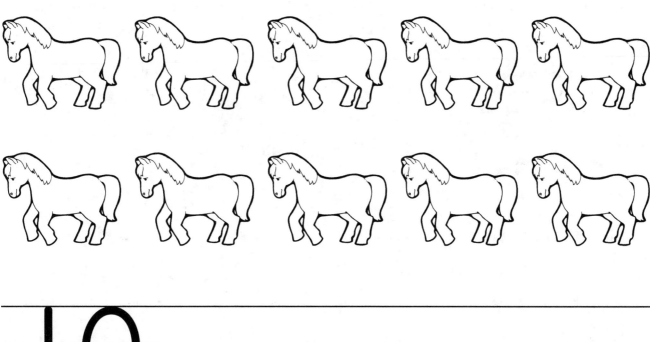

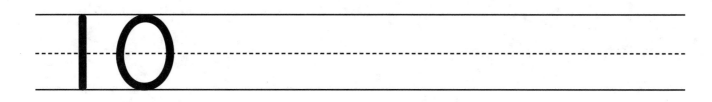

Zero in on Zero

Circle the dog with 0 spots.

Circle the cat with 0 stripes.

How many stripes
on the dog? _____

How many spots
on the cat? _____

How Many Berries?

Count the berries in the pail.

Write the number under the pail.

Color.

a.

_____

b.
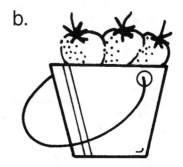

_____

c.

_____

d.

_____

e.

_____

f.

_____

How Many?

Count how many items are in each box. Write the number on the line.

a. _____

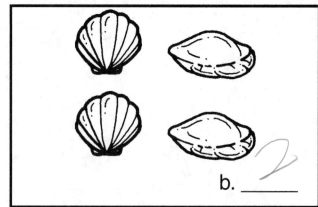

b. _____

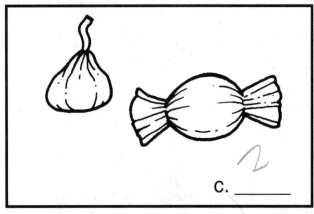

c. _____

d. _____

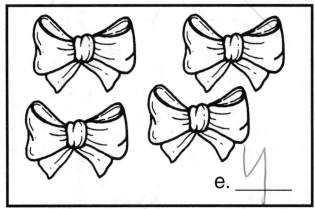

e. _____

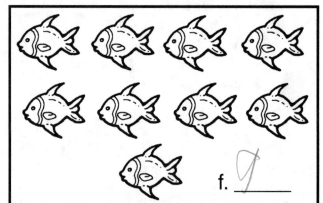

f. _____

g. _____

h. _____

Count the Library Books

Directions: Count the library books in each row. Then write the number in the box.

Count the Objects

Directions: Count the objects. Write the correct number in each box.

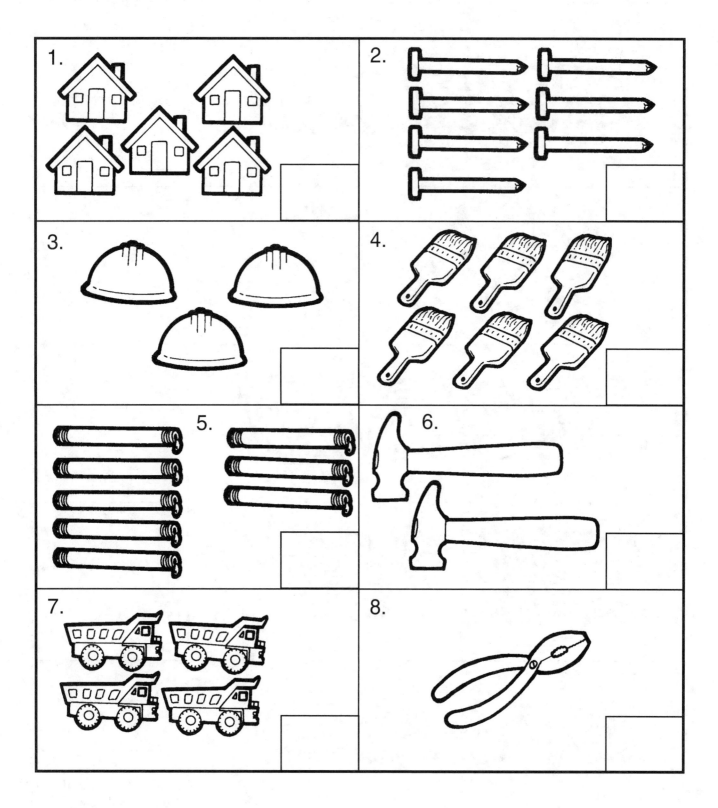

How Many Are There?

Directions: Write the correct numeral in each box.

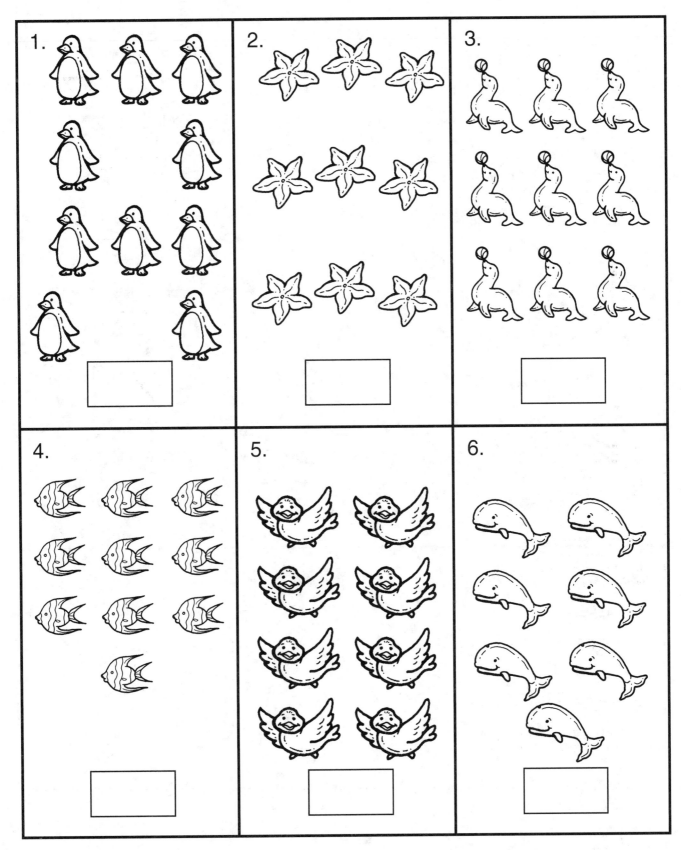

Beach Bears

Circle the numeral that tells how many.

	1	2	3			3	4	5
	2	3	4			2	3	4
	3	4	5			3	4	5
	1	2	3			1	2	3
	1	2	3			0	1	2

Coloring Fun

Color 3 stars yellow.

Color 2 balls red.

Color 1 bell blue.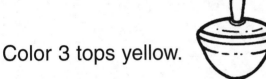

Color 3 tops yellow.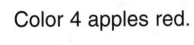

Color 4 apples red.

Color 5 hats blue.

1. How many things are yellow? _____ stars   + _____ tops = _____

2. How many things are red? _____ apples + _____ balls = _____

3. How many things are blue? _____ bell   + _____ hats = _____

Number Names

Match the names to the numbers.

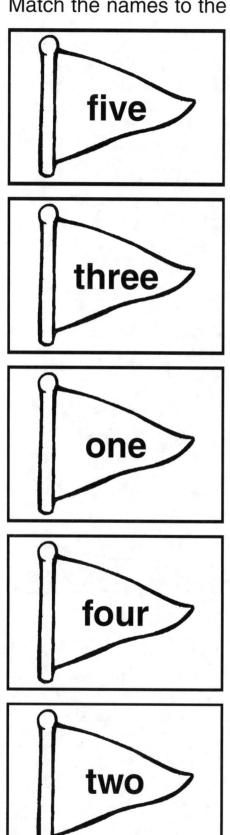

How Many Bees?

1. Count the bees.

2. Write the number in the box at the bottom of the page.

3. Color.

How many bees?

Snowflakes

1. Count the snowflakes.

2. Write the number in the box at the bottom of the page.

3. Color.

How many snowflakes?

Counting People

1. Count the people on or near the bus.
2. Write the number in the box.

Gingerbread House

Write the numerals from 1 to 100.

1	2	3				7	8	9	
11			14	15	16	17		19	20
21				25		27	28	29	30
31		33	34		36			39	
41		43			46	47		49	50
	52	53		55		57		59	
61	62		64		66		68		70
71		73	74		76	77		79	80
81		83			86		88	89	90
91		93	94			96	98		100

Draw It

1. Draw the pictures.
2. Color.

Snowmen

Draw buttons on the snowmen. Use the number to tell you how many buttons to draw.

Apple Trees

Draw apples on the trees. Use the number on the tree to tell you how many apples to draw.

Flying High

Draw bows on the kite strings. Use the number in the box to tell you how many bows to draw.

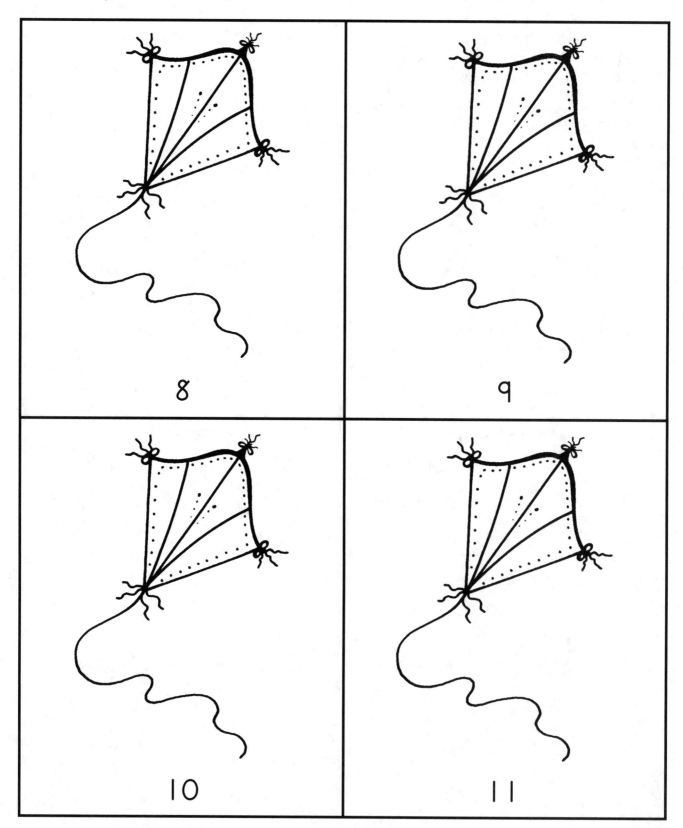

Which Has Fewer?

Circle the group that has fewer things in it.

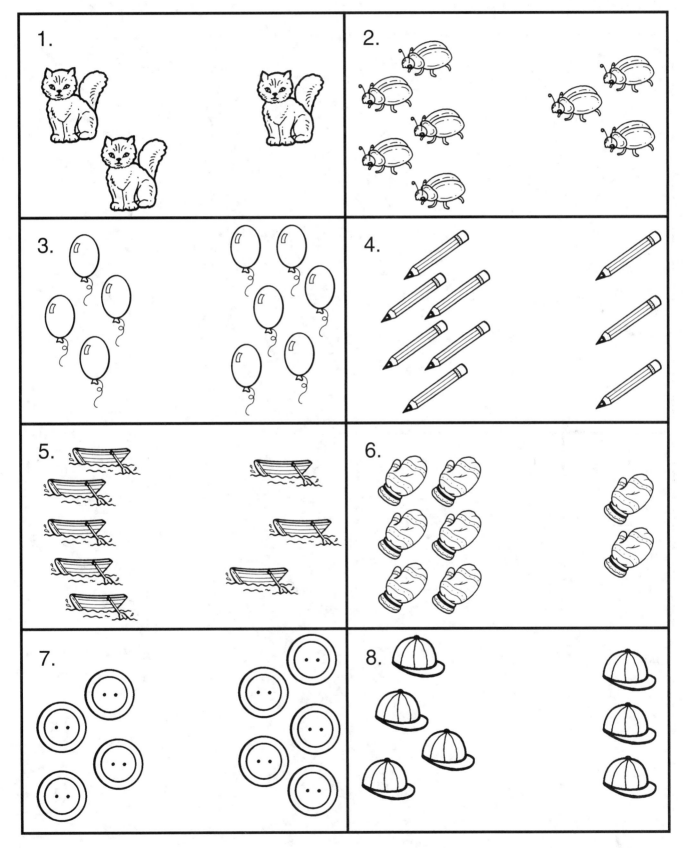

Which Has More?

Circle the group that has more things in it.

1.

2.

3.

4.

5.

6.

7.

8.

Matching Numbers

Draw a line to match the same numbers.

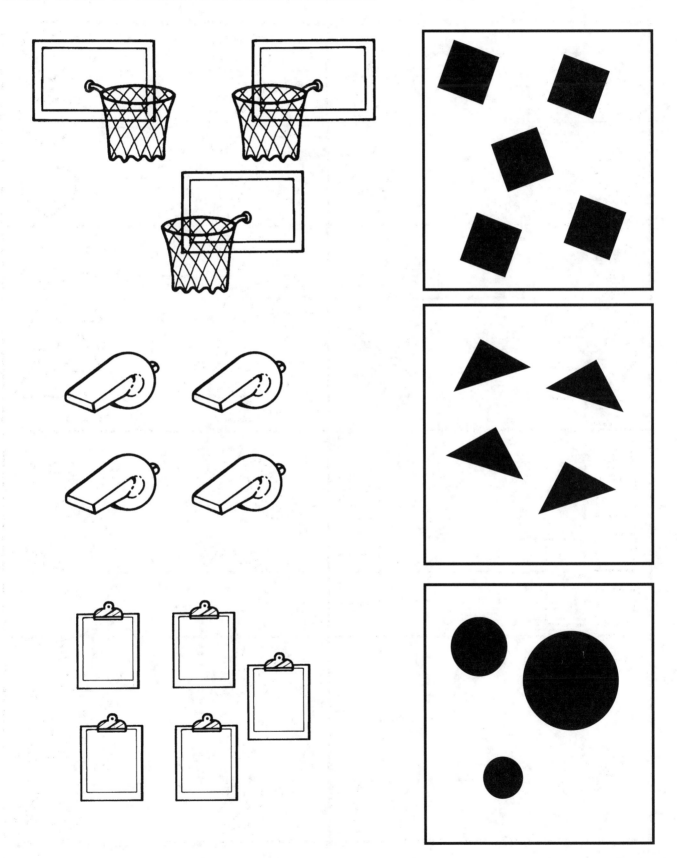

Same Numbers

Color the same number of shapes.

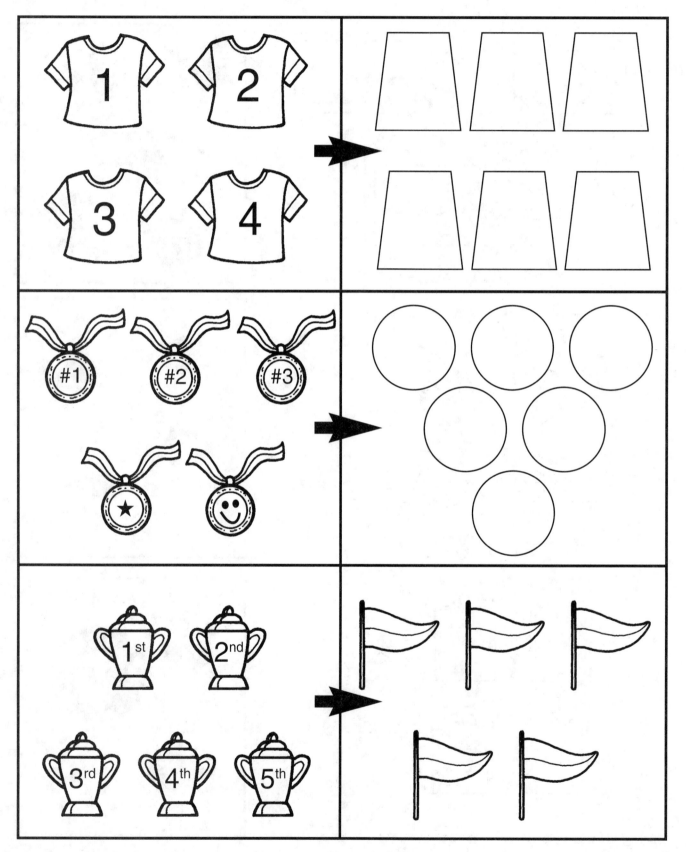

Equal Groups

Draw a line between the groups that have the same number of items in them.

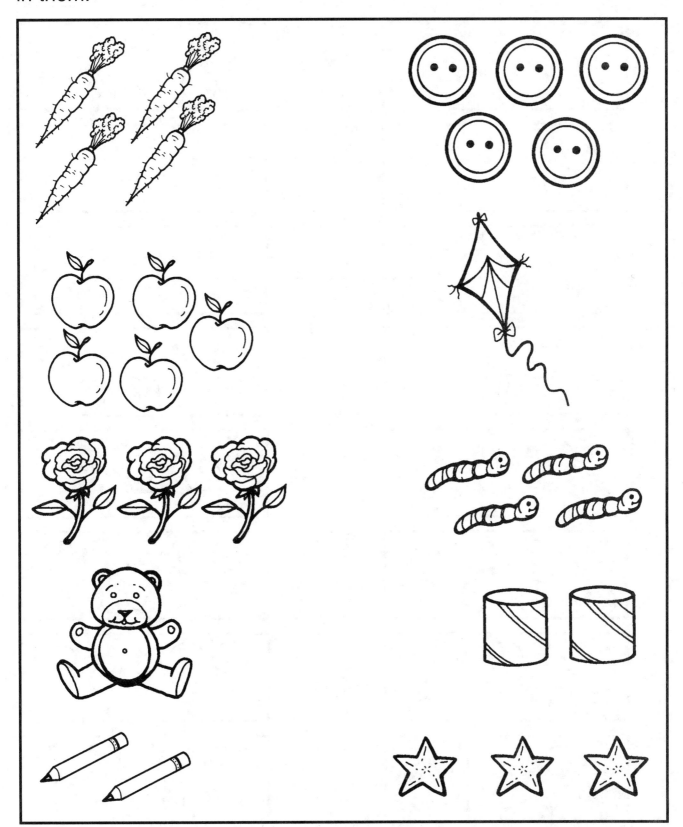

Matching Groups

Match sets that have the same number in them. Draw a line to equal groups.

1.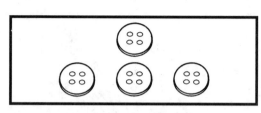

2.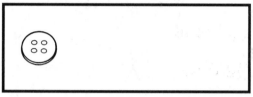

3.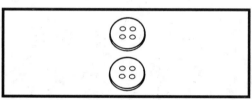

4.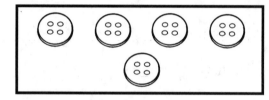

5.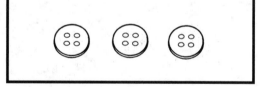

6.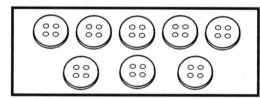

7.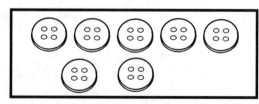

8.

Estimating in the Garden

Estimate how many are in each group. Write your estimate. Then count the items in each group. Write the true number.

1.

Estimate _____

Number _____

2.

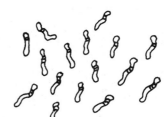

Estimate _____

Number _____

3.

Estimate _____

Number _____

4.

Estimate _____

Number _____

5.

Estimate _____

Number _____

6.

Estimate _____

Number _____

7.

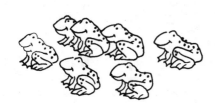

Estimate _____

Number _____

8.

Estimate _____

Number _____

Shortest

Directions: Color the shortest object in each row.

Longest

Directions: Color the longest object in each row.

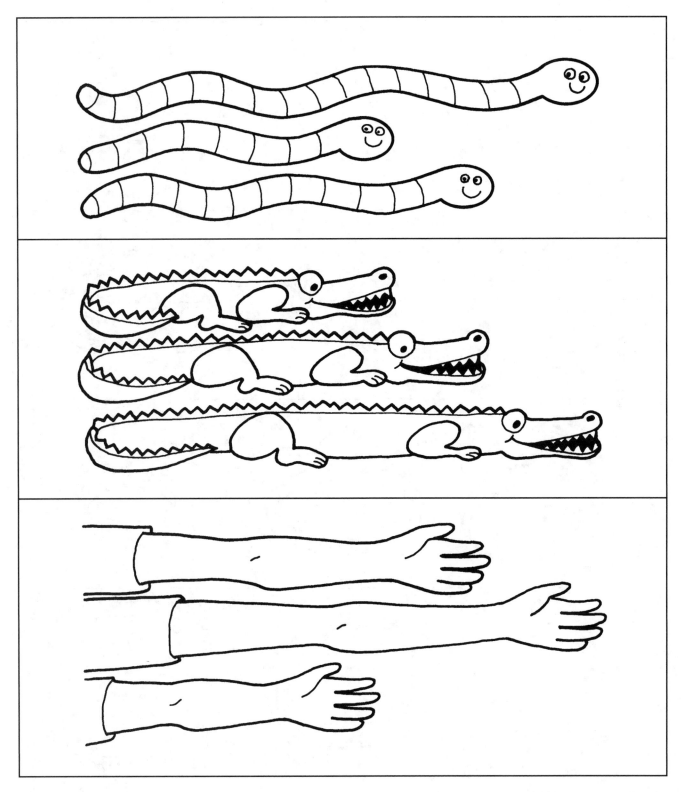

Smallest

Directions: Color the smallest object in each row.

Biggest

Directions: Color the biggest object in each row.

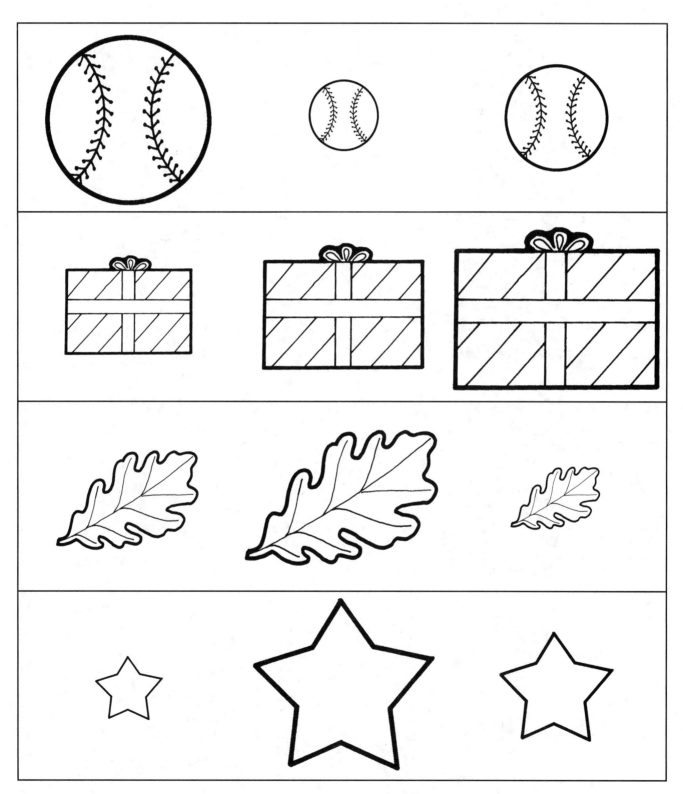

Matching Sizes

Match like big and small pictures. Color.

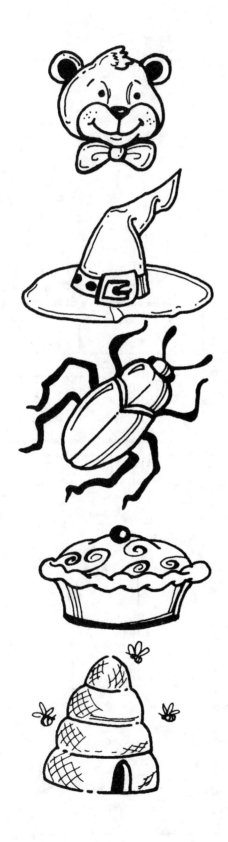

Turkeys

Draw a line to match the turkeys that are the same size.

What Comes Next?

Draw the next thing in each series.

1.

2.

3.

4.

5.

Colorful Beads

Continue each pattern.

Color the beads.

1. — blue — green — blue — green — blue — ◯

2. — orange — purple — orange — purple — orange — ◯

3. — red — red — blue — red — red — ◯

4. — black — white — black — white — ◯ — ◯

5. — brown — yellow — yellow — brown — yellow — ◯

6. — red — blue — blue — red — blue — ◯

Patterns with Letters and Numbers

Write the next letter or number in each series.

1. A B A B A B A B _____

2. A A B A A B A A _____

3. A B B A B B A B _____

4. 1 2 1 2 1 2 1 _____

5. X X X Y X X X Y X X X _____

6. 1 2 2 1 2 2 1 2 _____

7. A B C A B C A B _____

Patterning

Continue each pattern by drawing what comes next.

1.  ____ ____ ____

2.  ____ ____ ____

3.  ____ ____ ____

4.  ____ ____ ____

5.  ____ ____ ____

6. ____ ____ ____

Morning or Evening

Circle the word **morning** or **evening** to tell when you do each activity below.

1.

| morning   evening |

2.

| morning   evening |

3.

| morning   evening |

4.

| morning   evening |

5.

| morning   evening |

6.

| morning   evening |

Day or Night

Draw a picture of something you do during the day. Draw a picture of something you do at night.

Day	Night

Time Match

Match each clock to the written time by drawing a line.

1.    **3:00**

2.    **8:00**

3.    **5:00**

4.    **1:00**

5.    **11:00**

6.    **12:00**

Telling Time

Write the correct time under each clock. Use the bank to help you write the time correctly.

Bank					
2:00	10:00	4:00	7:00	6:00	9:00

1.

_____

2.

_____

3.

_____

4.

_____

5.
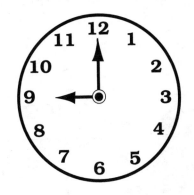

_____

6.

_____

Months of the Year

Write the names of the months on the lines.

January

February

March

April

May

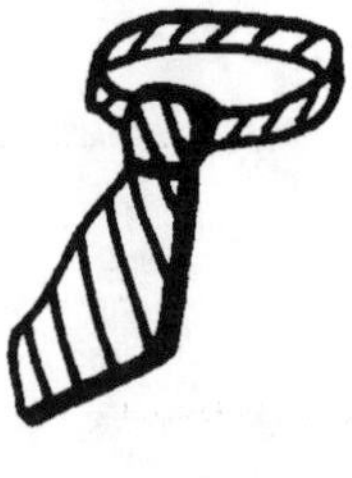

June

July

August

September

October

November

December

Rabbit Hop

Count forward to add. Put the rabbit forward two jumps on each number line. Write the number where he stops.

1.

2 + 2 = _____

```
0   1   2   3   4   5   6
|___|___|___|___|___|___|
```

2.

1 + 2 = _____

```
0   1   2   3   4   5   6
|___|___|___|___|___|___|
```

3.

3 + 2 = _____

```
0   1   2   3   4   5   6
|___|___|___|___|___|___|
```

4.

4 + 2 = _____

```
0   1   2   3   4   5   6
|___|___|___|___|___|___|
```

5.

0 + 2 = _____

```
0   1   2   3   4   5   6
|___|___|___|___|___|___|
```

School "Stuff"

Write the sums.

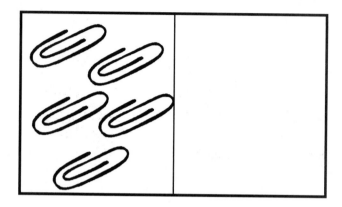

1. 5 + 0 = ____

2. 1 + 3 = ____

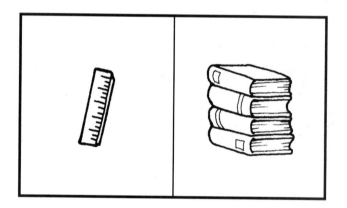

3. 1 + 4 = ____

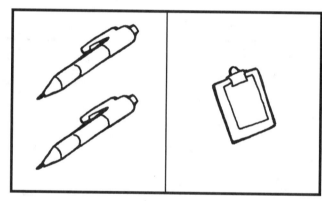

4. 2 + 2 = ____

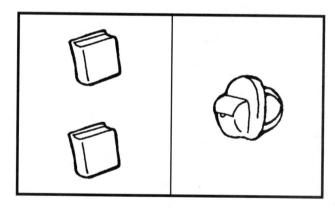

5. 2 + 1 = ____

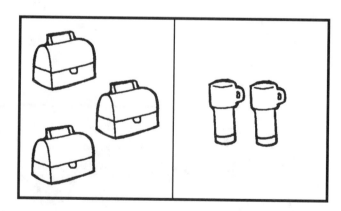

6. 3 + 2 = ____

It's Recess

Write the addition number sentences.

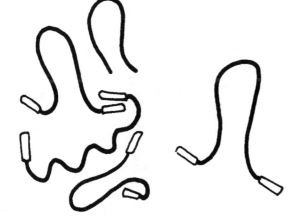
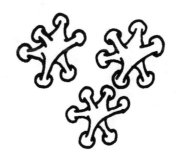

1. $\underline{4} + \underline{1} = \underline{5}$ 2. $\underline{} + \underline{} = \underline{}$

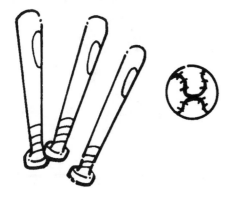
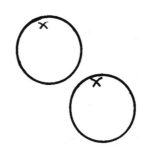

3. $\underline{} + \underline{} = \underline{}$ 4. $\underline{} + \underline{} = \underline{}$

5. $\underline{} + \underline{} = \underline{}$

Everything Counts!

Count the things in each box. Write the number sentence that tells how many in all.

1.

$$\underline{\ 2\ } + \underline{\ 3\ } = \underline{\ \ \ \ }$$

2.

$$\underline{\ \ \ \ } + \underline{\ \ \ \ } = \underline{\ \ \ \ }$$

3.

$$\underline{\ \ \ \ } + \underline{\ \ \ \ } = \underline{\ \ \ \ }$$

Add It Up!

Count the things in each box. Write the addition problems.

a.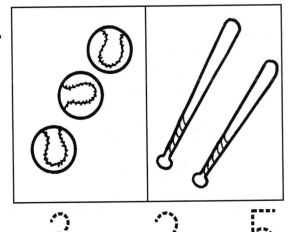

$$\underline{3} + \underline{2} = \underline{5}$$

b.

_____ + _____ = _____

c.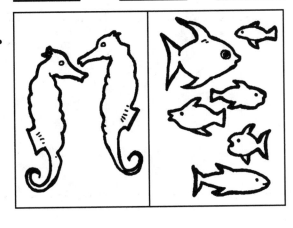

_____ + _____ = _____

d.

_____ + _____ = _____

e.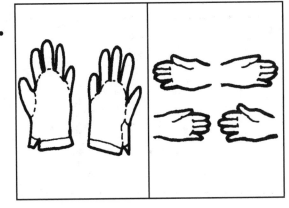

_____ + _____ = _____

f.

_____ + _____ = _____

More Add It Up!

Count the things in each box. Write the addition problems.

a.

$\vdots$ + 3 = ___

b.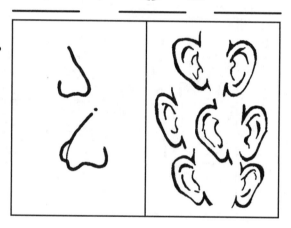

___ + ___ = ___

c.

___ + ___ = ___

d.

___ + ___ = ___

e.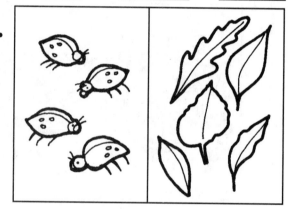

___ + ___ = ___

f.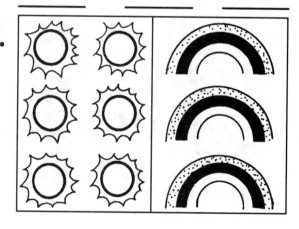

___ + ___ = ___

Addition

Count the things in each box. Write the addition problems.

a.

$$2 \;+\; 2 \;=\; \underline{\hspace{2cm}}$$

d.

$$\underline{\hspace{1.5cm}} \;+\; \underline{\hspace{1.5cm}} \;=\; \underline{\hspace{1.5cm}}$$

b.
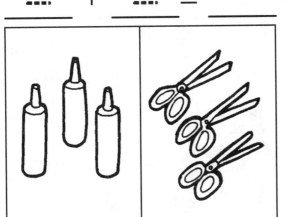

$$\underline{\hspace{1.5cm}} \;+\; \underline{\hspace{1.5cm}} \;=\; \underline{\hspace{1.5cm}}$$

e.

$$\underline{\hspace{1.5cm}} \;+\; \underline{\hspace{1.5cm}} \;=\; \underline{\hspace{1.5cm}}$$

c.
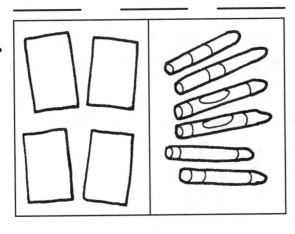

f.
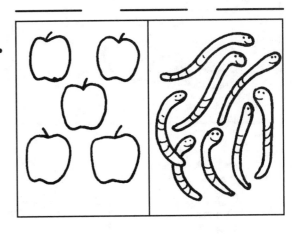

$$\underline{\hspace{1.5cm}} \;+\; \underline{\hspace{1.5cm}} \;=\; \underline{\hspace{1.5cm}}$$

$$\underline{\hspace{1.5cm}} \;+\; \underline{\hspace{1.5cm}} \;=\; \underline{\hspace{1.5cm}}$$

Adding One

Write the sums.

Bear Puzzle Math

1. Add.

2. Write the numeral.

3. Color using the color code.

4. Cut the pieces out and make a bear.

Color code			
brown	4	yellow	3
blue	2	red	1

Sailboats on the Sea

Write an addition number sentence to go with each set of pictures.

1. _____ + _____ = _____

2. _____ + _____ = _____

3. _____ + _____ = _____

Sun Catcher

Add.

Color the picture using the key.

Color Key	
4 = yellow	6 = red
7 = orange	12 = purple

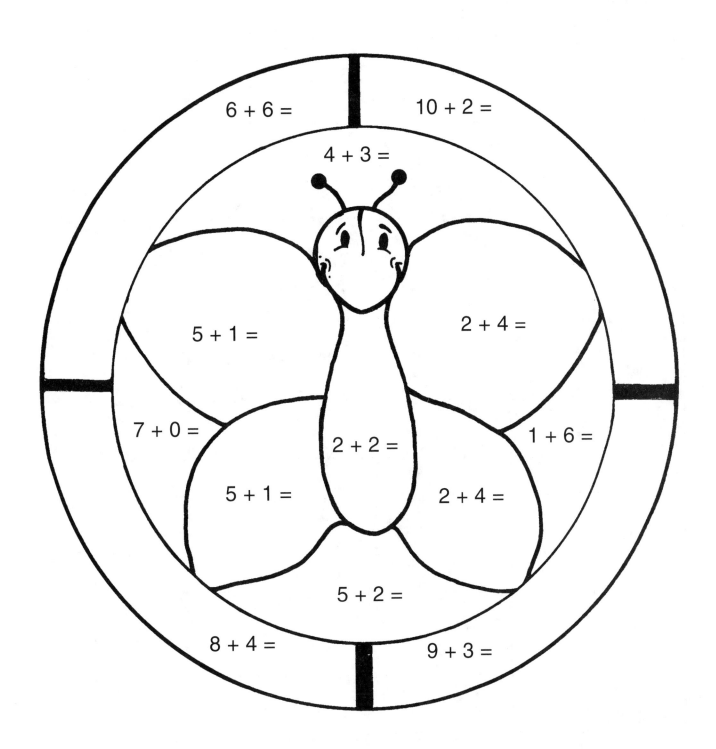

6 + 6 =

10 + 2 =

4 + 3 =

5 + 1 =

2 + 4 =

7 + 0 =

2 + 2 =

1 + 6 =

5 + 1 =

2 + 4 =

5 + 2 =

8 + 4 =

9 + 3 =

Circle the Number Words

Find the sum of the number pairs. Then circle the number words hidden in the letter maze. The words are written across.

Example: 0 + 0 = 0

3 + 2 = _____   8 + 3 = _____   5 + 4 = _____   4 + 3 = _____

2 + 1 = _____   5 + 1 = _____   6 + 6 = _____   6 + 2 = _____

1 + 0 = _____   9 + 1 = _____   1 + 1 = _____   3 + 1 = _____

zero
one
two
three
four
five
six
seven
eight
nine
ten
eleven
twelve

s	e	v	e	n	o	n	e
w	e	l	e	v	e	n	z
l	v	t	w	e	l	v	e
t	e	n	i	n	e	s	i
f	o	u	r	z	e	r	o
e	i	g	h	t	w	o	g
l	f	i	v	e	s	i	x
h	t	h	r	e	e	f	n

Subtraction in Action

a. Cross out 4 sandwiches.	b. Cross out 2 peanuts.	c. Cross out 1 pineapple.

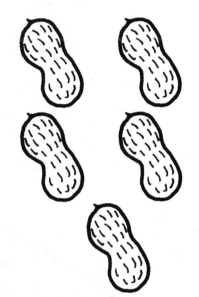

How many are left?____ | How many are left?____ | How many are left?____

d. Cross out 5 worms.	e. Cross out 3 shells.	f. Cross out 0 clocks.

How many are left?____ | How many are left?____ | How many are left?____

#3644 Practice and Learn

Wake Up, Sleepyhead!

Write how many are left.

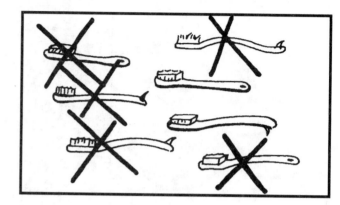

1.   6 – 2 = __

2.   7 – 5 = __

3.   8 – 3 = __

4.   6 – 1 = __

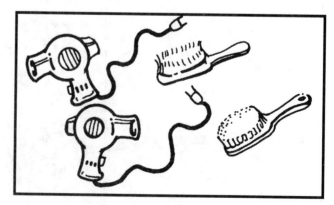

5.   5 – 1 = __

6.   4 – 0 = __

Subtraction

Use the pictures to solve these problems.

a.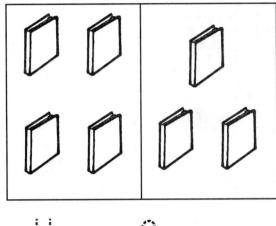

b.

4 - 3 = ____

____ - ____ = ____

c.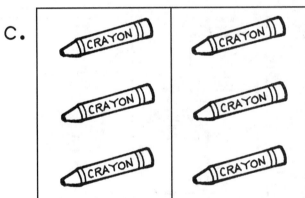

d.

____ - ____ = ____

____ - ____ = ____

e.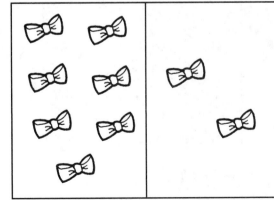

f.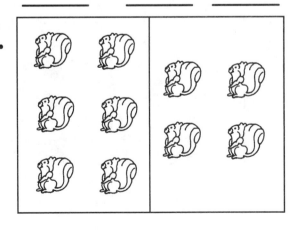

____ - ____ = ____

____ - ____ = ____

More Subtraction

Use the pictures to solve these problems.

a.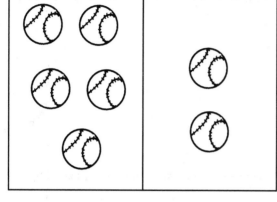

$$\underline{} 5 - \underline{} 2 = \underline{}$$

b.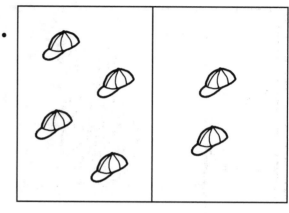

$$\underline{} - \underline{} = \underline{}$$

c.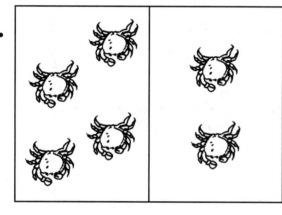

$$\underline{} - \underline{} = \underline{}$$

d.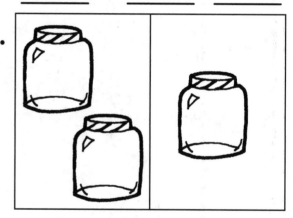

$$\underline{} - \underline{} = \underline{}$$

e.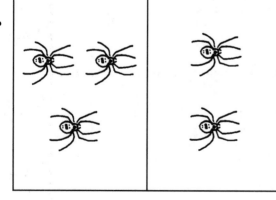

$$\underline{} - \underline{} = \underline{}$$

f.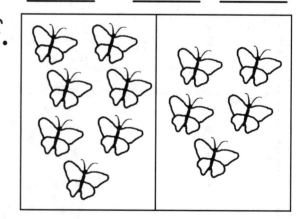

$$\underline{} - \underline{} = \underline{}$$

Walking a Tightrope

Trace each line with your finger, then a crayon.

Lost Mittens

1. Help each kitten find his mitten.

2. Trace the lines.

3. Color.

Bears and Buttons

Trace the lines from the buttons to the bears.

Write the number of the button on the line below the bear.

1　　2　　3　　4

Going to the Circus

Trace the path with your finger, then a crayon.

Maze

Help Officer Flossy catch Dingo Dog!

1. Follow the road with your pencil.   3. Color Officer Flossy blue.

2. Color Goldbug yellow.   4. Color Dingo Dog green.

Officer Flossy

Dingo Dog

Find the Ballerina

Help the soldier find the ballerina.

Color.

Find Your Way Home

Directions: Draw a line to help Poinsettia find her way home. Do not cross any lines.

Matching Parts

Color the first picture in each row. Color the other picture in the row that matches the part to the whole.

Wholes and Parts

Draw a line from the wholes to the parts. Color.

Hooves and Paws

Match the animal faces and feet. Color the pictures.

1.

A.

2.

B.

3.

C.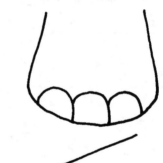

4.

D.

5.

E.

Make It Good As New

1. Fix these by drawing their missing parts.
2. Trace the words.

teddy bear

wagon

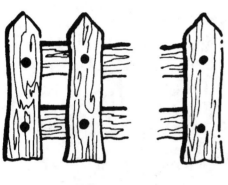

fence

fire engine

sandbox

swing

What's Missing?

Draw in the missing part of each picture from these things that go.

Car	Wagon
Wheel barrow	Bike
Ice skates	Airplane

Shadows

Draw a line from the object to the shadow.

Color the picture.

Matching Mittens

Draw lines to match each pair of mittens. Color the mittens. Use the same color for each pair.

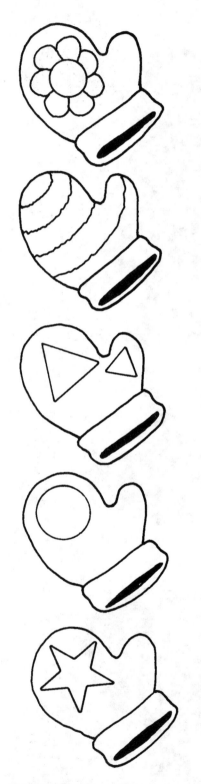

Challenge: Can you draw a matching hat for one pair of mittens?

Clothes Matching

Match the shirt to the hat.

Belonging

Can you tell which children belong to which parents? Color matching patterns the same color.

Down on My Tummy

Match the like seashells. Color.

Clown Clothes

Color the things a clown would wear.

Circus Act

Name the things in each ring. Then put an X on the one that doesn't belong. Tell why it doesn't belong.

Animals

Color the animals. Name the animals.

All Set?

Circle the things which belong in each set.

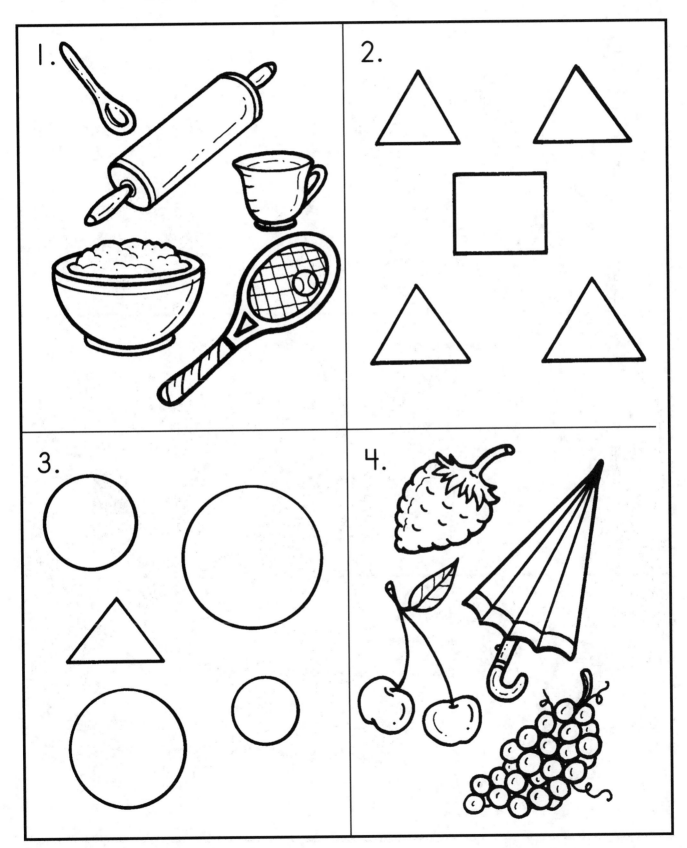

Which Belongs?

Circle things which belong in each set. Cross out things which do not belong.

Go Togethers

Match the things that go together. Draw lines to connect them.

What Goes Together?

Match the things that go together. Color the pictures.

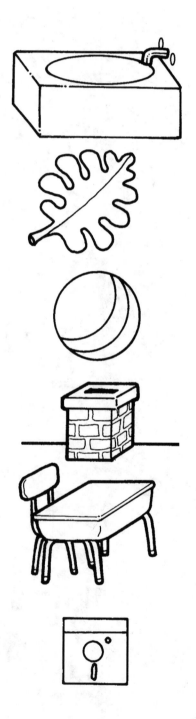

Make a Set

Match the things that go together. Color the pictures.

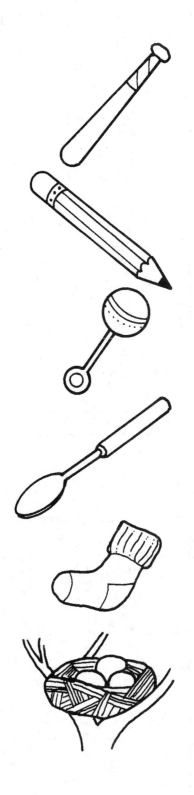

What Am I?

Color, cut, and glue pictures in the correct group.

people	animals
plants	**fish**

What Do We Wear?

Color everything that a person might wear.

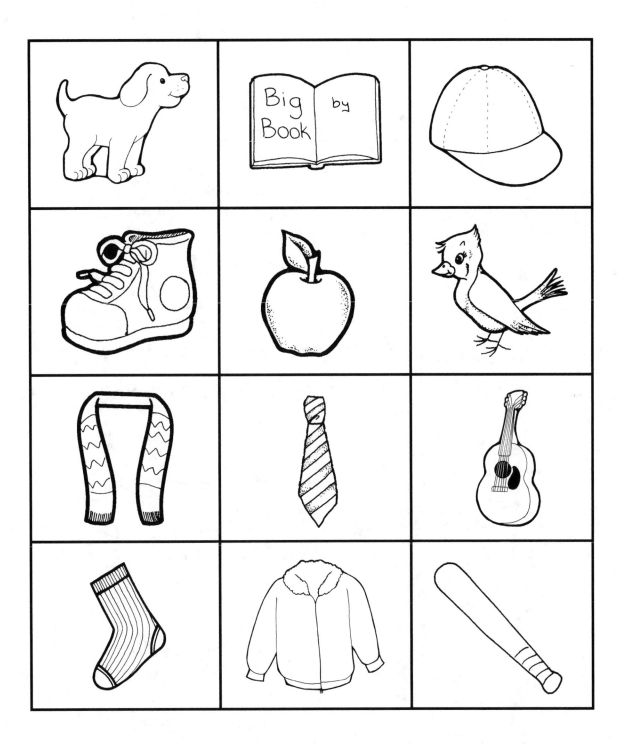

Can you find the opposites?

Circle the correct word and color the picture.

1. big   little

2. big   little

3. in   out

4. in   out

5. over   under

6. over   under

7. on   off

8. on   off

Find the Opposite

Look at the first picture in each row. Circle the opposites.

Animal Opposites

Draw a line from the picture on the left to the one on the right that shows the opposite.

Opposites

Draw a line to match the opposites.

1.    up

2.   hot

3.   happy

4.    day

5.    black

6.   full

7.   young

8.    open

sad

white

down

cold

old

night

closed

empty

More Opposites

Draw a line to match the opposites.

1. head
2. big
3. left
4. on
5. laugh
6. fire
7. sit
8. sun

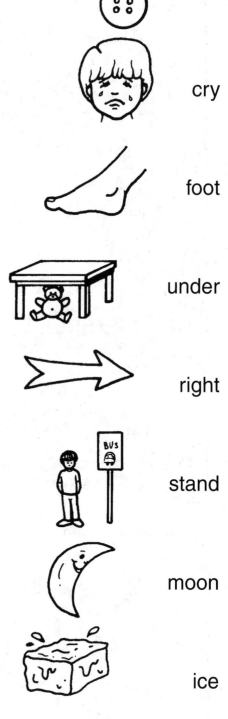

small

cry

foot

under

right

stand

moon

ice

Hidden Hats

1. Find the hidden hats.

2. Circle them and color the picture.

Hide and Go Seek

The teddy bears are playing hide and seek in their room. How many of them can you find? Color them.

Button, Button

How many buttons are in the picture? Color each one you find and count them all. Remember to look for the lost buttons!

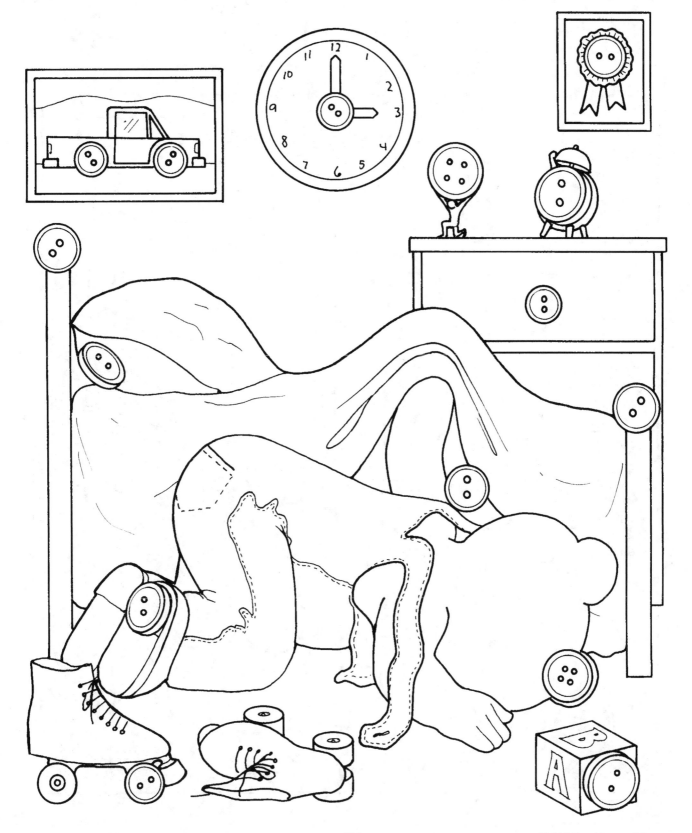

Hidden Pictures

1. Find the hidden pictures.

2. Circle and color the hidden pictures.

pail	spoon
T-shirt	shoe
bird	pie

Papa's Pig Pen

1. Read the letter "p" words in the box below.

2. Circle all the letter "p" pictures above.

3. Color the picture.

pencil	penny	picture	pizza
piggy bank	pie	pitcher	

My Own Zoo

1. Read the letter "z" words in the box below.

2. Circle all the letter "z" pictures above.

3. Color the picture.

zigzag	zoo	zebra	zero
zinnia	zipper	zucchini	

Clowning Around

Color the first clown in each row. Color the clown that is the same.

Which Are the Same?

Directions: Color the pictures in each row that are the same.

Musically the Same

Circle the picture that is different from the first picture in each row.
Color the pictures that are the same.

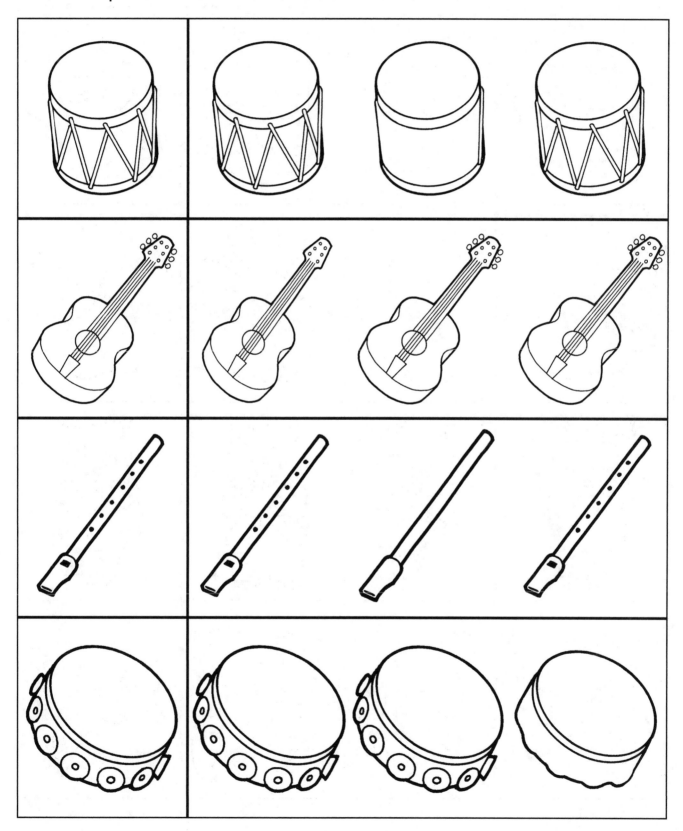

Clothes Match

Look at the first picture in the row. Color the one that is different.

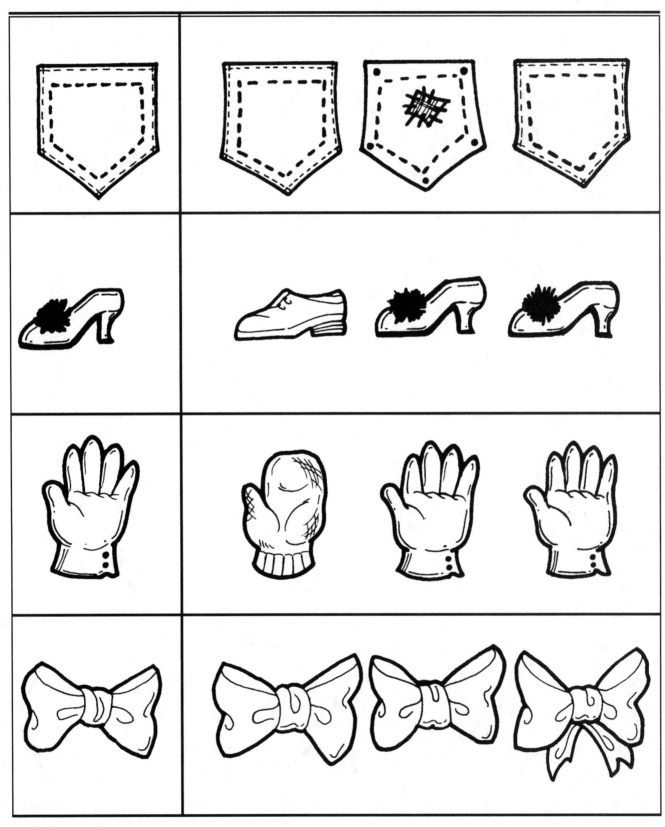

Important Things

1. Color the thing in each row whose number is different.

2. Write the number that is different in the box.

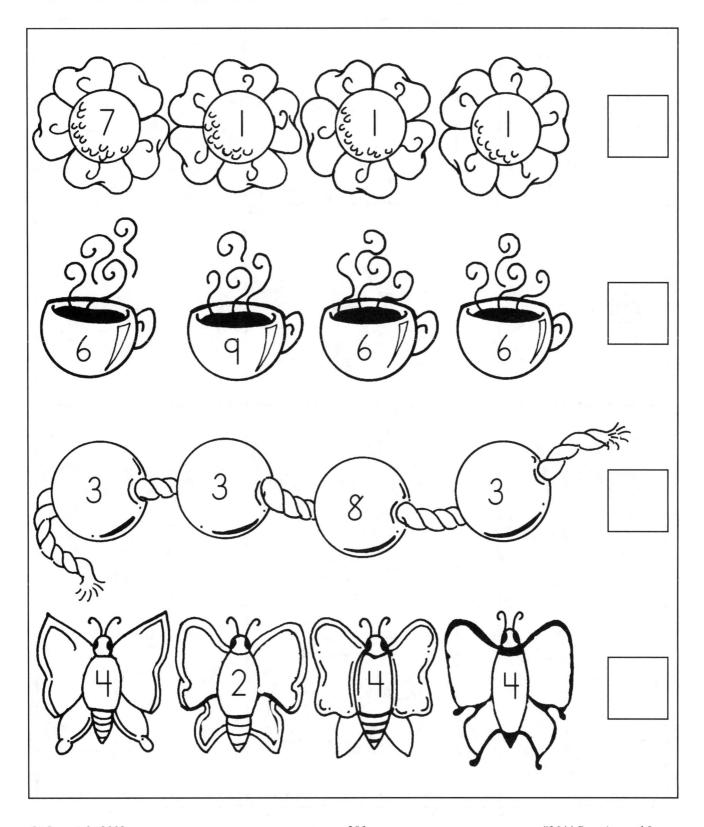

One Is Different

Put an X on the one that is different in each row. Color the ones that are alike.

One Is Different

Put an X on the one that is different in each row. Color the ones that are alike.

Building a Sandcastle

Show the order of the story by writing the numbers 1, 2, 3, and 4 in the correct boxes.

Flying a Kite

Show the order of the story by writing the numbers 1, 2, 3, and 4 in the correct boxes.

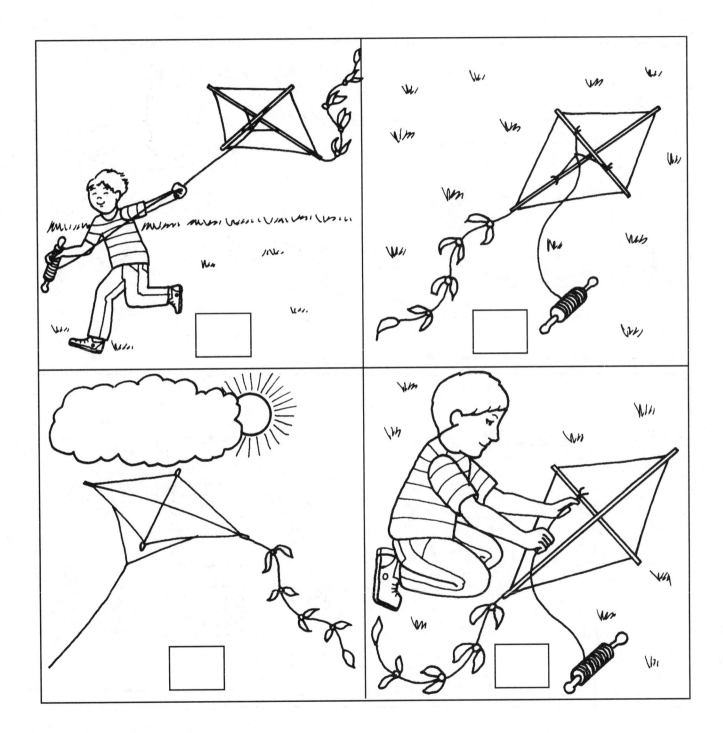

Making a Cake

Show the order of the story by writing the numbers 1, 2, 3, and 4 in the correct boxes.

Answer Key

Page 16 What Comes Next?

1. G	8. Z
2. M	9. O
3. S	10. I
4. Y	11. Z
5. H	12. V
6. N	13. P
7. T	14. J

Page 48 Celebrate the Way "A" Sounds
Color: alligator, ant

Page 49 Celebrate the Way "B" Sounds
Color: bear, blimp, bicycle, baseball, bananas, bird, broom, bubbles, bow, bees, bag, bottles, box, bell, bat, bulb, ball, balloons, buttons

Page 50 Celebrate the Way "C" Sounds
Circle: cat, camel, cow, car
Box: centipede, cereal

Page 52 Celebrate the Way "E" Sounds
egg, eagle, elephant

Page 55 Celebrate the Way "H" Sounds
horse, hippopotamus

Page 58 Celebrate the Way "K" Sounds
koala, kite, king, kiss, kitten

Page 59 Celebrate the Way "L" Sounds
lion, letter, ladder, leopard, lollipop

Page 62 Celebrate the Way "O" Sounds
Circle: octopus, octagon, owl, orangutan, orange, ostrich

Page 65 Celebrate the Way "S" Sounds
Circle: sun, snowman, seal, slide, snake, squirrels

Page 69 Celebrate the Way "X" and "Y" Sound
Box: yawn, yarn, yo-yo

Page 70 Celebrate the Way "Z" Sounds
Color: zebra, zipper, zoo, zig-zag

Page 71 Missing Letters

1. a	2. n	3. p
4. v	5. k	6. c
7. f	8. g	9. b

Page 72 More Missing Letters

1. b	2. f	3. r
4. s	5. d	6. f
7. l	8. v	9. c

Page 73 Ending Sounds

1. r	2. m	3. t
4. d	5. g	6. g
7. p	8. n	9. r

Page 74 More Ending Sounds

1. p	2. p	3. t
4. k	5. n	6. x
7. t	8. n	9. b

Page 75 Missing Vowels

1. i	2. o	3. o
4. a	5. e	6. u
7. a	8. i	9. a

Page 76 More Missing Vowels
1. a 2. e 3. e 4. i 5. i 6. u 7. u 8. u 9. a

Page 77 Sound It Out
1. top 2. leg 3. six 4. box 5. pen 6. fox 7. star 8. hand 9. flag

Page 78 More Sound It Out
1. jar 2. bed 3. ten 4. fan 5. web 6. pin 7. swim 8. drop or tear 9. nest or eggs

Page 79 Match and Rhyme
flag - bag, key - tree, shower - flower, dish - fish, note - boat

Page 80 Rhyme the Pictures
snake - cake, fly - tie, star - jar, heart - cart, clock - sock

Page 81 Find My Rhyming Pair
boat - goat, mouse - house, rain - train, ham - jam, dog - log

Page 82 What Am I?
can - man, fan, ran, let - met, set, get, jet - wet; take - make; hit - sit; mean - bean, seen, lean, clean, dean, queen; mop - top

Page 83 My Fat Cat
sat, mat, bat, rat, hat, fat

Page 84 My Pet, Jet
met, set, jet, let, get, wet

Page 85 Making Rhyming Words
1. cat – hat, bat 2. hog – log, dog 3. man – can, fan 4. pop – mop, top 5. dig – pig, wig 6. ten – pen, hen

Page 87 Above or Below
1. below 2. above 3. below 4. above

Page 88 Left or Right
1. right 2. left 3. left 4. right

Page 89 In or Out
1. in 2. out 3. in 4. out

Page 108 "Little Miss Muffet"
1. curds and whey 2. spider 3. no 4. frightened 5. ran away

Page 116 "Peter, Peter, Pumpkin Eater"
2, 1, 3

Page 121 He Stuck in His Thumb
And pulled out a plum

Page 123 Humpty Dumpty's Fall
4, 2, 1, 3

Answer Key (cont.)

Page 128 "Jack Be Nimble"
jet, jacket, jack o'lantern, jar

Page 129 "Pease Porridge"
Blue: ice cube, ice-cream cone, snowman; Red: soup, sun, candle

Page 197 How Many Berries?
a. 2 b. 2 c. 4 d. 5 e. 6 f. 7

Page 198 How Many?
a. 1 b. 4 c. 2 d. 8 e. 4 f. 9 g. 10 h. 6

Page 199 Count the Library Books
5, 2, 4, 3, 6

Page 200 Count the Objects
1. 5 2. 7 3. 3 4. 6 5. 8 6. 2 7. 4 8. 1

Page 201 How Many Are There?
1. 10 2. 9 3. 9 4. 10 5. 8 6. 7

Page 202 Beach Bears
1 sand castle, 3 birds, 3 bears, 2 pails, 1 ball, 3 boats, 2 shovels, 3 umbrellas, 1 sun, 0 rafts

Page 203 Coloring Fun
1. 6 yellow things 2. 6 red things 3. 6 blue things

Page 204 Number Names
five – 5, three – 3, one – 1, four – 4, two – 2

Page 205 How Many Bees?
15 bees

Page 206 Snowflakes
12 snowflakes

Page 207 Counting People
1. 2	2. 5
3. 8	4. 1
5. 3	6. 4
7. 10	8. 6
9. 7	10. 9

Page 213 Which Has Fewer?

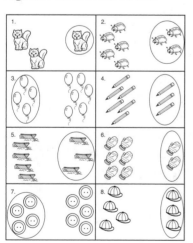

Page 214 Which Has More?

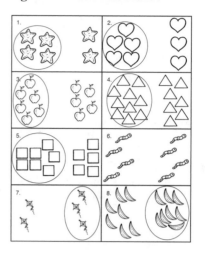

Page 215 Matching Numbers

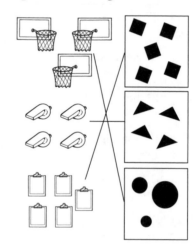

Page 216 Same Numbers

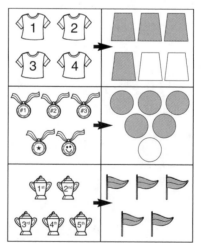

Answer Key (cont.)

Page 217 Equal Groups

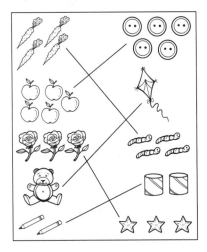

Page 218 Matching Groups

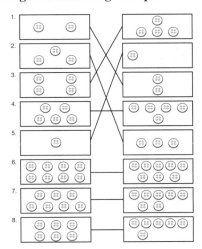

Page 219 Estimating in the Garden

1. 10 2. 16 3. 20 4. 12 5. 5 6. 25 7. 7 8. 1

Page 220 Shortest

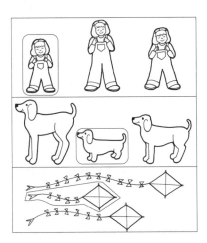

Page 221 Longest

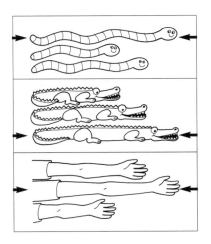

Page 222 Smallest

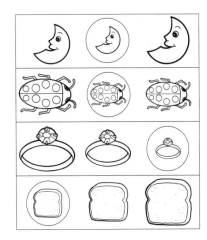

Page 223 Biggest

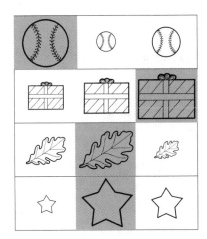

Answer Key (cont.)

Page 224 Matching Sizes

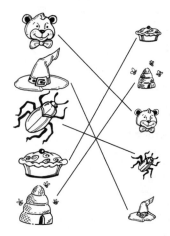

Page 225 Turkeys

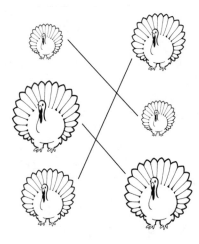

Page 226 What Comes Next?
1. heart 2. triangle 3. heart 4. triangle 5. square

Page 227 Colorful Beads
1. green 2. purple 3. blue 4. black, white 5. yellow 6. blue

Page 228 Patterns with Letters and Numbers
1. A 2. B 3. B 4. 2 5. 6. Y 6. 2 7. C

Page 229 Patterning
1. button, button, needle 2. bee, hive, bee 3. milk, cookie, cookie 4. mitten, mitten, mitten 5. kite, balloon, kite 6. crayon, paper, paper

Page 230 Morning or Evening
1. morning 2. evening 3. morning 4. evening 5. morning 6. evening

Page 232 Time Match
1. 3:00 2. 5:00 3. 8:00 4. 11:00 5. 12:00 6. 1:00

Page 233 Telling Time
1. 7:00 2. 2:00 3. 4:00 4. 6:00 5. 9:00 6. 10:00

Page 235 Rabbit Hop
1. 4 2. 3 3. 5 4. 6 5. 2

Page 236 School "Stuff"
1. 5 2. 4 3. 5 4. 4 5. 3 6. 5

Page 237 It's Recess
1. $4 + 1 = 5$ 2. $3 + 2 = 5$ 3. $3 + 1 = 4$
4. $2 + 0 = 2$ 5. $3 + 2 = 5$

Page 238 Everything Counts!
1. $2 + 3 = 5$ 2. $1 + 2 = 3$ 3. $3 + 2 = 5$

Page 239 Add It Up!
a. $3 + 2 = 5$ b. $4 + 1 = 5$ c. $2 + 6 = 8$
d. $5 + 3 = 8$ e. $2 + 4 = 6$ f. $3 + 7 = 10$

Page 240 More Add It Up!
a. $1 + 3 = 4$ b. $2 + 7 = 9$ c. $5 + 3 = 8$
d. $4 + 3 = 7$ e. $4 + 5 = 9$ f. $6 + 3 = 9$

Page 241 Addition
a. $2 + 2 = 4$ b. $3 + 3 = 6$ c. $4 + 6 = 10$
d. $5 + 1 = 6$ e. $0 + 7 = 7$ f. $5 + 8 = 13$

Page 242 Adding One
1. 4 2. 3 3. 5 4. 2 5. 4

Page 244 Sailboats on the Sea
1. $3 + 2 = 5$
2. $1 + 3 = 4$
3. $4 + 2 = 6$

Page 246 Circle the Number Words
$3 + 2 = 5$ $5 + 3 = 11$ $5 + 4 = 9$ $4 + 3 = 7$
$2 + 1 = 3$ $5 + 1 = 6$ $6 + 6 = 12$ $6 + 2 = 8$
$1 + 0 = 1$ $9 + 1 = 10$ $1 + 1 = 2$ $3 + 1 = 4$

Page 247 Subtraction Action
a. 1 b. 3 c. 3 d. 1 e. 3 f. 5

Page 248 Wake Up, Sleepyhead!
1. 4 2. 2 3. 5 4. 5 5. 4 6. 4

Page 249 Subtraction
a. $4 - 3 = 1$ b. $9 - 5 = 4$ c. $3 - 3 = 0$
d. $10 - 3 = 7$ e. $7 - 2 = 5$ f. $6 - 4 = 2$

Page 250 More Subtraction
a. $5 - 2 = 3$ b. $4 - 2 = 2$ c. $4 - 2 = 2$
d. $2 - 1 = 1$ e. $3 - 2 = 1$ f. $7 - 5 = 2$

Page 260 Hooves and Paws
1. C 2. D 3. E 4. B 5. A

Page 268 Clown Clothes
Color the following: shirt, pants, belt, big shoe, hat

Page 269 Circus Act
Put an X on the following: the shoe, the wagon, the leaf

Page 270 Animals
Color everything in the picture except the man.

Page 271 All Set?
Circle: 1. the spoon, the rolling pin, the measuring cup, the bowl 2. the triangles 3. the circles 4. the strawberries, cherries, grapes

Answer Key (cont.)

Page 272 Which Belongs?
Circle: 1. octopus, fish, whale 2. ice-cream cone, popsicle, sundae 3. screw, saw, hammer, screwdriver, pliers, nail

Page 273 Go Togethers
flower – pot, baby – crib, raincoat – umbrella, crayon – drawing, chair – table, comb – brush

Page 274 What Goes Together?
house – chimney, duck – bathtub, tree – leaf, computer – disk, school – desk, boy – ball

Page 275 Make a Set
fork – spoon, ball – bat, baby – rattle, bird – nest, paper – pencil, shoe – sock

Page 277 What Do We Wear?
Color: hat, shoe, scarf, tie, sock, jacket

Page 278 Can you find the Opposites?
1. big 2. little 3. in 4. out 5. under 6. over 7. on 8. off

Page 279 Find the Opposite

Page 280 Animal Opposites

Page 281 Opposites

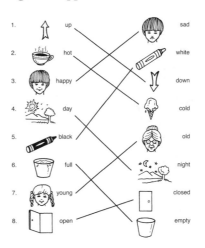

Page 282 More Opposites

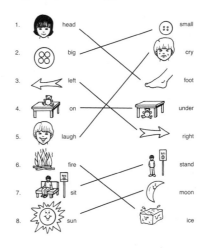

Page 283 Hidden Hats

Answer Key (cont.)

Page 284 Hide and Go Seek

Page 285 Button, Button

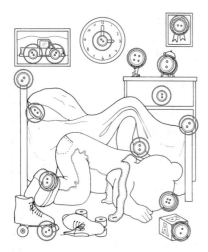

Page 286 Hidden Pictures

Page 287 Papa's Pig Pen

Page 288 My Own Zoo

Page 296 Building a Sandcastle
4, 2, 1, 3

Page 297 Flying a Kite
3, 2, 4, 1

Page 298 Making a Cake
3, 1, 4, 2

Practice
and
Learn

Part 2

Table of Contents
Part 2

Language Arts
    The Alphabet 307
    Phonics 310
    Phonemic Awareness 347
    Spelling 363
    Grammar and Usage 369

Reading Skills 388

Writing 412

Math
    Numbers 427
    Addition 463
    Subtraction 479
    Mixed Practice 489
    Money 494
    Measurement 497
    Geometry 506
    Directions and Patterns 510
    Fractions 515
    Problem Solving (Word Problems) 517

Social Studies
    Transportation 523
    Homes 526
    Careers 529
    City/Country 530
    Sense of Time 531
    Holidays and Symbols 532
    Maps 534
    Social Skills 542

Science/Health and Safety
    Life Science 544
    Earth Science 556
    Physical Science 563
    Dental Health 569
    Personal Safety 571

The Arts
    Visual Art/Color 576
    Music/Sound 581

Critical Thinking/Logic
    Logic 583
    Visual Discrimination 593
    Following Directions 595

Answer Key 599

Alpha Buttons

Write the missing capital letter.

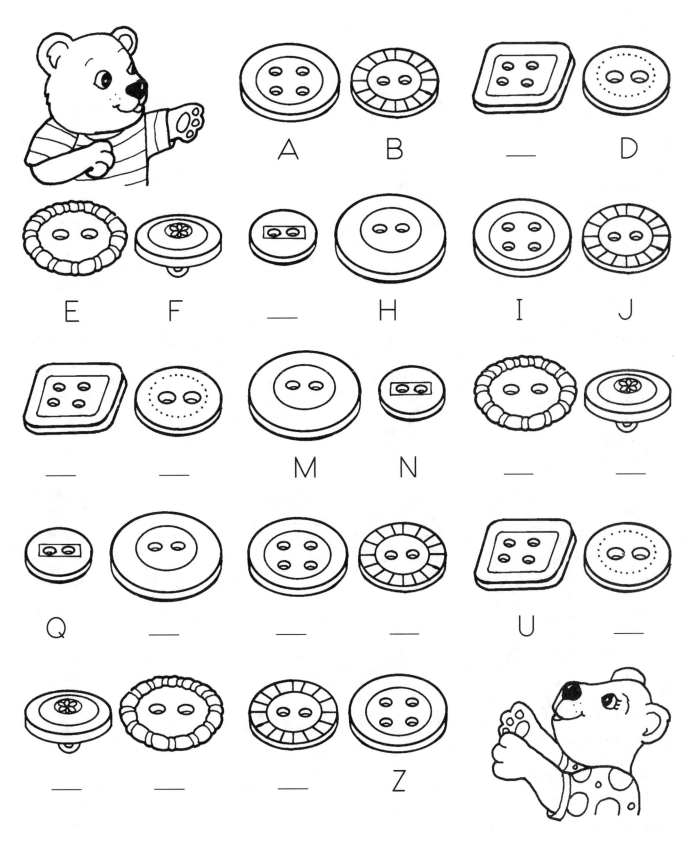

A   B   __   D

E   F   __   H   I   J

__   __   M   N   __

Q   __   __   __   U   __

__   __   __   Z

#3644 *Practice and Learn*

A Bee C's

Write the missing lowercase letter.

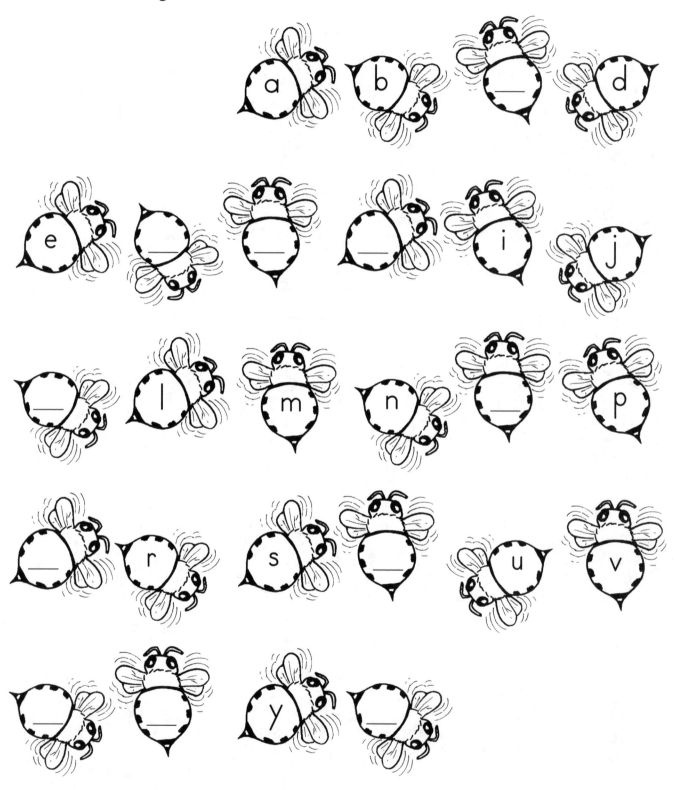

The Mouse Ran Up The Clock

Connect the dots.

Ballerina Begins With "Bb"

Color the "b" sound pictures.

Printing Practice

Cowboy Begins With "Cc"

Color the "c" sound pictures.

Printing Practice

Daisy Begins With "Dd"

Color the pictures in each row that start with the same sound as the first picture.

Printing Practice

Fiddle Begins With "Ff"

Color the "f" sound pictures.

Printing Practice

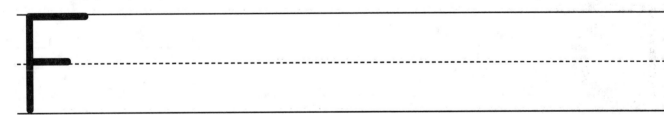

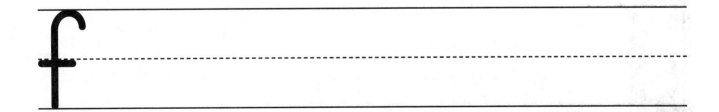

Gorilla Begins With "Gg"

Color the 🐱 if the three pictures in each row start with the "g" sound.

Color the 🐱 if the three pictures in each row do not start with the "g" sound. Color the "g" pictures.

Printing Practice

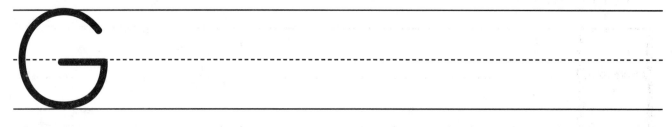

Hamster Begins With "Hh"

Find the babies that belong to the father. Each baby has a picture sound on its body. If the sound of the picture's first letter matches the sound of the father's letter, draw a line from the baby to the father.

Printing Practice

Jewelry Begins With "Jj"

Circle and color the "j" pictures.

Printing Practice

Kangaroo Begins With "Kk"

Color the "k" sound pictures.

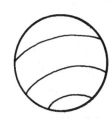  

Printing Practice

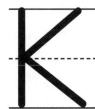

K

k

Licorice Begins With "Ll"

Look at the pictures in each box. Color the pictures that begin with the same sound.

a.

b.

c.

d.
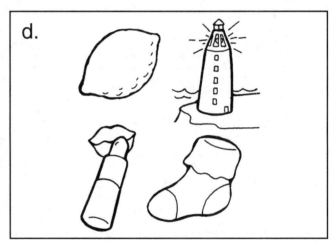

Printing Practice

Mushroom Begins With "Mm"

Color the "m" sound(s) in each box.

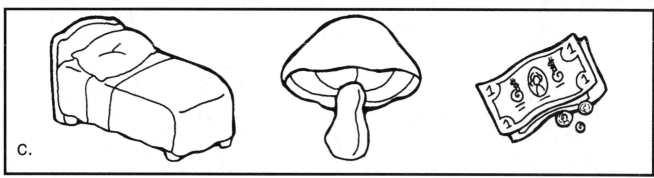

Printing Practice

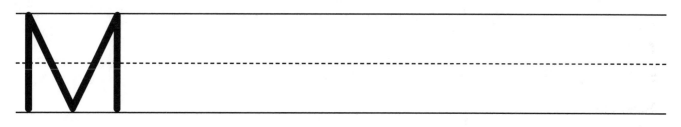

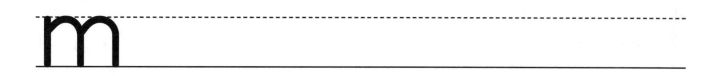

Nickel Begins With "Nn"

Look at the picture in the square. Color the pictures in the box that begin with the same sound.

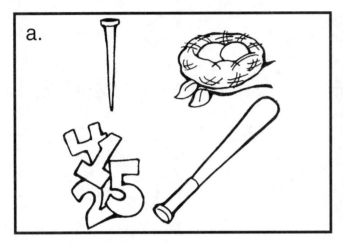

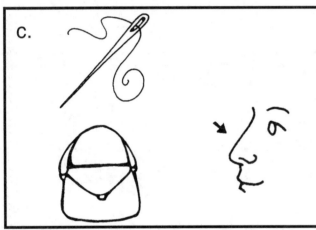

Printing Practice

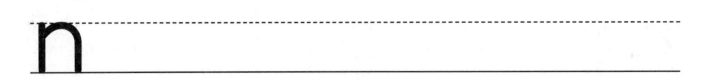

Pancake Begins With "Pp"

Circle and then color the four "p" things in each row.

Printing Practice

Quail Begins with "Qq"

Find the babies that belong to the mother. Each baby has a picture sound on its body. If the picture sound matches the mother's sound, draw a line from the baby to the mother.

Printing Practice

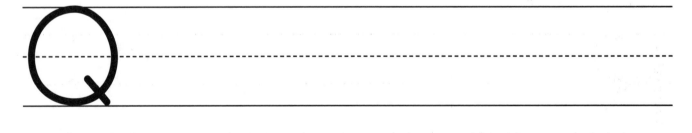

Robot Begins With "Rr"

Color the "r" sound(s) in each box.

Printing Practice

R

r

Sausage Begins With "Ss"

Color the three "s" sounds in each box.

Printing Practice

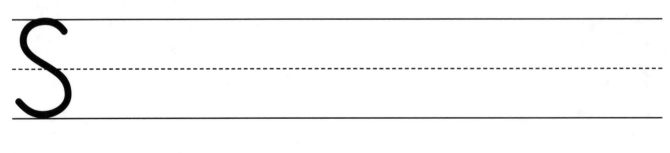

Telescope Begins With "Tt"

Circle and then color the pictures in each row that start with the same sound as the first picture.

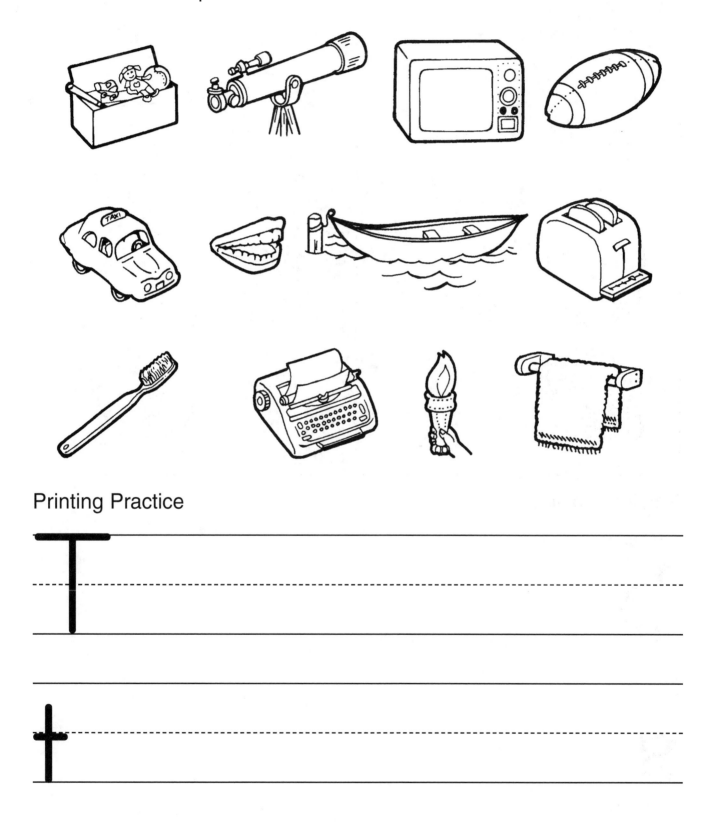

Printing Practice

Vulture Begins With "Vv"

Color the "v" sound pictures.

Printing Practice

Web begins With "Ww"

One of the pictures in each box starts with the "w" sound. Color the "w" picture in each box.

Printing Practice

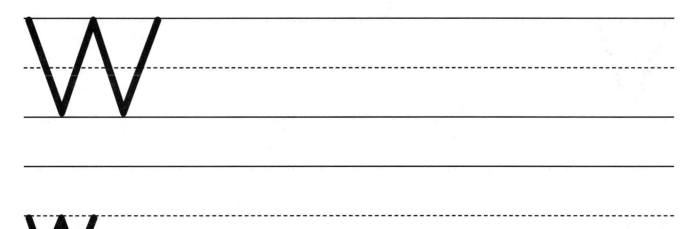

X-Ray Begins With "Xx"

Color the pictures that **do not** begin with "x."

Printing Practice

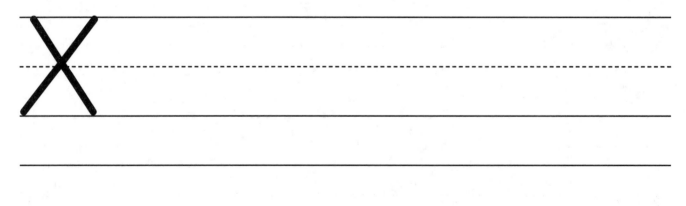

Yogurt Begins With "Yy"

Color the "y" pictures.

Printing Practice

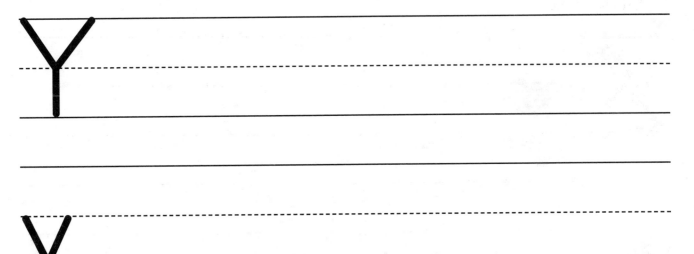

Zebra Begins With "Zz"

Color the "z" pictures.

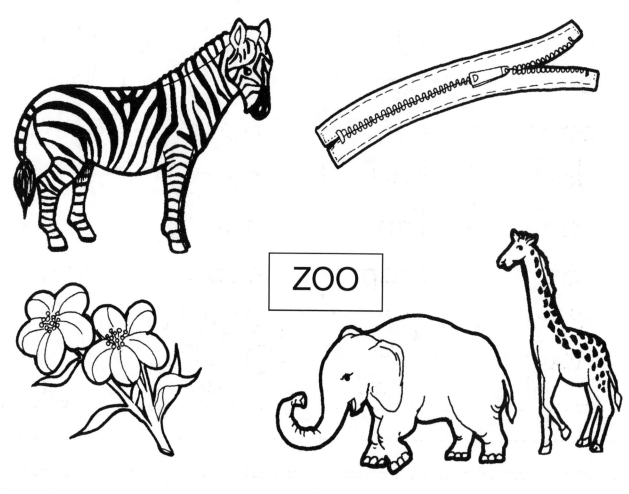

ZOO

Printing Practice

Short Vowel-"Aa"

Write the words in the correct word family. Fill in the letter under the picture.

lap	van	tap	mat
bat	slap	man	lad
can	cat	bad	sat
dad	had	mad	pan
ran	fan	hat	sad
rat	map	cap	nap

__ at

__ ad

__ an

__ ap

Short Vowel-"Ee"

Finish each word with "et" or "en." Color the pictures.

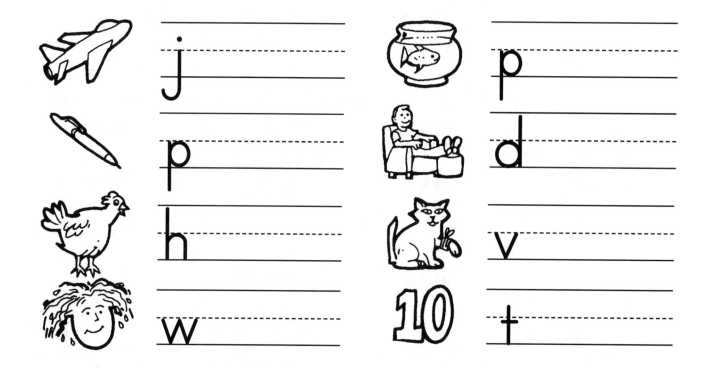

j

p

h

w

p

d

v

t

Finish each word with "est" or "ell." Color the pictures.

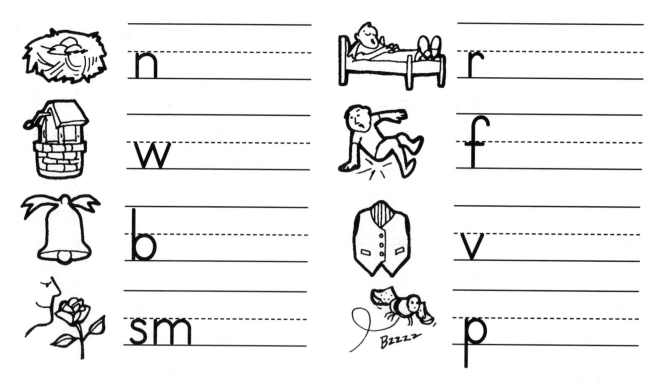

n

w

b

sm

r

f

v

p

Short Vowel-"Ii"

Unscramble the words. Write them correctly on the lines.

lip	swim	mill	sit
hit	flip	grin	pill

llim _____

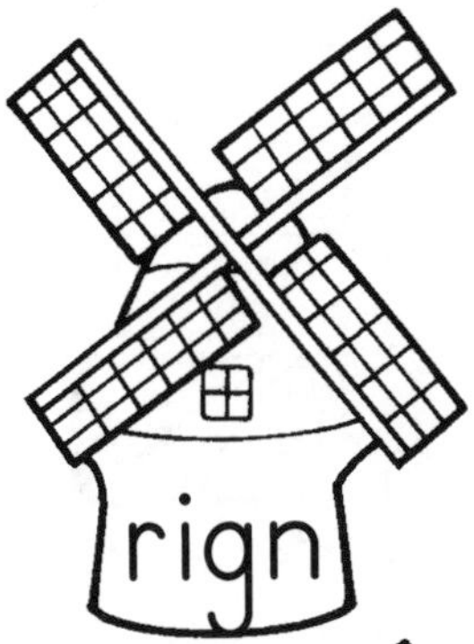

rign _____

tih _____

llip _____

pli _____

tis _____

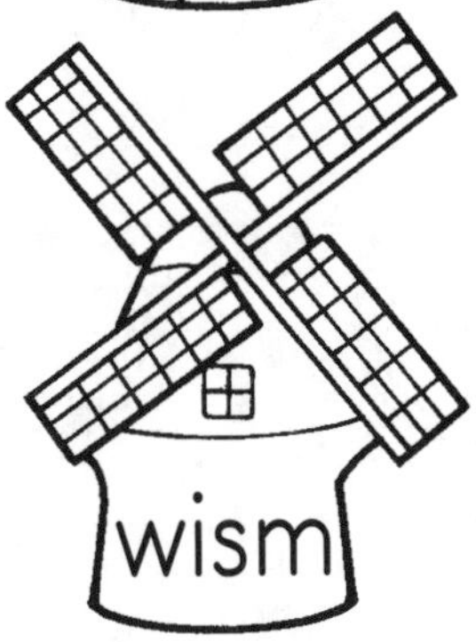

wism _____

plif _____

Short Vowel-"Oo"

Fill in the crossword blocks with the correct short "o" words. Use the words below.

dock	lock	frog
pop	clock	sock
log		
dog		

1.

2.

3.

4.

5.

6.

7.

8.

Short Vowel-"Uu"

The pup is pulling the sheet! Unscramble the short "u" words. Write them on the lines.

phmu _____

ppu _____

umpj _____

mdpu _____

pcu _____

uppm _____

pu _____

mupl _____

cup   jump

pup   lump

up   pump

dump

hump

Long Vowel-"Aa"

Write the long "a" words in the correct word family. Fill in the letter under the picture.

trace	Kate	jay	space
hay	day	bay	bake
skate	may	cake	gate
lake	Jake	say	race
grace	lace	wake	face
ate	make	date	late

___ay   ___ake   ___ate   ___ace

Long Vowel-"Ee"

Finish each word with "ee" or "ea."

w___d   m___t

tr___   s___

h___t   w___k

k___p   n___t

n___d   f___d

wh___t   bl___d

sh___p   sh___t

b___   sp___d

Long Vowel-"Ii"

Look at the pictures. Use the words to name the objects.

1.  _____

5. _____

2.  _____

6.  _____

3.  _____

7. _____

4. _____

8.  _____

dice   rice   mice   pine

night   dine

ice      vine

Long Vowel-"Oo"

Finish each word with "old" or "oat."

g _____

thr _____

f _____

g _____

b _____

c _____

s _____

c _____

Finish each word with "oke" or "ow."

r _____

sm _____

b _____

bl _____

arr _____

thr _____

br _____

w _____

Long Vowel-"Uu"

Unscramble the words. Write the long "u" words on the lines.

cube	Duke	huge	tube
cure	dune	mule	tune

gueh _____

lume _____

ebtu _____

dneu _____

keuD _____

eutn _____

becu _____

ucre _____

"Bl" and "Br" Blends

Color the pictures that begin either with the "bl" or "br" sound.

"St" Starfish Stories

Read the words on the starfish that begin with the "st" sound. Circle the word that names the picture.

"Tr" Words

Color the pictures that begin with the "tr" sound.

Charlie the "Ch" Chick

Charlie the Chick is hatching from his egg. Color the pictures on his egg that begin with the "ch" sound. Color the chick yellow.

A Shocking "Sh" Shark

Use the pictures on the shark's teeth to help you unscramble the words that begin with the "sh" sound. Write them on the dashed lines.

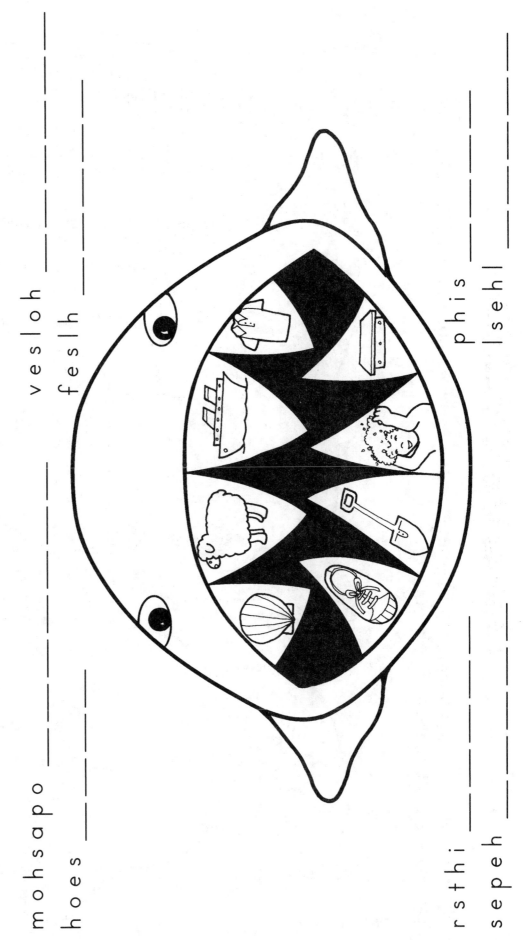

v e s l o h ___ ___ ___ ___ ___ ___

f e s l h ___ ___ ___ ___ ___

p h i s ___ ___ ___ ___

l s e h l ___ ___ ___ ___ ___

m o h s a p o ___ ___ ___ ___ ___ ___ ___

h o e s ___ ___ ___ ___

r s t h i ___ ___ ___ ___ ___

s e p e h ___ ___ ___ ___ ___

Who-o-o Can Read the "Th" Words?

Read the words on the owl's body that begin with the "th" sound. Write them on the blank lines to finish the sentences. Color the owl.

I like _____ milkshakes.

The rose _____ is very sharp.

Mom uses a _____ when she sews.

Ted wants to _____ everyone.

thick   think

thief   thorn

thank   thumb

thing   thimble

The _____ stole the money.

I _____ I can sleep now.

Dad hit his _____ with a hammer.

I have one more _____ to do.

Initial Consonants

Fill in the correct letters. Use the picture word bank below to complete the words in the story.

MY FARM

I live on a farm. There are ____ows, ____eep, ____ens, and many ____orses. We all have jobs to do. ____other milks the cow. I feed the ____ickens. The animals live in a ____arn. It is fun to live on a farm.

Picture Word Bank

sheep

barn

Mother

chickens

hens

cows

horses

Birds or Bears or Bugs

Use the letter bank below to help you listen for the missing sound. On the line, write the letter or letters that make that sound.

Birds soar.

Lions ____ oar.

Elephants walk.

Parrots ____ alk.

Dogs lick.

Kangaroos ____ ick.

Bears growl.

Wolves ____ owl.

Monkeys swing.

Birds ____ ing.

Letter Bank

t   k   s   r   h

Beginning Letters

Write the letter that begins each word. Color the pictures.

letter _____

letter _____

letter _____

letter _____

letter _____

letter _____

letter _____

letter _____

letter _____

letter _____

letter _____

letter _____

Missing Sounds in Animal Names

Use the picture of the animal to help you listen for the missing sound.
On the line, write the letter or letters that make that sound.

_____ ish

_____ ouse

_____ eep

_____ ider

_____ ion

_____ at

_____ urtle

_____ ig

Onsets and Rimes

Make a new word from an old word by changing the beginning letter.

1. Change   <u>can</u> into   _____.

2. Change   <u>corn</u> into   _____.

3. Change   <u>log</u> into   _____.

4. Change   <u>dish</u> into   _____.

5. Change   <u>ten</u> into   _____.

6. Change   <u>bag</u> into   _____.

7. Change   <u>band</u> into   _____.

8. Change   <u>cake</u> into   _____.

Missing Vowels

Say the picture names.

Write the missing vowels.

1. b___t	5.  r___ck
2. n___t	6. b___x
3. 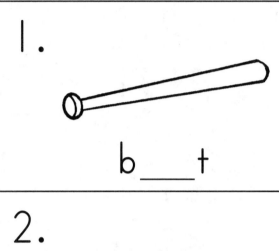 d___c___	7.  m_____t
4. 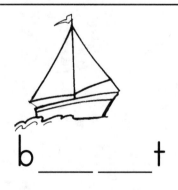 b_____t	8.  t___m___

Short Vowel Sound Quilt

Listen for the short vowel sound in each word. Color the spaces this way:

short a = purple   short e = blue

short i = red   short o = yellow

short u = green

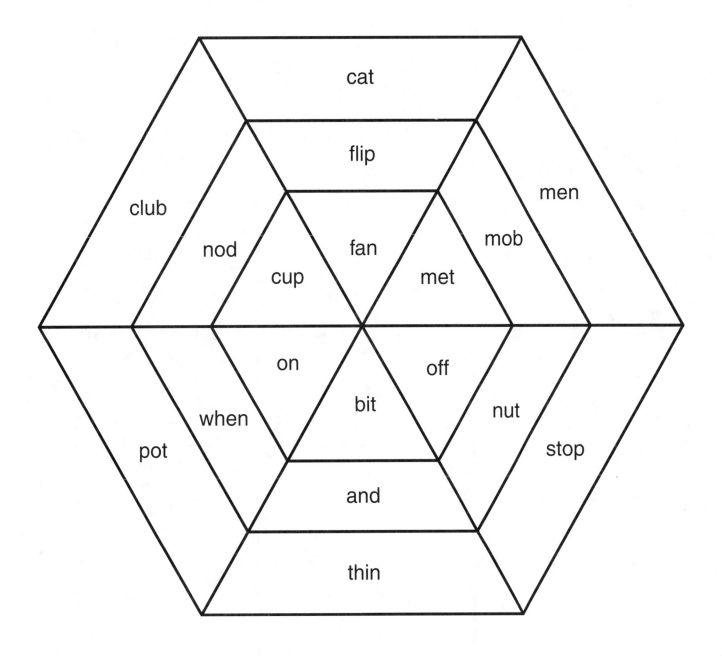

Long Vowel Sound Quilt

Listen for the long vowel sound in each word. Color the spaces this way:

long a = red   **long e = purple**   **long i = yellow**

long o = green   **long u = blue**

mind

seem

find

you   fuse

treat

he

meet

tape   open   whale

show   eat   nice   name   bee   so

table   huge   ate

free

she

team

cube   rule

mine

try

sleep

Identifying Final Sounds

Circle the word in each box that has the same ending sound as the picture.

look far spoon	the run cap	not dog doll	pass hat can
will what bus	this then book	door dirt girl	jam coat lion
pen room big	fair hand bag	foot ring light	sun bar hug

What Letter Is Last?

1. Look at the animal pictures and say each animal name.
2. Listen to the ending sound.
3. Write the correct letter to complete the animal words.
4. Use lowercase letters.

do____

pi____

duc____

shee____

he____

goa____

rabbi____

What Letter Must Be Last?

1. Look at the food pictures and say each name.

2. Listen to the ending sound.

3. Print the correct letter to complete the food words.

4. Use uppercase letters.

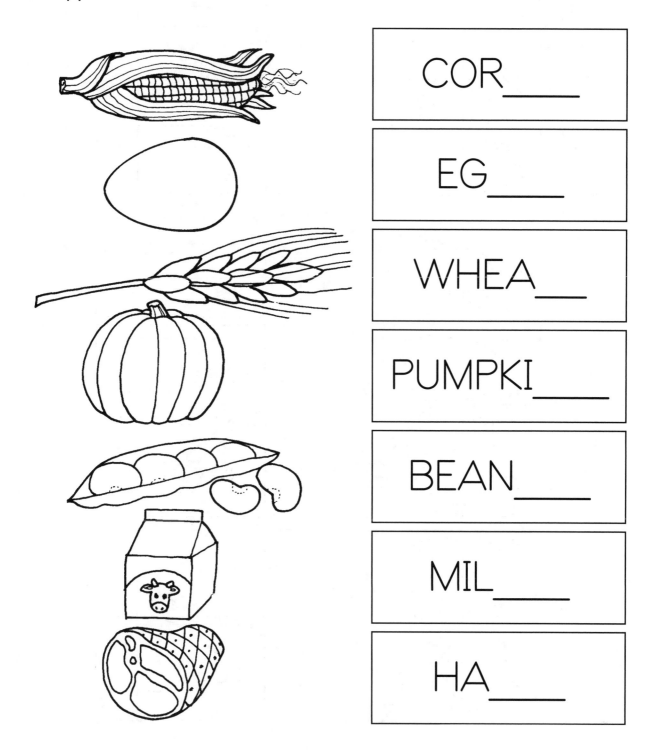

COR___

EG___

WHEA___

PUMPKI___

BEAN___

MIL___

HA___

Word Families—Sounds Alike

Say the name of each picture. Draw a circle around the pictures that have the same ending sound as the first picture in each row.

clock	block	lock	cat
cat	bat	hat	hen
cake	man	rake	hat
can	pan	bat	pig

Word Families - Sounds Different

Say the name of each picture. Make an **X** over the word in each row that does not have the same ending sound as the others.

can	man	fan	fish
coat	rock	goat	boat
cake	cat	hat	bat
pen	hen	ten	car
car	star	fish	jar

Rhyming Pairs

If the word pairs below rhyme, color the happy face. If they do not rhyme, color the sad face.

1. mouse   house   ☺   ☹

2. sill   hill   ☺   ☹

3. dream   sleeve   ☺   ☹

4. wait   late   ☺   ☹

5. part   dark   ☺   ☹

6. big   bit   ☺   ☹

7. hot   dot   ☺   ☹

8. snarl   howl   ☺   ☹

9. street   heat   ☺   ☹

10. box   socks   ☺   ☹

More Onsets and Rhymes

Please Feed the Animals!

The zoo animals are hungry. Help fill up their tummies. Use the word parts on their favorite foods to write the picture words on their tummies.

Rhyme Time

Write all the words you can think of that rhyme with the words below.

cake

man

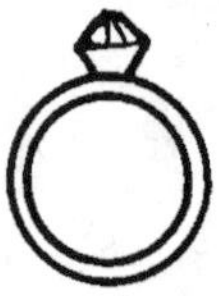

ring

cat

tree

light

book

A Perfect Pair

To discover some compound words, write a word for each picture. The last picture in each row will be a compound word that joins the first two words in each row.

1.

_____   _____   _____

2.

 +  =

_____   _____   _____

3.

 +  =

_____   _____   _____

4.

 +  =

_____   _____   _____

Compound Words

 Add a word from the word box to each word below to make a new word.

bath	cow	foot	star	tooth
butter	flower	sail	sun	water

1. _____ boat

2. _____ shine

3. _____ pot

4. _____ light

5. _____ fall

6. _____ boy

7. _____ brush

8. _____ ball

9. _____ tub

10. _____ cup

Con "trap" tions

Help the mouse get to the cheese before he gets trapped! Draw a line from the mouse hole to the correct contraction on the trap.

1.  is not   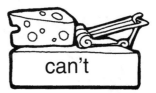 can't

2.  let us    we've

3.  cannot   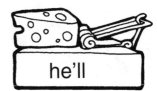 he'll

4.  he will    isn't

5.  are not   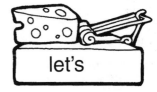 let's

6.  we have    aren't

Blooming With Contractions

The contraction for "not" is "**n't**." Write a contraction on each flower, using the word in the center plus the contraction for "not".

1.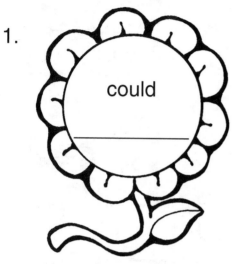

could
_____

2.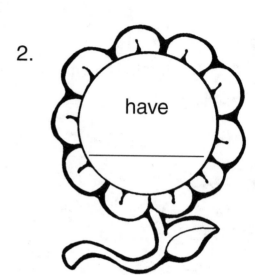

have
_____

3.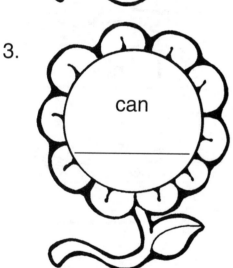

can
_____

4.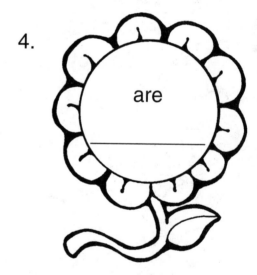

are
_____

5.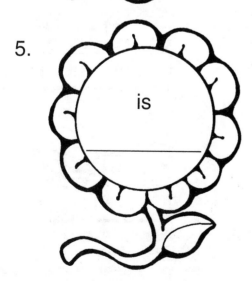

is
_____

6.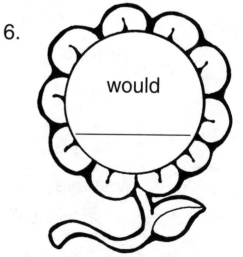

would
_____

Pet Contractions

Write the contraction for the two words given:

- **I'm**
- **he's**

- **can't**
- **you'd**

- **it's**
- **you're**

- **we're**
- **isn't**

she will

she'll

Example

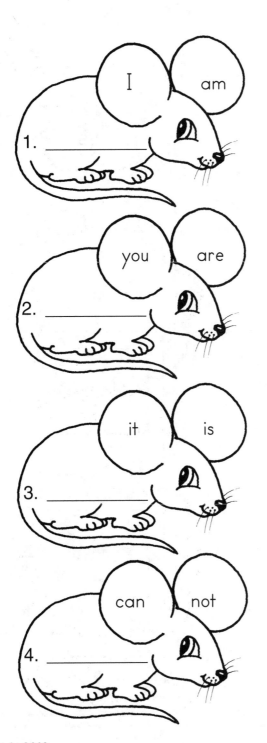

1. _____

2. _____

3. _____

4. _____

5. _____

6. _____

7. _____

8. _____

Shopping for Contractions

Write the contraction for the two words on each shopping bag.

you'll	wasn't	couldn't
it's	that's	won't
we'll	didn't	

Example: let us — let's	did not — _____	we will — _____
it is — _____	could not — _____	that is — _____
will not — _____	you will — _____	was not — _____

The Word "I"

The word *I* is always capitalized. Practice writing the word *I* on the lines below.

1. _____ lost my tooth.

2. _____ like to play on the swings.

3. _____ have six dollars.

4. _____ have a dog as a pet.

5. _____ read a good book.

6. Today _____ am going to the park.

7. _____ went to the library yesterday.

8. May _____ have a drink?

9. Tom and _____ played ball at recess.

10. _____ like to ride my bike.

Start Right!

The first word in every sentence begins with a capital letter. The first word to each sentence below is written under the line. Practice capitalizing the first word in each sentence by writing it on the line.

1. _____ favorite color is yellow.
   my

2. _____ we play now?
   can

3. _____ helped us make a cake.
   she

4. _____ like to eat pizza.
   i

5. _____ are going to see a movie.
   we

6. _____ you coming with us?
   are

7. _____ are eggs in the nest.
   there

Tell It Like It Is

Practice writing a period at the ends of these sentences.

1. My family has a pet dog

2. I watched cartoons on Saturday

3. We had pizza for dinner

4. Tim rides a blue bike

5. I know a lot about dinosaurs

6. Mom asked me to help her clean

7. The hamster got out of his cage

8. I wrote a letter to my grandma

Now it is your turn. Write your own telling sentences on the lines below. Use a period at the end of each sentence.

1. _____

_____

2. _____

Nouns—Naming Words

 Underline each word that names a person.

1. The dancer jumped in the air.
2. The boy watched television.
3. Mr. Smith teaches our class.
4. The baby cried.

 Underline each word that names a place.

5. We walked down our street.
6. My school is great.
7. They play in the park.
8. We shopped at the store.

 Underline each word that names a thing.

9. The dog ate its bone.
10. I opened the present.
11. We found our missing toy.
12. The bird flew from its cage.

More Naming Words

A noun is a word that names a person, a place, or a thing.

 Write each word under the correct heading.

jacket	branch	room	teacher
Lisa	field	soda	school
China	flower	water	town
mother	girl	father	

Person

_____

- - - - - - - - - - - -

_____

- - - - - - - - - - - -

_____

- - - - - - - - - - - -

_____

- - - - - - - - - - - -

_____

- - - - - - - - - - - -

_____

Place

_____

- - - - - - - - - - - -

_____

- - - - - - - - - - - -

_____

- - - - - - - - - - - -

_____

- - - - - - - - - - - -

_____

- - - - - - - - - - - -

_____

Thing

_____

- - - - - - - - - - - -

_____

- - - - - - - - - - - -

_____

- - - - - - - - - - - -

_____

- - - - - - - - - - - -

_____

- - - - - - - - - - - -

_____

Animal Actions

Circle the verbs (or action words) in each sentence.

1. That cat purred.
2. His dog wagged his tail.
3. The brown cat meowed.
4. The horse nuzzled his head against my hand.
5. Kitty jumped up on Mom's lap.
6. His ears perked up.
7. The puppy ran after the boy.
8. The gerbil raced around his cage.
9. The dog barked at the stranger.
10. He growled at the mailman.

Write the names of six animals from above:

_____   _____   _____

- - - - - - - - - - - - - - - - - - -   - - - - - - - - - - - - - - - - - - -   - - - - - - - - - - - - - - - - - - -

_____   _____   _____

- - - - - - - - - - - - - - - - - - -   - - - - - - - - - - - - - - - - - - -   - - - - - - - - - - - - - - - - - - -

_____   _____   _____

Verbs

Underline one word in each sentence that tells what someone or something does.

1. Alice rode her bike.

2. The girl swam in the pool.

3. I drew a picture of my dog.

4. The kitten played with the ball.

5. My teacher read a story to us.

6. The leaves blew in the wind.

7. The team ate a pizza after the game.

8. James caught the ball.

9. The clown danced at the party.

10. The rabbit hopped across the field.

11. I talked on the phone.

12. The hen sat on its eggs.

More Verbs

Write **is**, **am**, or **are** in each sentence.

1. Mr. Jones _____ a tall man.

2. I _____ a good student.

3. Where _____ they going?

4. Who _____ at the door?

5. We _____ at the park.

6. Bob and Bill _____ eating

   grapes.

7. Where _____ I?

8. They _____ eating pizza.

Describe It

Adjectives can be used to describe any noun.

Think of 3 adjectives that describe you.

_____   _____   _____

Think of 3 adjectives that describe the sun.

_____   _____   _____

Think of 3 adjectives that describe an apple.

_____   _____   _____

Circle the adjectives in the sentences below.

1. The yellow pencil is on the desk.

2. I like to eat black licorice.

3. My favorite aunt came to visit my family.

4. My dad says I have beautiful eyes.

5. My dog just had nine puppies.

6. At recess, I play on the high bar.

7. Sarah has brown hair.

8. My mom made me a chocolate cake for my birthday.

9. Mrs. Jeeno read us a long chapter book.

10. After playing in the sun, I drank two glasses of cold water.

Word Plurals

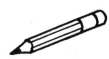

Add the letter **s** to each word to make it more than one.
Write the whole word.

1. jar _____

2. dog _____

3. hill _____

4. kite _____

5. card _____

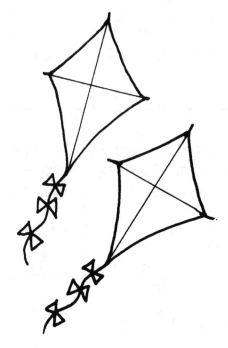

Add the letters **es** to each word to make it more than one.

6. fox _____

7. dress _____

8. glass _____

9. class _____

10. brush _____

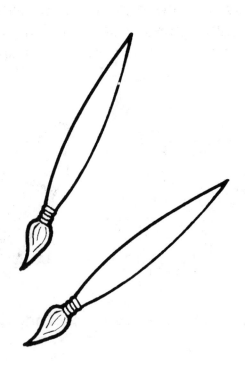

More Than One

Write a noun for each picture below.

_____   _____   _____   _____

You wrote the *singular* form of each of these nouns because there is only one of each item. The singular form of a noun shows there is only one. One way to show the *plural* (more than one) is to add an **s** to the end of the word.

book   books   tree   trees

Try writing the plural forms of the nouns you wrote above.

_____   _____   _____   _____

By adding an **s** to the end of most nouns you make the noun plural and show there is more than one item. Now it is your turn to try some more. Write singular nouns under the pictures that show only one. Write plural nouns under the pictures that show more than one.

_____   _____   _____   _____

Word Endings

Write the word in the sentence. Add **s** if it is needed.

play   1. The baby _____ with its
        toy.

swim   2. She _____ across the pool.

jump   3. He _____ over the fence.

roar   4. A lion _____ for its
        dinner.

eat   5. Alex _____ an apple.

like   6. He _____ to play
        baseball.

Word Roundup

This cowboy is roping base words and endings. Help him with his word roundup. Put base words and endings together to make new words. Write the new words in the word corral.

Word Corral

Base Words

talk
stay
box
fish

Endings

ed
s
ing
es

Root Words and Endings

Draw lines to match each word below with its root word.

1. smiled   • ant

2. talking   • judge

3. judges   • pet

4. friends   • long

5. ants   • smile

6. called   • call

7. pets   • talk

8. longest   • friend

9. leaving   • leave

10. walked   • show

11. showed   • pin

12. slowest   • brag

13. bragged   • walk

14. pinned   • search

15. passed   • pass

16. searched   • slow

Homophones

Write the correct word in each blank.

1. I will give _____

cookies _____ you.

2. The _____ wants

to _____ in its hive.

3. She ate a _____

while I put on my

_____ of socks.

4. I did not _____ you

come in _____ .

Synonyms

 Draw a line to match the words that mean the same thing.

plane	dish
sea	jet
small	ocean
loud	mitt
hat	cap
plate	tiny
look	noisy
glove	see

Antonyms

An antonym is a word that means the opposite of another word. Examples: hot—cold, soft—hard

Use the word bank to find words that are opposites. Print the opposite word in the space below and draw a picture to show the meaning.

Word Bank			
laugh	asleep	day	large
smile	rain	dark	straight

crooked	**light**	**frown**	**night**
shine	**cry**	**awake**	**small**

385

Opposites

List the opposites.

1. hot   _____
2. dark   _____
3. off   _____
4. over   _____
5. high   _____
6. in   _____
7. far   _____
8. curly   _____
9. up   _____
10. empty   _____
11. happy   _____
12. wet   _____
13. soft   _____
14. tall   _____
15. clean   _____

More Opposites

1. Read the sentence.
2. Look at the picture.

3. Circle the correct word or words.
4. Color each picture the correct color.

Pigs are _____ a red car.

in   out of

Pigs are _____ the black car.

in   out of

This blue car is going _____.

up   down

This pink car is going _____.

up   down

His green bike is _____.

fast   slow

Her yellow bike is _____.

fast   slow

This brown car is _____.

old   new

This orange car is _____.

old   new

Alphabetical Order

Put the words in alphabetical order.

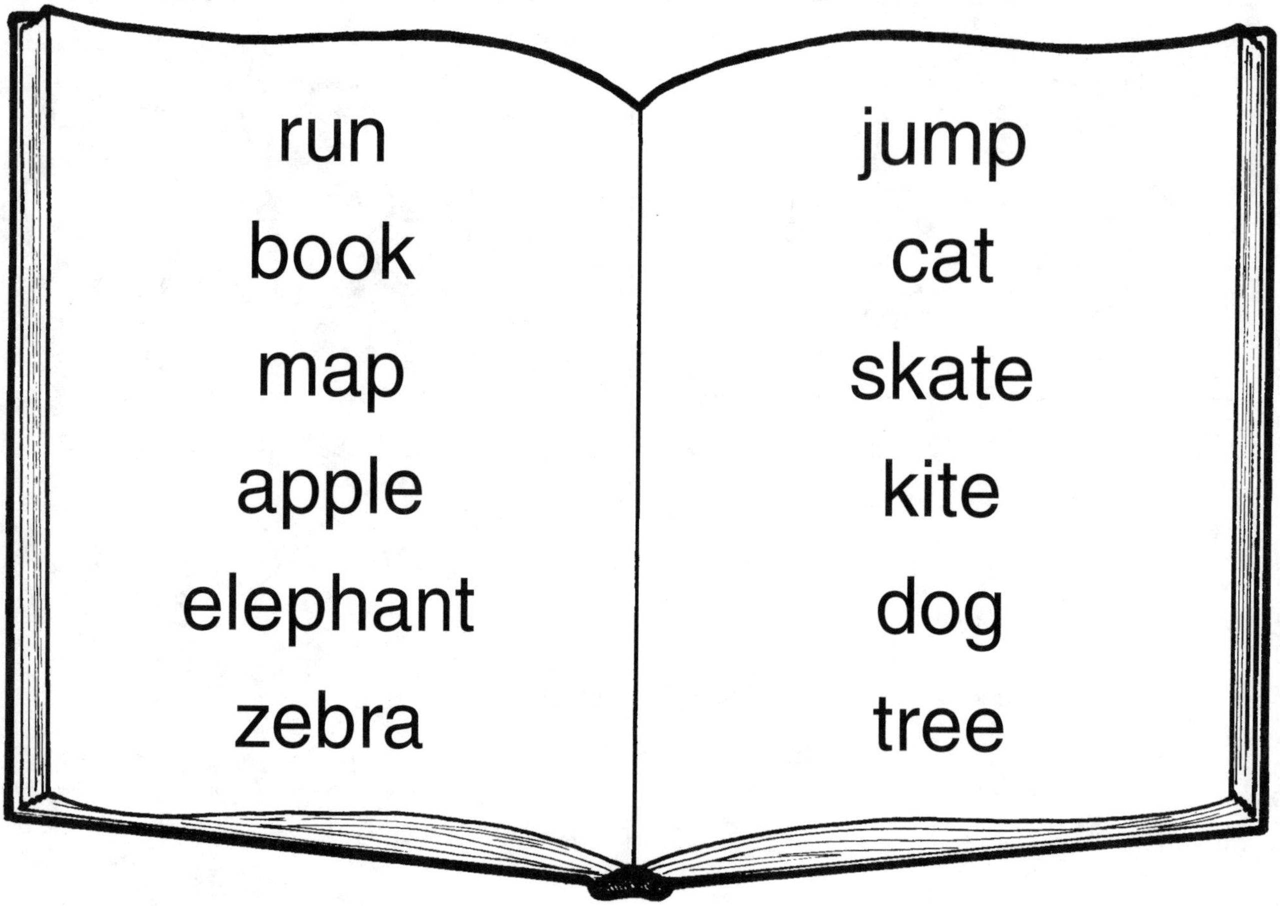

run	jump
book	cat
map	skate
apple	kite
elephant	dog
zebra	tree

1. _____

2. _____

3. _____

4. _____

5. _____

6. _____

7. _____

8. _____

9. _____

10. _____

11. _____

12. _____

Alphabetical Animals

Write the following words in alphabetical order on the cat.

ant	fish	horse	monkey	zebra
dog	bat	lion	goat	cat

1. _____   6. _____

2. _____   7. _____

3. _____   8. _____

4. _____   9. _____

5. _____   10. _____

Leo Lion's Sight Words

Leo is a strange lion. When he roars, only sight words come out!
Find and circle the sight words across or down.

```
a  m  o  f  i  n  d  w
b  a  r  w  l  o  o  h
o  n  t  h  a  t  w  o
u  y  h  a  d  h  n  w
t  o  e  t  i  e  o  i
b  u  i  o  d  y  w  t
u  r  r  o  o  n  e  h
```

on	what	find	no	now
their	who	they	you	of
that	had	not	too	did
down	how	many	about	one
or	with	your	an	out

Myrtle Turtle's Sight Words

Myrtle is a sight word turtle. She had to hide in her shell in a hurry.
She scrambled her sight words. What a mess! Write the sight words
correctly on her shell.

have   this   get   people

said   she   me   make

been   and   some   which

these   first   bike   because

Sam Snake's Sight Words

Sam Snake slid over some rocks and scrambled his sight word scales.
Can you unscramble them for him? Write the sight words correctly.

her	use	more	in
them	can	so	like
way	we	than	do
its	long	when	be
him	time	know	

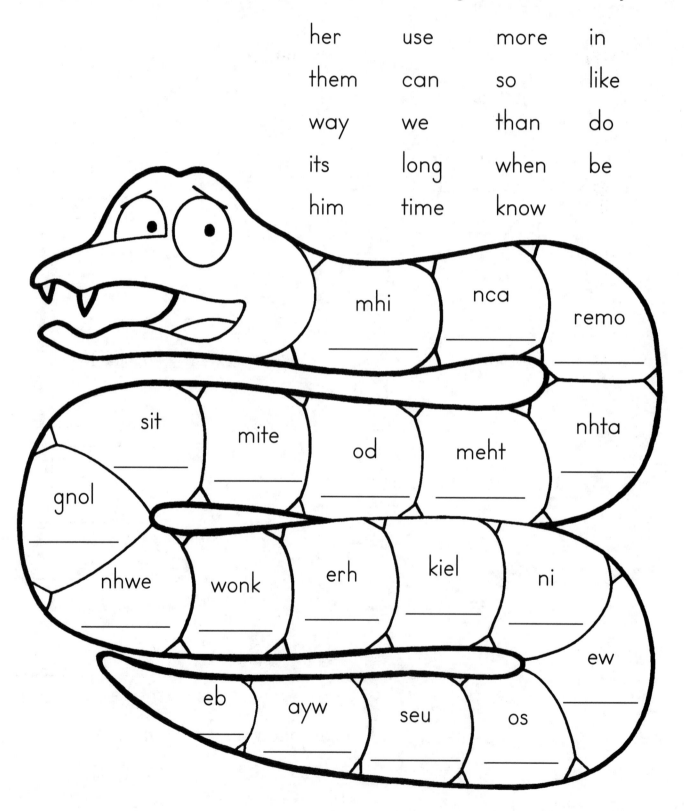

Picture Words

Write the words that go with the pictures.

 1.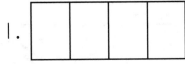

 2.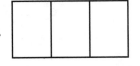

 3.

 4.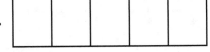

 5.

 6.

 7.

 8.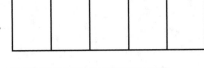

 9.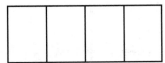

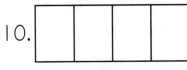 10.

 11.

 12.

 13.

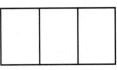 14.

 15.

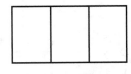 16.

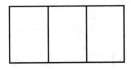 17.

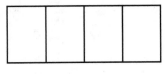 18.

bee	flute	mice	pail	vine
cake	goat	mow	seed	woke
eat	green	mule	suit	
five	sun	old	tube	

Beary Good Words

From the word box below, choose the word that matches the picture.
Write it on the line.

_____

too _____

_____

too _____

just _____

too _____

_____

too _____

_____

Word Box

bears	cottage	hot	cold	soft
hard	Golidlocks	home	right	

The Cat and the Fiddle Context Clues

Find and write the words from "The Cat and the Fiddle" that make sense in the sentences.

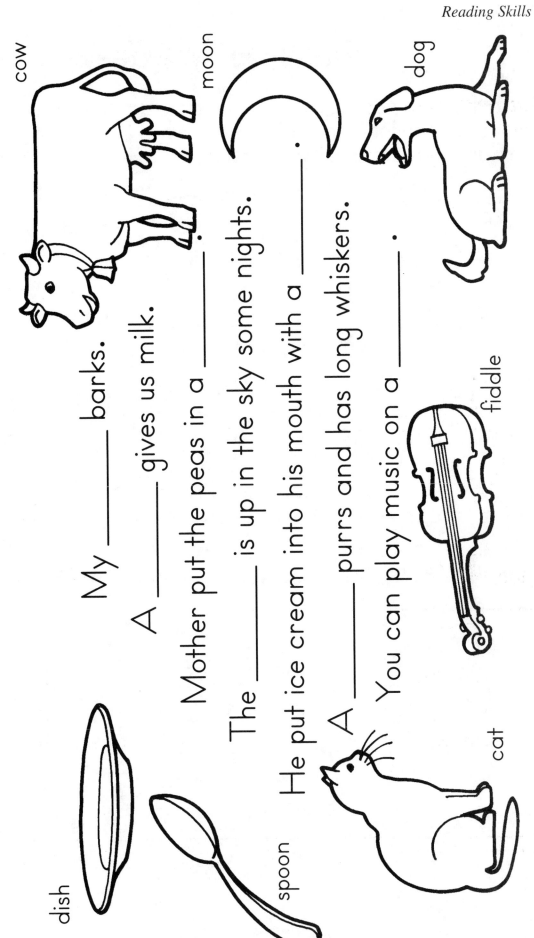

cow

moon

dog

My _____ barks.

A _____ gives us milk.

Mother put the peas in a _____.

The _____ is up in the sky some nights.

He put ice cream into his mouth with a _____.

A _____ purrs and has long whiskers.

You can play music on a _____.

dish

spoon

fiddle

cat

What Do You Hear?

Read the sentence. Look at the three words under each sentence.
Choose one of the words that makes sense in the sentence. Circle
the word and write it in the sentence.

1. Frogs _____ at me.

   croak　　　bark　　　roar

2. Birds _____ to me.

   hiss　　　moo　　　sing

3. Chickens _____ at me.

   sing　　　growl　　　cluck

4. Cats _____ at me.

   purr　　　bark　　　roar

5. Snakes _____ at me.

   roar　　　hiss　　　sing

6. Ducks _____ at me.

   sing　　　quack　　　squeal

7. Pigs _____ at me.

   purr　　　squeal　　　cluck

8. Cows _____ at me.

   moo　　　quack　　　bark

What Do You See?

Read the sentences. Choose the words that make sense in the sentences. Write them on the lines.

bird

duck

frog

fish

horse

sheep

A _____ has soft feathers and webbed feet.

We put the saddle on the _____.

The pretty _____ swims in the water.

We get fluffy wool from the _____.

I saw the _____ fly to her nest.

The little green _____ jumped on the rocks.

What Color Is It?

Color the crayons the color they say. Read the sentences. Choose the color words on the crayons that make sense in the sentences. Write the color words on the lines.

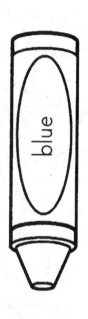

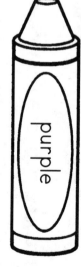

1. We saw the bright _____ fire truck.
2. The grass is nice and _____ .
3. The ground was _____ with snow.
4. There were no clouds in the _____ sky.
5. It is _____ outside at night.
6. The monkey ate a yummy _____ banana.
7. I drink _____ grape juice for breakfast.

Context Clues

Read the sentences. Find and write the words that make sense in the sentences.

1. We clean the floor when we _____ it with a _____.

2. Mom looks at herself in the _____ when she brushes her long _____ .

3. I like to drink a _____ of milk and eat a yummy _____ .

4. It is fun to draw _____ on paper and cut them out with _____ .

5. I put my head on my _____ and cover up with my _____ when I take a nap.

glass	story	blanket	cookie
pillow	hair	mirror	broom
sweep	scissors	pictures	

Matching Pictures With Text

Circle the sentence that tells about each picture.

The lion roars.

Lions eat meat.

Lions sleep a lot.

The alligator swims.

Two alligators rest.

The alligator sleeps.

The bear dives into the water.

The bear eats a fish.

The bear rolls in the grass.

Ice cream is a nice treat.

Cupcakes are good.

I had spaghetti for lunch.

Baking a Cake

Look at the picture. Read the story.

I baked a cake in my oven. I made a mistake. The cake was strange. I ate the cake anyway.

Read the questions. Circle the correct pictures.

1. What was baked?

2. Where was it baked?

3. Who ate the cake?

Lawn Care

Look at the picture. Read the story.

Joe mows the grass that grows near his home. Then he hoes the rows in his garden. Next, he uses the hose to water everything. Joe is a good gardener.

Read the questions. Circle the correct pictures.

1. What does Joe mow?

2. What does Joe hoe?

3. What does Joe water?

My Pet Dog

Look at the picture. Read the story.

My pet can fetch an egg from a hen.
The hen may peck, but my pet can
run like a jet!

Fill in the missing word in each sentence.

1. The _____ can fetch an egg.

2. The _____ can peck.

3. The _____ can run like a jet!

A Bath

Look at the picture. Read the story.

I scrub myself in the tub. A bug
looks at me. I splash on the rug.
The bug jumps in the tub.

 Fill in the missing word in each sentence.

1. The person is in the _____.

2. The person splashes on the _____.

3. The _____ jumps in the tub.

Jack and Jill

Look at the picture. Read the poem.

Jack and Jill
  Went up a hill
To fetch a pail of
  water;
Jack fell down,
  And broke his crown,
And Jill came tumbling
  after.

 Answer the questions.

1. Who went up a hill?

_____

2. Why did they go up a hill?

_____

3. What happened to Jack?

_____

Bedtime

Read the story.

At bedtime, my father reads a story to me and tucks me in my covers. Then we tell each other about our day. He says that he is proud of me. I always have sweet dreams!

 Draw a picture to illustrate the story.

 Answer the questions.

1. What is the first thing the father does?

   _____

   _____

2. What does the child tell the father?

   _____

   _____

3. How does the child sleep?

   _____

   _____

Draw the Picture!

Show that you understand the words on this page by drawing the pictures to explain them.

	One of the balloons had popped. It was not the same color as the others.
	The rectangle is larger than the square.
	One of the candles has been blown out.
	Six different colors are marked on the wall.
	One of the balls is different.

Sequencing

Show the correct order by writing **1**, **2**, **3**, or **4** in each box.

Brushing my hair

Before my hair is brushed.

Now my hair is brushed.

Turn out the light.

Go upstairs.

Say "good night."

Say your prayers.

Sequencing Pictures

Indicate the correct order of the pictures in each row by putting a **1**, **2**, or **3** in each circle.

Worth Repeating

Color the parrot only if the two sentences *parrot* each other—that is, mean the same thing.

1. Sue is happy. Sue is glad.	
2. Bill has practice on Saturday. Bill's practice is the day after Monday.	
3. Before you color, fold the paper. Fold your paper first, and then color it.	
4. We went shopping yesterday. The day before today we shopped.	
5. The black dog's collar is big. The big dog's collar is black.	
6. The TV program starts before lunch. That TV program is on in the morning.	
7. Amy came to the party late. Amy was not on time for the party.	

Sense or Nonsense?

Circle YES or NO to answer each question:

1.	Could a stray cat follow you home?	YES	NO
2.	Could a stray elephant come to your house for dinner?	YES	NO
3.	Could you see your reflection in a store window?	YES	NO
4.	Could a man grow a mustache out of ice cream?	YES	NO
5.	Could you put on a show for your friends?	YES	NO
6.	Could a cat dance on a frog?	YES	NO
7.	Could a dog be taller than a building?	YES	NO
8.	Could a dog chase a cat?	YES	NO
9.	Could a cat tear a paper bag?	YES	NO
10.	Could a cat play the violin?	YES	NO
11.	Could ice cream be green?	YES	NO
12.	Could ice cream be hot?	YES	NO
13.	Could a friend wait for you?	YES	NO
14.	Can a wall walk?	YES	NO
15.	Could a dog jump?	YES	NO
16.	Could a horse jump?	YES	NO

❑ Write a real sentence of your own that makes sense:

_____

_____

❑ Write a nonsense sentence of your own:

_____

_____

Sentence Match

 **Draw a line to match each sentence half.**

The bird

is my favorite food.

My blue hat

whizzed by my house.

The cup

jumped over each other.

A fast train

flew high in the sky.

Pizza

fell and broke.

The puppies

matches my blue coat.

Complete the Sentence

 **Write a word from the word box to complete each sentence.**

blue	count	shark	wet
camp	licks	sun	

1. We put up a tent at our _____ .

2. The _____ swam in the ocean.

3. The sky is big and _____ .

4. He _____ the ice cream cone.

5. I can _____ to one hundred.

6. The _____ is bright today.

7. I got _____ in the rain.

More Complete the Sentence

 **Write a word from the word box to complete each sentence.**

egg	city	friend
mile	river	

1. We walked for one _____ .

2. The _____ flowed down the hill.

3. There were many tall buildings in the _____ .

4. I found an _____ in the nest.

5. My _____ and I played in the yard.

Unscramble the Sentences

**Unscramble these words to make a sentence.
Put a period at the end of each sentence.**

1. roof cat The is on the

_____

_____

2. I candy the ate

_____

_____

3. swim pond the in Fish

_____

_____

4. write I my can name

_____

_____

5. book good This a is

_____

_____

Cracked Egg Sentences

The words in each egg can be put together to make a sentence. Write each sentence on the lines next to its egg. Be sure to use the correct sentence punctuation.

1.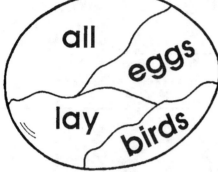

1. _____
   _____
   _____

2.

2. _____
   _____
   _____

3.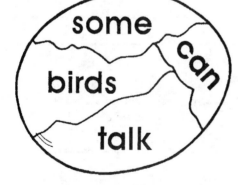

3. _____
   _____
   _____

4.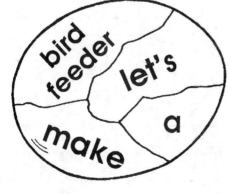

4. _____
   _____
   _____

Writing Sentences

 **Write each group of words as a sentence by making the first letter capital and putting a period at the end.**

1. my friend is at the door

_____

_____

2. a chicken ate the corn

_____

_____

3. your hat is on the table

_____

_____

4. the actor was in a play

_____

_____

Write a Sentence

Write a sentence for each picture.

1. _____

   _____

2. _____

   _____

3. _____

   _____

4. _____

   _____

5. _____

   _____

6. _____

   _____

7. _____

   _____

Writing More Sentences

Write a sentence for each word.

ant
_____
- -
_____

catch
_____
- -
_____

boy
_____
- -
_____

see
_____
- -
_____

wave
_____
- -
_____

green
_____
- -
_____

pet
_____
- -
_____

hot
_____
- -
_____

Design a Car or Truck

1. Finish drawing a funny car or truck.
2. Draw yourself in the seat driving.
3. Give it a funny name.
4. Fill in the story blanks below.

This is a_____.
                    (car / truck)

It can go _____.   It is _____.
            (fast / slow)   (big / little)

It has four _____ and two _____.
            (wheels / doors)   (wheels / doors)

Its color is _____.   It is _____!
(The color word is on your marker or crayon.)   (super/great/silly)

Some Silly Sentences

Fill in the blanks with two of the animal names. Then draw a picture for that sentence.

ant	canary	cat	parrot	frog
fish	puppy	dog	turtle	goldfish

❑ The _____ helped the _____
eat pizza one afternoon.

❑ The _____ and the _____
read a book on the beach.

Giggles Story Starter

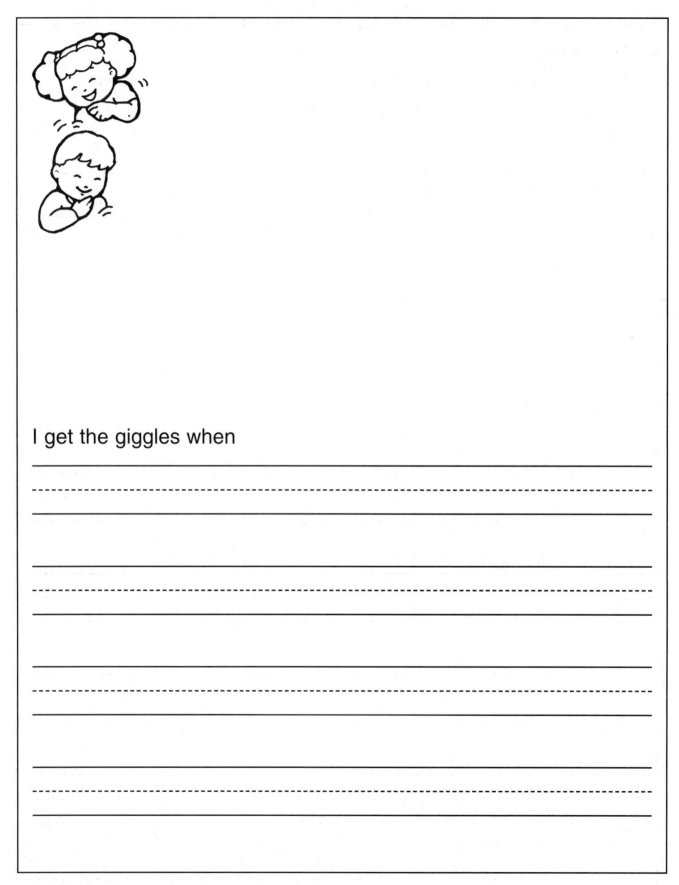

I get the giggles when

Play Story Starter

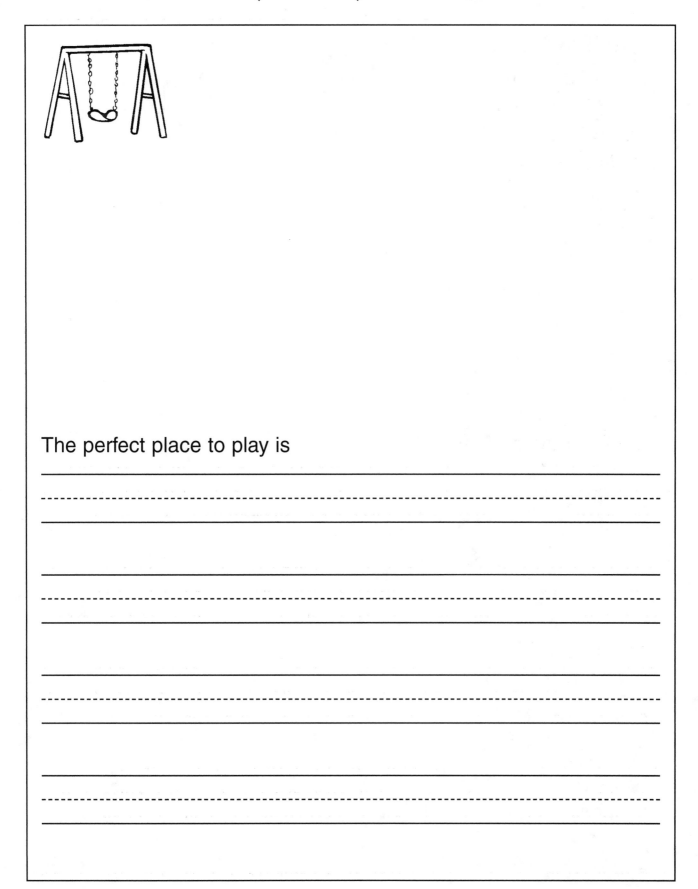

The perfect place to play is

_____

- -

_____

_____

- -

_____

_____

- -

_____

_____

- -

_____

Zoo Story Starter

If I lived at the zoo, I would be

_____

_____

_____

_____

Feelings Faces

I am happy when _____

_____

_____

I am sad when _____

_____

_____

I am worried when _____

_____

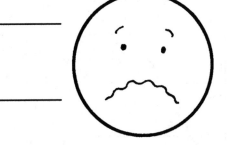

_____

My Monster

Where does your monster like to hide?

_____

- -

_____

What does your monster like to do?

_____

- -

_____

What is your monster afraid of?

_____

- -

_____

What do you do about your monster?

_____

- -

_____

Draw your monster here.

School Numbers

Draw lines matching each number to the bus with that many children.

5

2

4

6

3

1

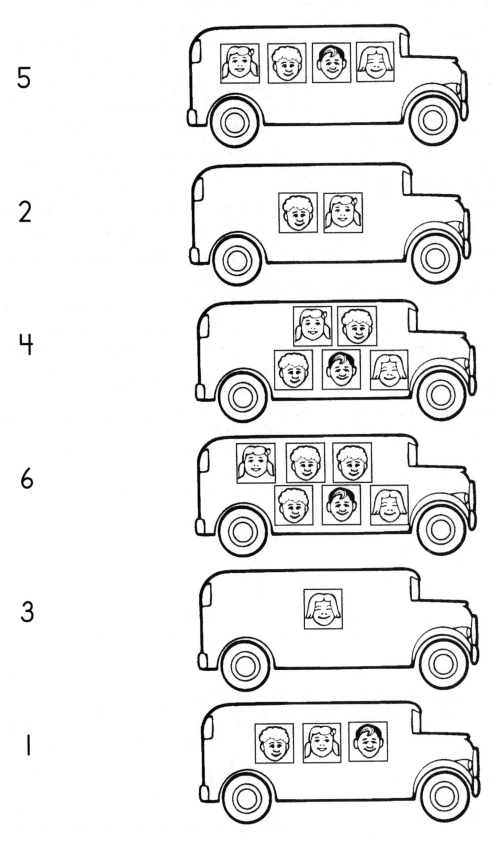

Counting Leaves and Flowers

• **Count the leaves and write the numbers.**

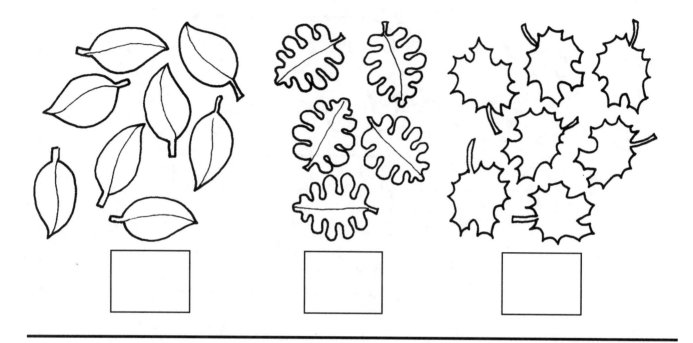

• **Read the numbers and draw that many flowers.**

| 6 | 4 | 9 |

Mrs. Pig's Garden

Directions: Draw a line from each group of pigs to the matching group of flowers.

How Many?

Color the pictures. Cut them out. Glue the pictures in the right box.
Count the pictures in each box. Write the number in the blank spaces.

Hats	**Boots**
There are _____ hats.	There are _____ boots.
Scarves	**Vests**
There are _____ scarves.	There are _____ vests.

Count and Draw

1. Write how many suitcases.

2. Write how many plants.

3. Write how many bananas.

4. Draw 5 watermelons.

5. Draw 9 ears of corn.

6. Draw 7 paint cans.

Night Numbers

Color the correct number of stars in each row.

0	☆ ☆ ☆ ☆ ☆ ☆ ☆ ☆ ☆ ☆
1	☆ ☆ ☆ ☆ ☆ ☆ ☆ ☆ ☆ ☆
2	☆ ☆ ☆ ☆ ☆ ☆ ☆ ☆ ☆ ☆
3	☆ ☆ ☆ ☆ ☆ ☆ ☆ ☆ ☆ ☆
4	☆ ☆ ☆ ☆ ☆ ☆ ☆ ☆ ☆ ☆
5	☆ ☆ ☆ ☆ ☆ ☆ ☆ ☆ ☆ ☆
6	☆ ☆ ☆ ☆ ☆ ☆ ☆ ☆ ☆ ☆
7	☆ ☆ ☆ ☆ ☆ ☆ ☆ ☆ ☆ ☆
8	☆ ☆ ☆ ☆ ☆ ☆ ☆ ☆ ☆ ☆
9	☆ ☆ ☆ ☆ ☆ ☆ ☆ ☆ ☆ ☆
10	☆ ☆ ☆ ☆ ☆ ☆ ☆ ☆ ☆ ☆

Beach Bears

Circle the numeral that tells how many.

(sandcastle)	1 2 3		(sailboat)	3 4 5
(seagull)	2 3 4		(shovel)	2 3 4
(bear face)	3 4 5		(umbrella)	3 4 5
(bucket)	1 2 3		(sun)	1 2 3
(beach ball)	1 2 3		(inner tube)	0 1 2

A "Mazing" Bear

Help the bear find the honey.

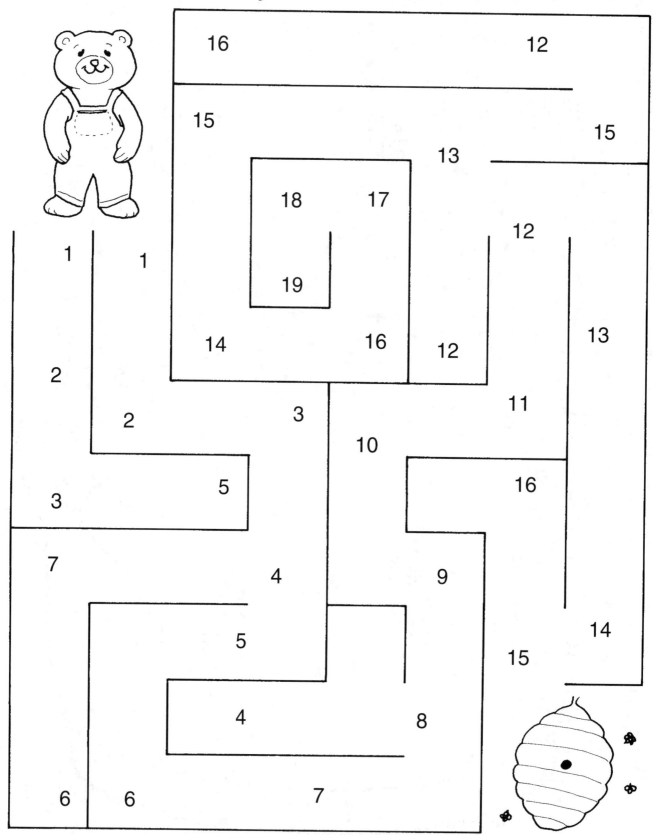

The Surprise

Connect the dots to see the surprise. Color it.

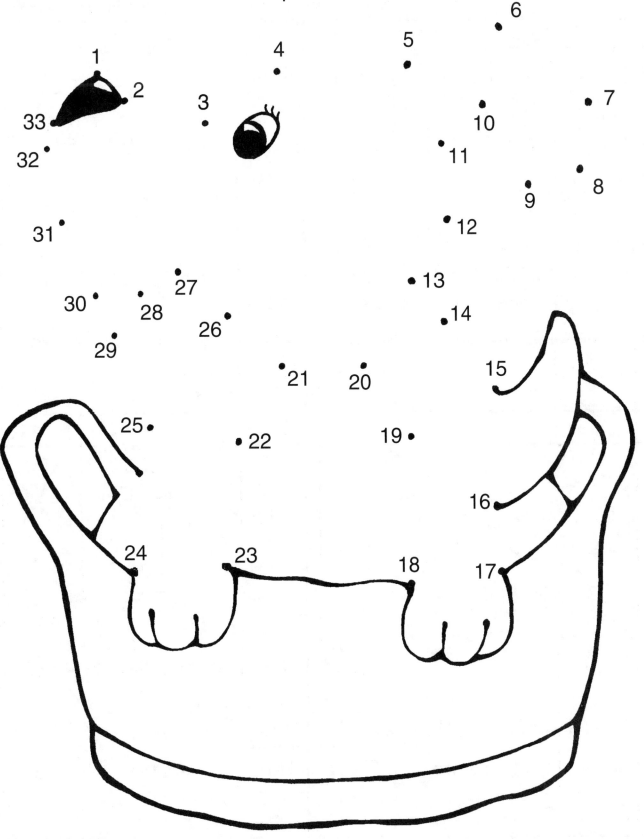

How Many?

Complete the pictures.

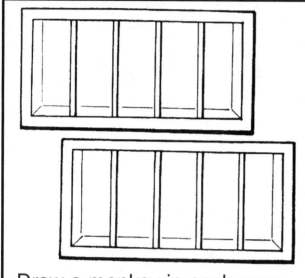

Draw a monkey in each cage.

How many monkeys are there?

_____

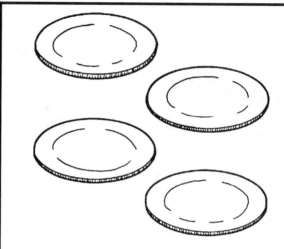

Draw a piece of cake on each plate.

How many pieces are there?

_____

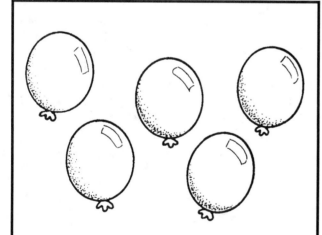

Draw a string on each balloon.

How many strings are there?

_____

Draw a scarf on each snowman.

How many scarves are there?

_____

Snakes are Sensational

Snakes are reptiles. They have no legs and no ears. Most snakes hatch from eggs. Snakes stick out their tongues to help them smell and to feel things. Their eyesight is not good. If you stand still, a snake may not even notice you. Snakes are cold-blooded. They hibernate during the cold winter. They move when the weather is warmer. Connect the dots.

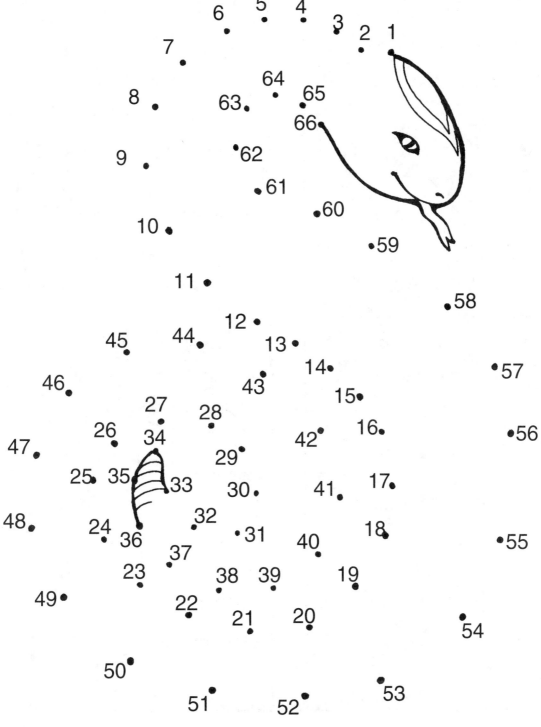

Gumball Machine

Write the missing numerals. Count from 0 to 100. Color the picture.

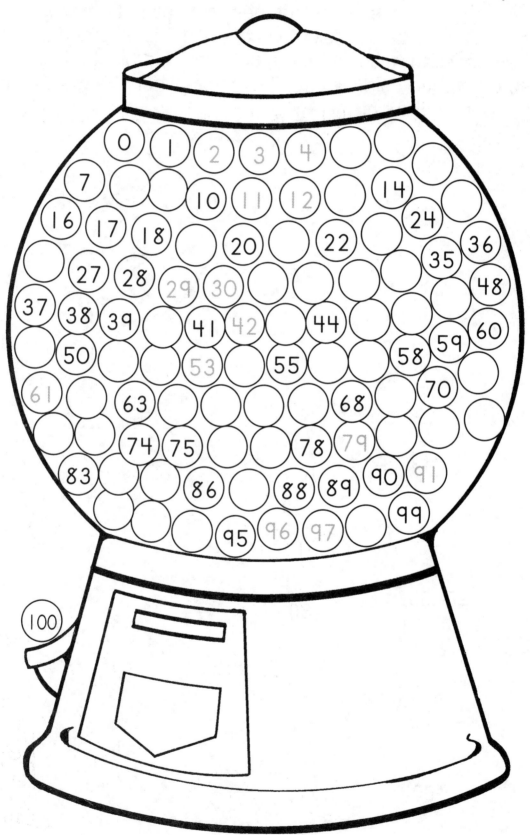

Candy Lane

To get to the gingerbread house, write the missing numerals from 0 to 100.

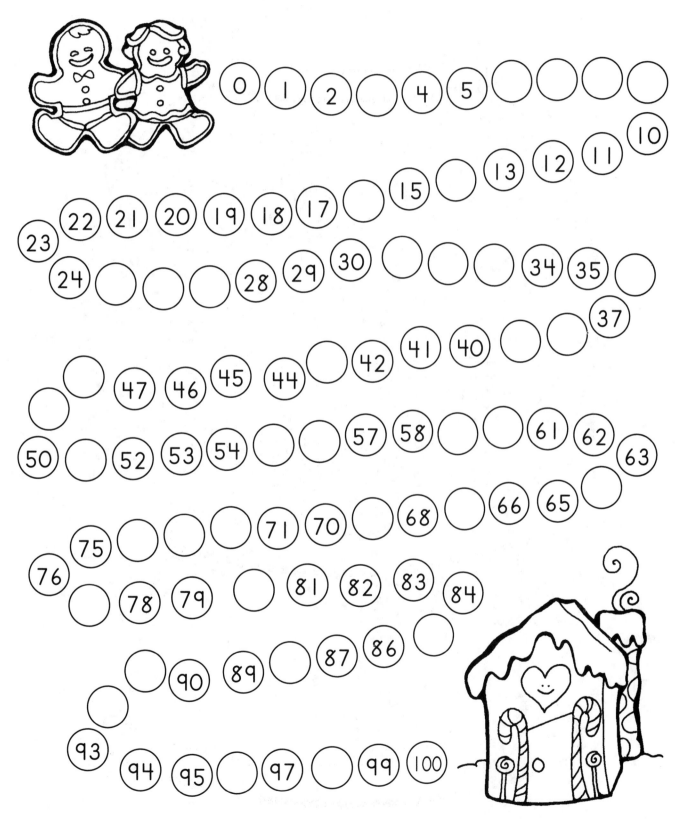

Counting Dot-to-Dot

Draw a line to connect the dots from 1 to 100. Color the picture.

Missing Numbers

Write the correct numeral in each blank.

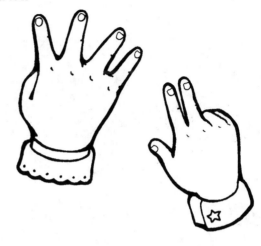

1. 3, 4, 5, _____

2. 9, 10, _____

3. 14, 15, _____

4. 21, 22, _____

5. 31, 32, _____

6. 36, _____, 38

7. 40, _____, 42

8. 47, _____, 49

9. 50, _____, 52

10. _____, 57, 58

11. 74, 75, _____

12. 80, _____, 82

13. 89, 90, _____

14. 98, _____, 100

15. 98, 99, _____

In the space below, make up some of your own counting puzzles.

Two by Two

Count by two's to fill in the blank.

2	4	—	8
10	—	14	—
—	20	—	24
—	28	—	32
—	—	38	40

Nifty Fifty

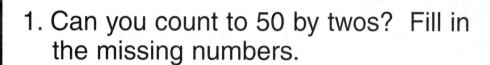

1. Can you count to 50 by twos? Fill in the missing numbers.

   2, 4, 6, ___ , 10, 12, ___ , 16, 18, ___ , 22, ___ , 26, 28, 30, ___ , 34, 36, ___ , ___ , 42, 44, ___ , 48, ___

2. Can you count to 50 by fives? Fill in the missing numbers.

   5, 10, ___ , 20, ___ , ___ , 35, 40, 45, ___

3. Can you count to 50 by tens? Fill in the missing numbers.

   10, ___ , 30, ___ , 50

Number Names

Match the names to the numbers.

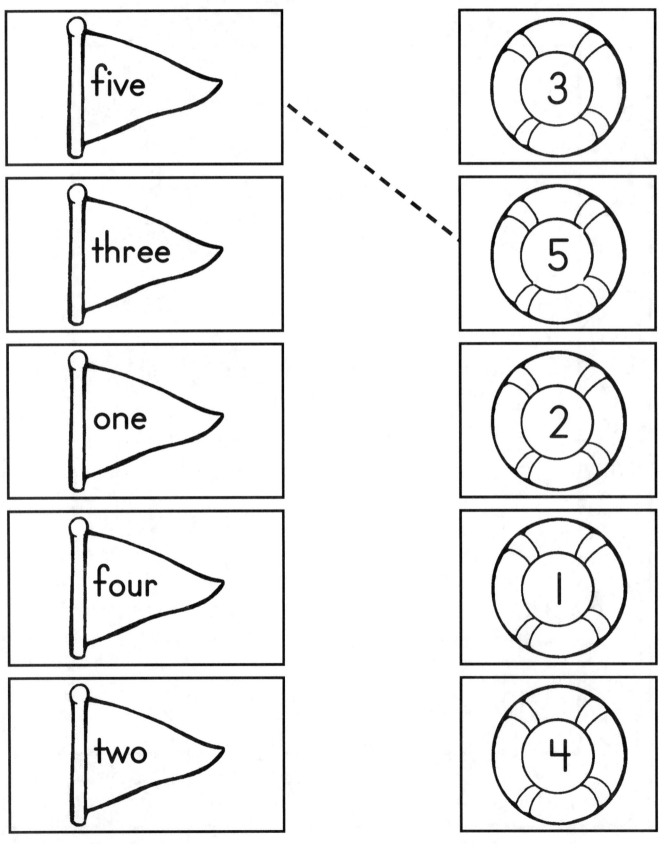

Words and Numerals

Draw a line to connect each rabbit to the word that names the numeral.

Watermelon Wagon and Flying Fish

Follow the directions:

1. Count how many fish. _____
   Draw one more.
   Write how many now. _____

2. Count how many watermelons. _____
   Draw one more.
   Write how many now. _____

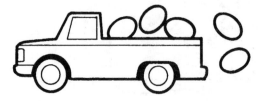

3. Count how many fish. _____
   Draw one more.
   Write how many now. _____

4. Count how many watermelons. _____
   Draw one more.
   Write how many now. _____

5. Count how many fish. _____
   Draw one more.
   Write how many now. _____

6. Count how many watermelons. _____
   Draw one more.
   Write how many now. _____

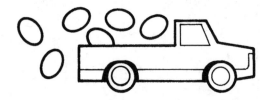

It's Music—More or Less

Write the number that is 1 less or 1 more.

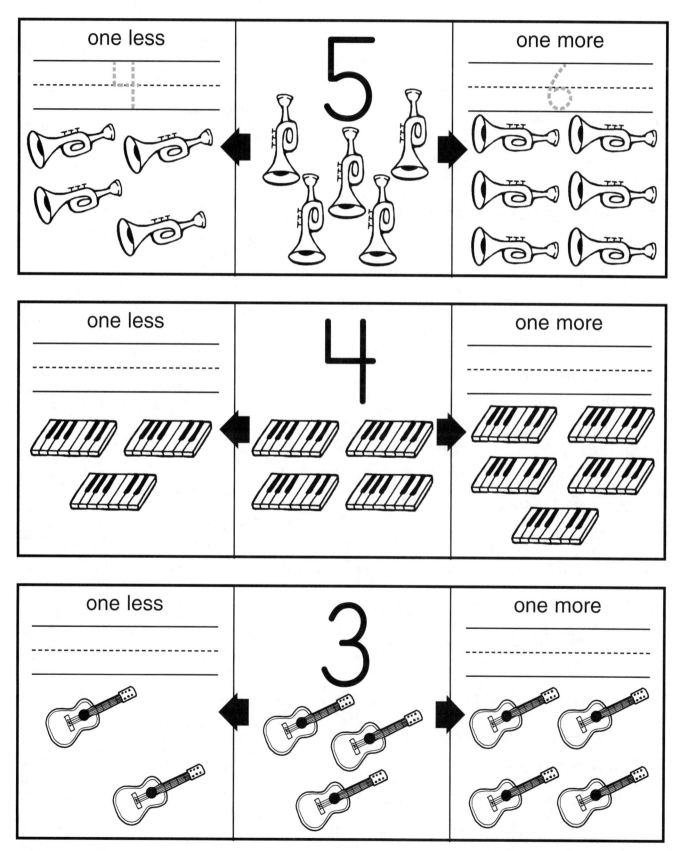

Different Drum

Draw a group of circles to show 1 more than each group of instruments.

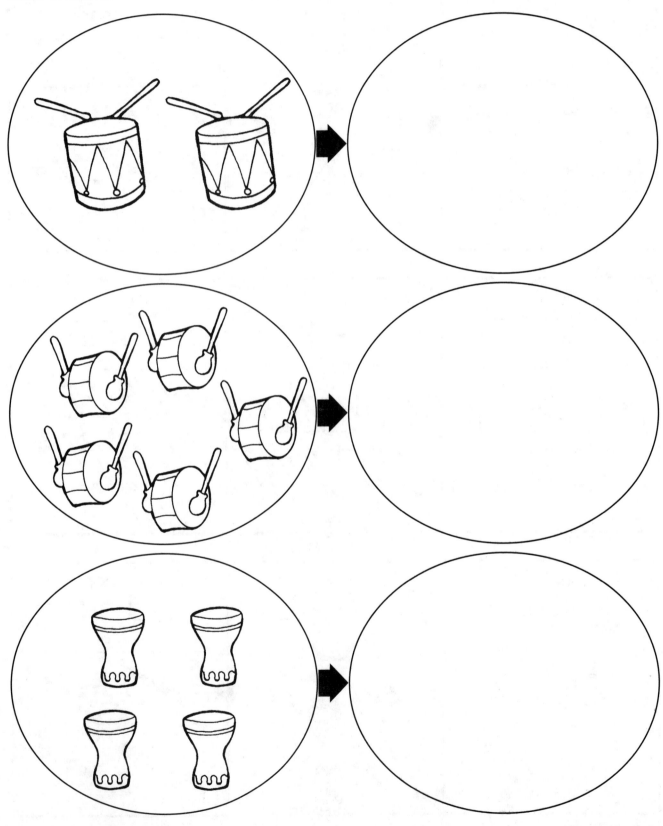

Making All Things Equal

Circle things to show = sets.

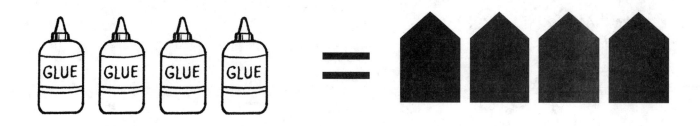

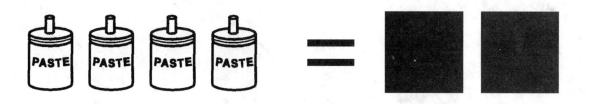

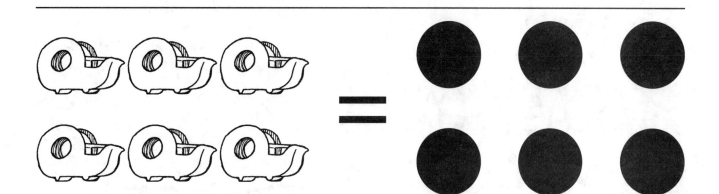

Falling Leaves

Write a numeral in each leaf to make each number sentence true.

Which Is More?

Write the numerals that show the number of things in each group.
Color the group that has more in each row.

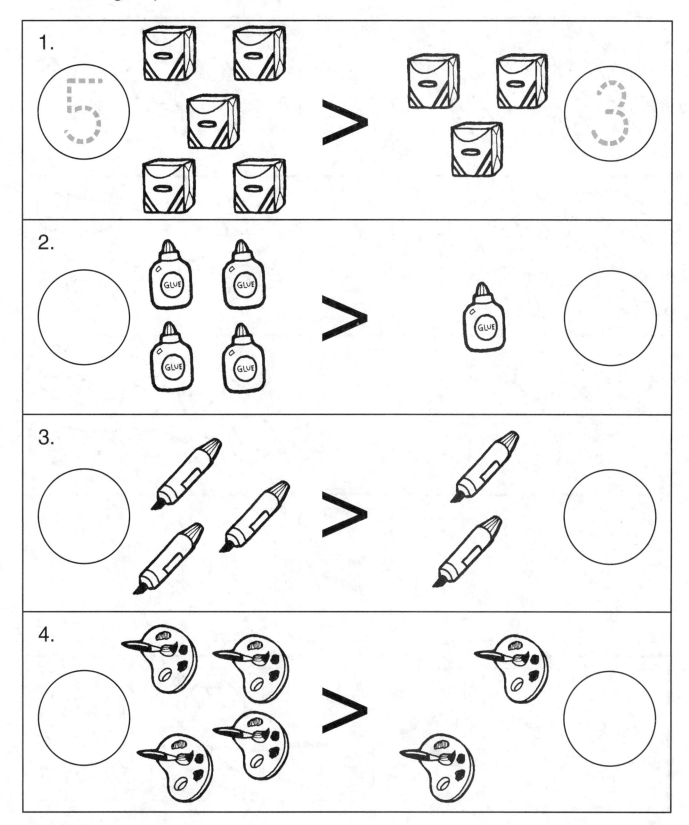

Make It Right!

Draw the correct symbol in each box. Use the symbols in the bank below.

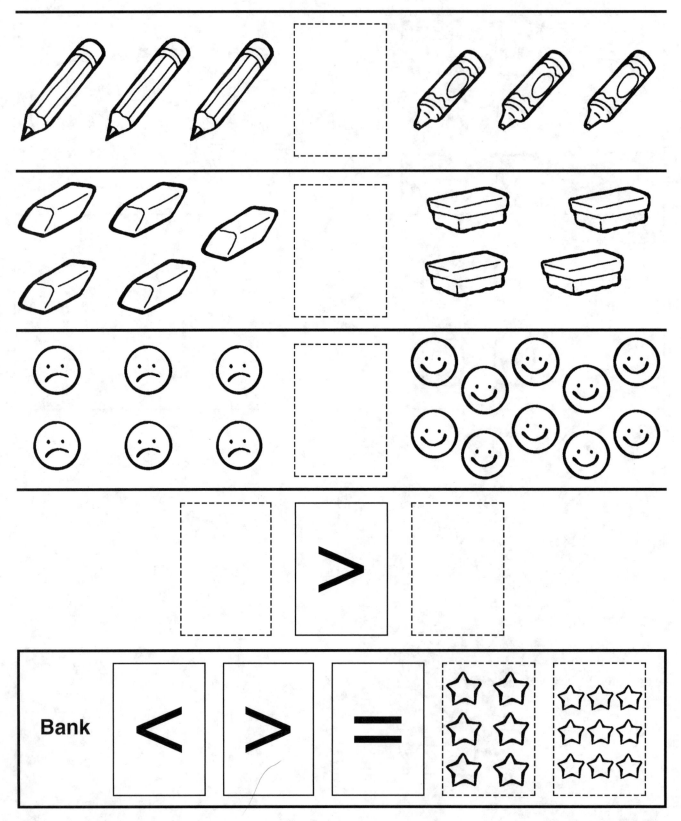

Shining Stars

Write a numeral in each star to make each number sentence true.
Sometimes there are many correct answers.

1.  ☆ (20)   >   1

2.  ☆ (20)   >   9

3.  ☆ (1)   <   2

4.  ☆ (1)   <   12

Everything in Order

Write the correct symbol in each box to make each number sentence true.

1.  ⬜

2. 3 ⬜ 3

3.  ⬜ 5

4. 6 ⬜ 8

5. 12 ⬜ 10

| > | = | < | > | < |

Sets of Ten

Complete each set to make a set of ten items. Color the pictures.

Counting Tens and Ones

Count how many tens (⌷) and ones (▫). Write the number of each in the boxes. Write the number on the line.

1. ⌷⌷ ▫ ▫ ▫

tens	ones

_____

2. ⌷⌷⌷⌷ ▫▫▫▫ / ▫▫▫▫

tens	ones

_____

3. ⌷⌷⌷⌷⌷⌷⌷ ▫ ▫ ▫ ▫

tens	ones

_____

4. ⌷⌷⌷ ▫ ▫ ▫ ▫ ▫ ▫

tens	ones

_____

5. ⌷ ▫ ▫ ▫ ▫ ▫ ▫ ▫ ▫ ▫

tens	ones

_____

6. ⌷⌷⌷⌷ ▫ ▫ ▫ ▫ ▫ ▫ ▫

tens	ones

_____

7. ⌷⌷⌷⌷ ▫ ▫ ▫ ▫ ▫

tens	ones

_____

8. ⌷⌷⌷⌷⌷⌷⌷⌷ ▫

tens	ones

_____

9. ⌷⌷⌷⌷ ▫ ▫ ▫ ▫

tens	ones

_____

10. ⌷⌷⌷⌷⌷ ▫ ▫

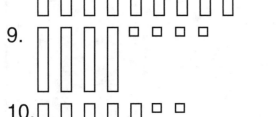

tens	ones

_____

Tens and Ones

Read how many tens and ones. Write the number on the line.

1. 2 tens 6 ones _____   2. 5 tens 4 ones _____

3. 3 tens 1 one _____   4. 8 tens 4 ones _____

5. 6 tens 8 ones _____   6. 9 tens 2 ones _____

7. 7 tens 5 ones _____   8. 1 ten 6 ones _____

9. 4 tens 9 ones _____   10. 4 tens 7 ones _____

Draw a line to match the pictures with the tens (⎕) and ones (▫).

1. 5 tens 2 ones   a.

2. 3 tens 1 one   b.

3. 7 tens 9 ones   c.

4. 2 tens 5 ones   d.

5. 6 tens 3 ones   e.

6. 4 tens 8 ones   f.

7. 1 ten 6 ones   g.

8. 4 tens 2 ones   h.

Place Value Practice

 = 10    = 1

Find the number each group of moths and silkworms represents.

1.    = _____

2.    = _____

3.    = _____

4.    = _____

5.    = _____

6.   = _____

Graph

Look at these pictures of Joe, Spud, Helena, and Joanna. Count them to complete the graph.

	1	**2**	**3**	**4**	**5**	**6**	**7**
a. Joe							
b. Joanna							
c. Spud							
d. Helena							

Hide and Seek

Look at the picture below. Find the faces and plot them on the graph. Then, answer the questions.

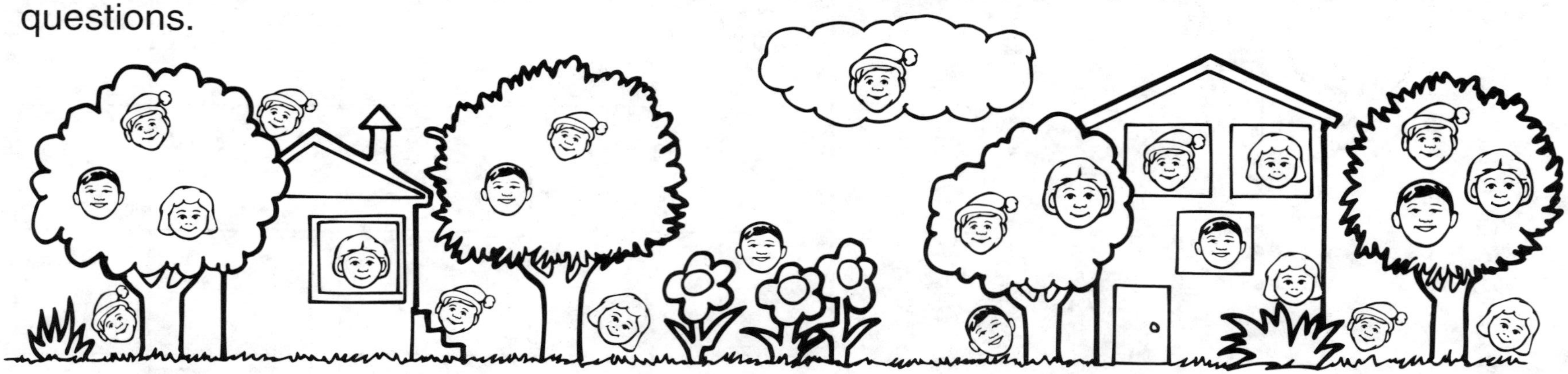

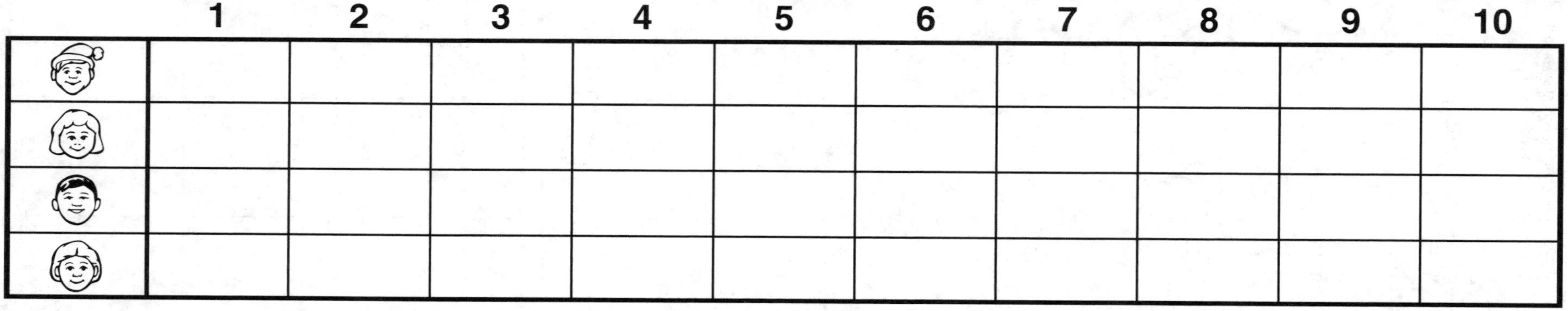
1
2
3
4
5
6
7
8
9
10

How many?

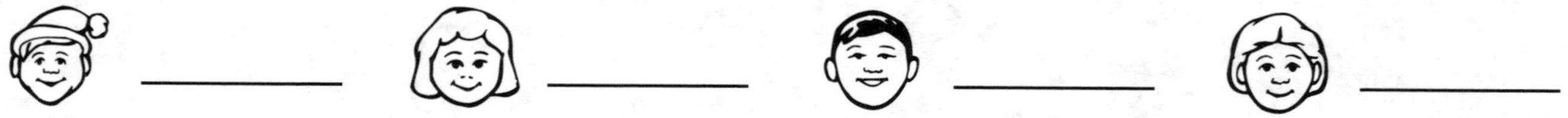

Circle the correct picture.

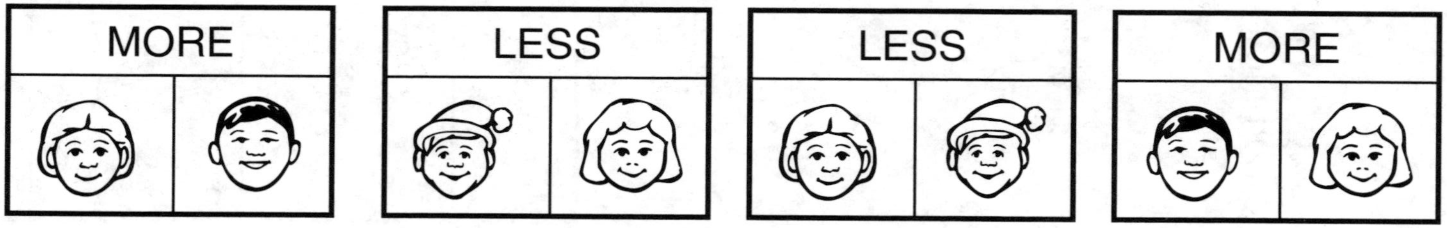
MORE
LESS
LESS
MORE

Everything Counts

Count how many. Color the pictures.

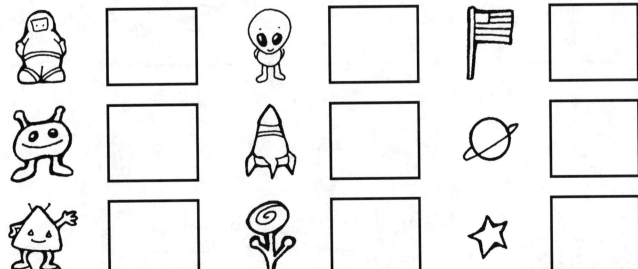

Underwater World

Write the numeral on the lines to show how many of each thing are in the picture.

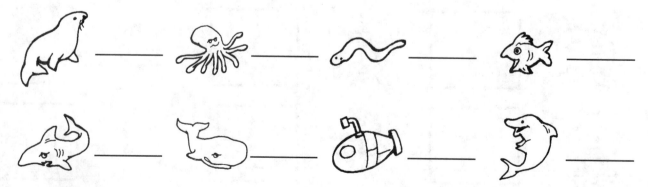

Animal Math

Count. Write a number sentence.

1.

$4 + 3 = 7$

2.

_____

3.

_____

4.

_____

5.

_____

6.

_____

Food Facts

Add the numbers together by counting the vegetables. Write the answer on the pot.

1. 3 + 4 =

2. 2 + 3 =

3. 4 + 2 =

4. 3 + 5 =

5. 2 + 2 =

6. 4 + 5 =

I Can Add!

1. Count the chocolate chips.

3. Add.

2. Print the number under the cookie.

4. Color.

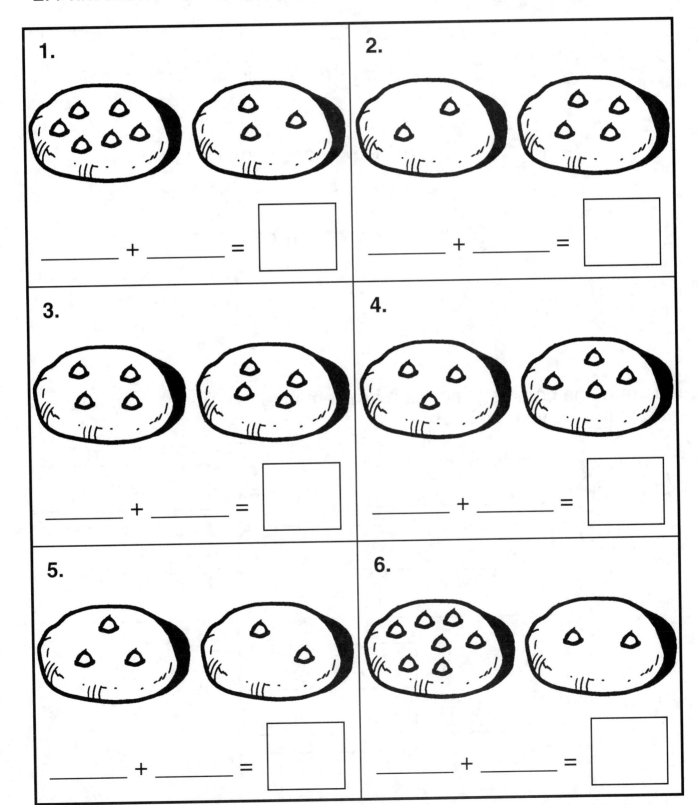

Farm Facts

1. [cats] + [cats] = How many cats in all?_____

2. [chickens] + [chicks] = How many chickens in all?_____

3. [pumpkins] + [pumpkins] = How many pumpkins in all?_____

4. [cow] + [lamb] = How many cows in all?_____

5. [ducks] + [ducks] = How many ducks in all?_____

Illustrate and complete the math problems below. Think about a farm when drawing your pictures.

6. 3
   +3

7. 2
   +3

8. 4
   +1

School "Stuff"

Write the sums.

1.
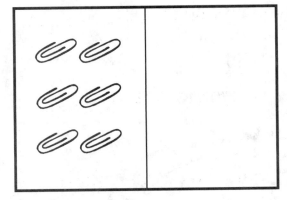

$6 + 0 = \underline{\hspace{1cm}}$

2.

$4 + 3 = \underline{\hspace{1cm}}$

3.
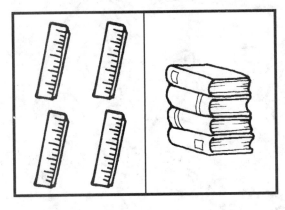

$4 + 4 = \underline{\hspace{1cm}}$

4.

$2 + 2 = \underline{\hspace{1cm}}$

5.
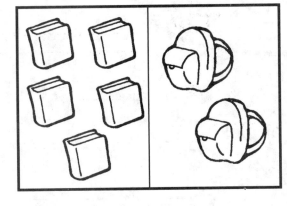

$5 + 2 = \underline{\hspace{1cm}}$

6.
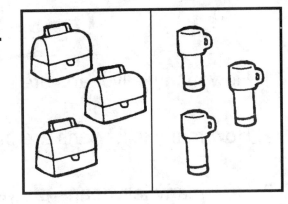

$3 + 3 = \underline{\hspace{1cm}}$

Jellybeans Add Up!

Color the jellybeans.

3 red   2 brown
1 purple   4 pink
5 orange   6 green
8 black   7 yellow

1. How many jellybeans are red or green? _____ + _____ = _____
                                          red   green

2. How many jellybeans are orange or pink? _____ + _____ = _____
                                           orange   pink

3. How many jellybeans are yellow or brown? _____ + _____ = _____
                                            yellow   brown

4. How many jellybeans are purple or black? _____ + _____ = _____
                                            purple   black

Fill the Jellybean Jars

Follow the directions. Then write the missing number.

1. Draw 10 jellybeans in the jar.

   Color 6 jellybeans red.

   Color the other jellybeans yellow.

   Complete the addition sentence.

   6 + _____ = 10

2. Draw 8 jellybeans in the jar.

   Color 5 jellybeans blue.

   Color the other jellybeans orange.

   Complete the addition sentence.

   5 + _____ = 8

3. Draw 12 jellybeans in the jar.

   Color 2 jellybeans pink.

   Color the other jellybeans green.

   Complete the addition sentence.

   2 + _____ = 12

Adding Palm Trees

Add the numbers on each tree. Add the top 2 numbers first. Then add the bottom number to the sum of the first 2 numbers.

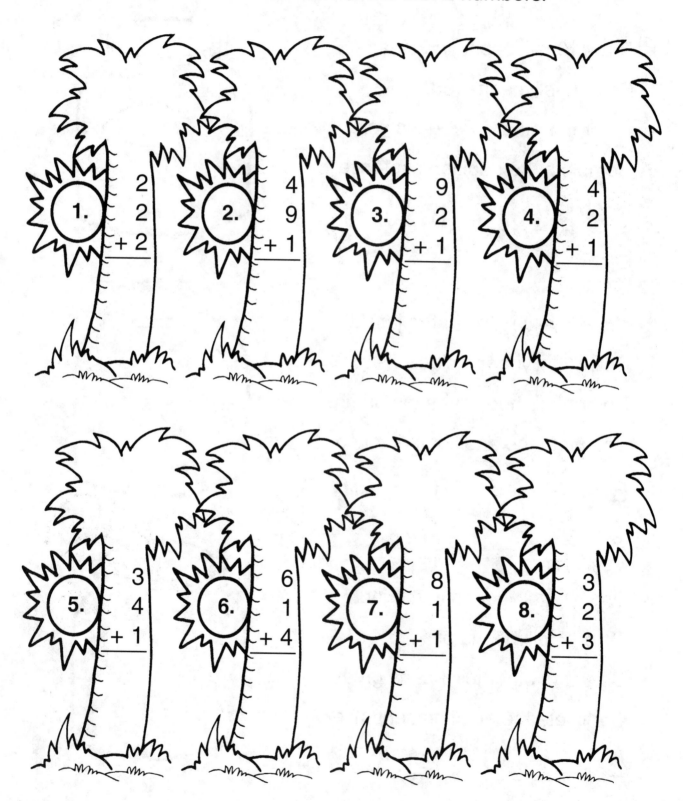

1.
```
  2
  2
+ 2
___
```

2.
```
  4
  9
+ 1
___
```

3.
```
  9
  2
+ 1
___
```

4.
```
  4
  2
+ 1
___
```

5.
```
  3
  4
+ 1
___
```

6.
```
  6
  1
+ 4
___
```

7.
```
  8
  1
+ 1
___
```

8.
```
  3
  2
+ 3
___
```

The Great Snowball Fight

Add the numbers on the snowballs.

1.
2
4
+ 9

2.
2
6
+ 6

3.
1
2
+ 8

4.
5
3
+ 5

5.
7
2
+ 6

6.
5
4
+ 7

What Is It?

To discover a secret shape, follow the directions. Find the sums. Then connect the answers with a line. Connect the first answer with the second answer and the second answer with the third answer. Continue until you finish the shape.

1.
```
  17
+ 22
_____
```

2.
```
  54
+ 21
_____
```

3.
```
  76
+ 22
_____
```

4.
```
  18
+ 31
_____
```

5.
```
  70
+ 20
_____
```

6.
```
  11
+ 11
_____
```

7.
```
  51
+ 27
_____
```

8.
```
  19
+ 10
_____
```

9.
```
  62
+ 22
_____
```

10.
```
  35
+ 21
_____
```

39

98 •   75   56   84

49 •   • 29

22

90 •   • 78

Sailing Into Addition

What a great day to go sailing! Solve the problems on each sailboat, and you will go far!

$$10 + 87$$
1. =

$$54 + 22$$
2. =

$$21 + 47$$
3. =

$$50 + 28$$
4. =

$$85 + 14$$
5. =

$$73 + 13$$
6. =

$$24 + 21$$
7. =

What Is the Secret Number?

To discover the secret number, find the sums and follow the directions.

1.

```
  21
+ 18
------
```

2.

```
  31
+ 16
------
```

3.

```
  31
+ 21
------
```

4.

```
  41
+ 31
------
```

5.

```
  12
+ 12
------
```

6.

```
  10
+ 17
------
```

1. It is not number 24. Cross it out.

2. It is not number 39. Cross it out.

3. It is not number 52. Cross it out.

4. It is not number 72. Cross it out.

5. It is not number 47. Cross it out.

What is the secret number? _____

Twenty

Directions: Follow all of the leaves that when added up equal 20 to get the ladybug home to its friends.

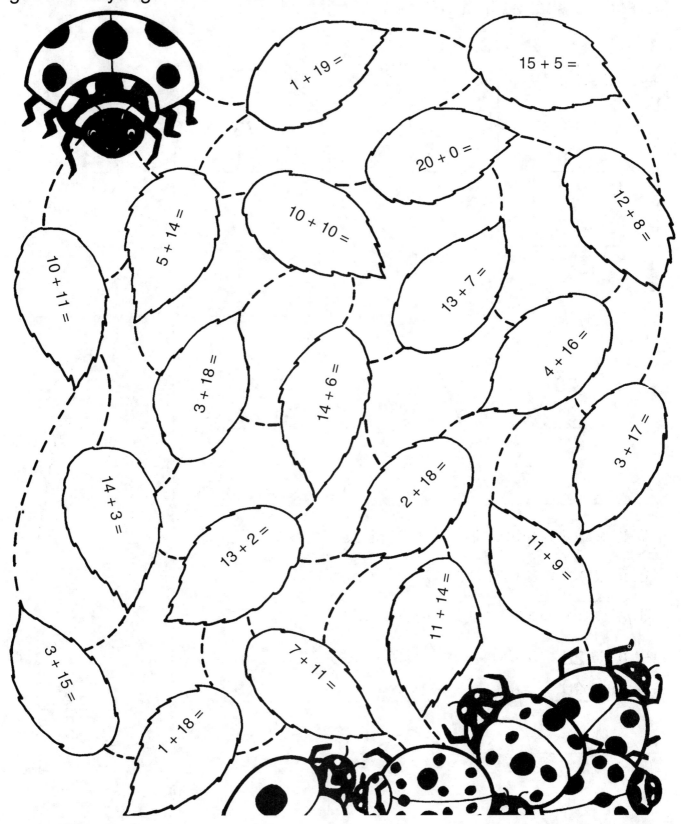

The Shape of Things

Solve the problems on each shape. Can you name each one?

Color the shapes that you can identify.

1.

$$\begin{array}{r} 17 \\ + \ 11 \\ \hline \end{array}$$

2.

$$\begin{array}{r} 24 \\ + \ 41 \\ \hline \end{array}$$

3.

$$\begin{array}{r} 72 \\ + \ 11 \\ \hline \end{array}$$

4.

$$\begin{array}{r} 10 \\ + \ 10 \\ \hline \end{array}$$

5.

$$\begin{array}{r} 25 \\ + \ 31 \\ \hline \end{array}$$

6.

$$\begin{array}{r} 19 \\ + \ 40 \\ \hline \end{array}$$

7.

$$\begin{array}{r} 42 \\ + \ 32 \\ \hline \end{array}$$

8.

$$\begin{array}{r} 81 \\ + \ 11 \\ \hline \end{array}$$

9.

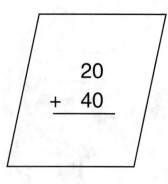

$$\begin{array}{r} 20 \\ + \ 40 \\ \hline \end{array}$$

10.

$$\begin{array}{r} 12 \\ + \ 35 \\ \hline \end{array}$$

11.

$$\begin{array}{r} 80 \\ + \ 19 \\ \hline \end{array}$$

12.

$$\begin{array}{r} 54 \\ + \ 23 \\ \hline \end{array}$$

The Pumpkin Patch

Solve the problems on the pumpkins. Draw a face on the pumpkin without a problem.

1.
$$19$$
$$+\ 12$$

2.
$$72$$
$$+\ 19$$

3.
$$15$$
$$+\ 16$$

4.
$$47$$
$$+\ 35$$

5.
$$68$$
$$+\ 26$$

6.
$$42$$
$$+\ 19$$

7.
$$23$$
$$+\ 17$$

Hidden Treasure

Solve the problems by adding.

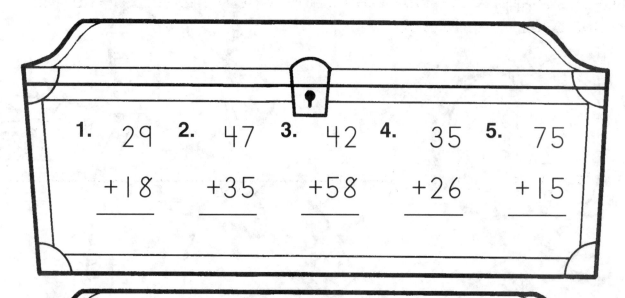

1. 29
   +18
   ___

2. 47
   +35
   ___

3. 42
   +58
   ___

4. 35
   +26
   ___

5. 75
   +15
   ___

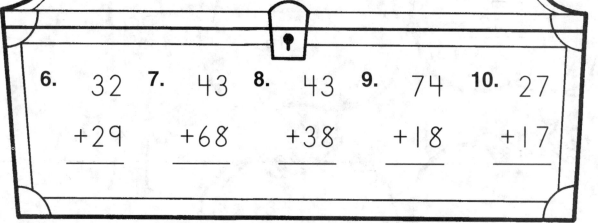

6. 32
   +29
   ___

7. 43
   +68
   ___

8. 43
   +38
   ___

9. 74
   +18
   ___

10. 27
    +17
    ___

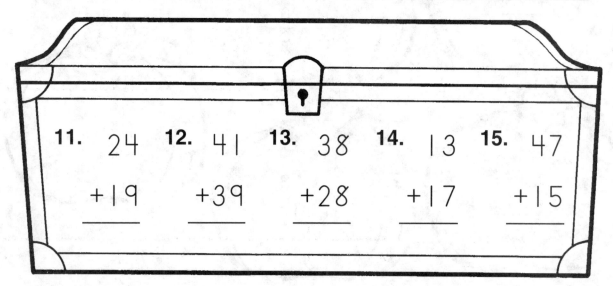

11. 24
    +19
    ___

12. 41
    +39
    ___

13. 38
    +28
    ___

14. 13
    +17
    ___

15. 47
    +15
    ___

Bouncing Back One

Subtraction is counting backwards. Put the kangaroo back one jump on each number line. Write the number where she stops. The first one has been done for you.

1.　5 - 1 = **4**

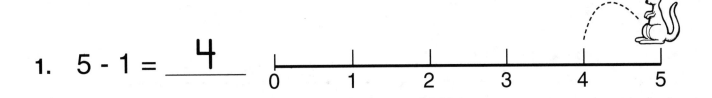

2.　4 - 1 = _____

3.　3 - 1 = _____

4.　2 - 1 = _____

5.　1 - 1 = _____

Hopping Down the Line

Follow Freddie Frog as he hops along the number line.

1. How many hops did Freddie Frog hop?

6 - 3 = 3

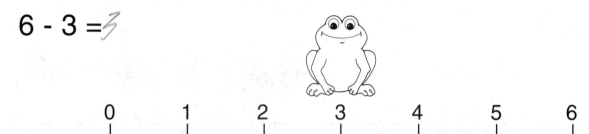

2. How many hops did Freddie Frog hop?

6 - 2 = 4

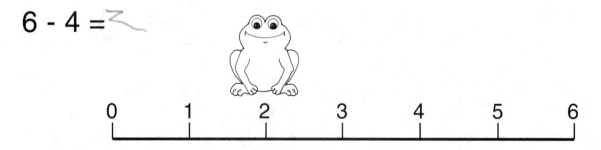

3. How many hops did Freddie Frog hop?

6 - 4 = 2

4. How many hops did Freddie Frog hop?

6 - 5 = 1

Take Away Toys

Subtract. Write how many are left.

1.

$$5$$
$$- \ 1$$

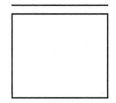

2.

$$6$$
$$- \ 4$$

3.

$$3$$
$$- \ 1$$

4.

$$3$$
$$- \ 2$$

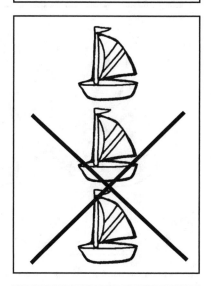

5.

$$4$$
$$- \ 1$$

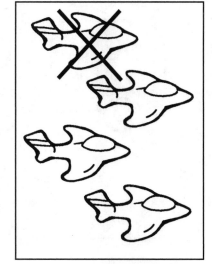

6.

$$2$$
$$- \ 0$$

Get Ready!

Write how many are taken away and how many are left.

1.

$$7 - \underline{\hspace{2cm}} = \underline{\hspace{2cm}}$$

2.

$$4 - \underline{\hspace{2cm}} = \underline{\hspace{2cm}}$$

3.

$$6 - \underline{\hspace{2cm}} = \underline{\hspace{2cm}}$$

4.

$$4 - \underline{\hspace{2cm}} = \underline{\hspace{2cm}}$$

5.

$$7 - \underline{\hspace{2cm}} = \underline{\hspace{2cm}}$$

Let's Go!

Cross out the things that are taken away. Write how many are left.

1.

6 - 2 = _____

2.

9 - 6 = _____

3.

6 - 0 = _____

4.

4 - 3 = _____

Subtraction Rainbow

Complete each subtraction problem. Then use the color code to color the rainbow.

5 = purple	4 = blue	3 = green
2 = yellow	1 = orange	0 = red

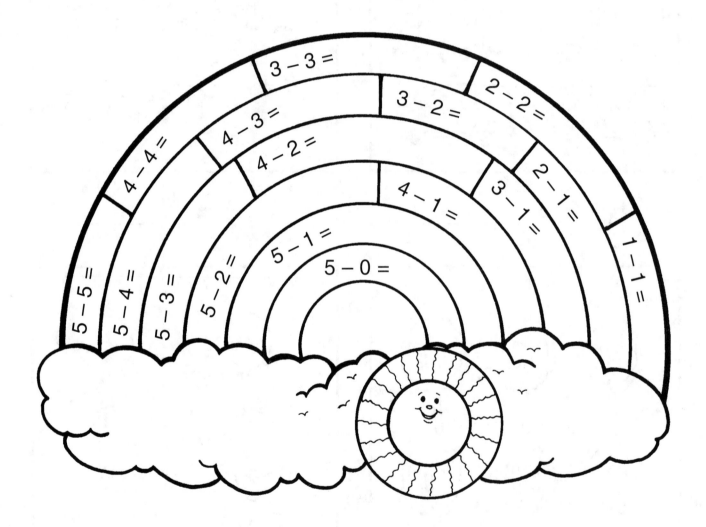

Dots

Finish the subtraction sentences. Write the answer. Draw the number of dots.

1. 6 dots take away 4 dots = _____ dots

2. 6 dots take away 2 dots = _____ dots

3. 6 dots take away 1 dot = _____ dots

4. 6 dots take away 3 dots = _____ dots

5. 6 dots take away 5 dots = _____ dot

6. 6 dots take away 6 dots = _____ dots

Subtraction

1. $\begin{array}{r} 3 \\ -\ 1 \\ \hline \end{array}$	**2.** $\begin{array}{r} 4 \\ -\ 2 \\ \hline \end{array}$	**3.** $\begin{array}{r} 2 \\ -\ 2 \\ \hline \end{array}$	**4.** $\begin{array}{r} 5 \\ -\ 3 \\ \hline \end{array}$	**5.** $\begin{array}{r} 3 \\ -\ 3 \\ \hline \end{array}$
6. $\begin{array}{r} 5 \\ -\ 1 \\ \hline \end{array}$	**7.** $\begin{array}{r} 3 \\ -\ 2 \\ \hline \end{array}$	**8.** $\begin{array}{r} 4 \\ -\ 3 \\ \hline \end{array}$	**9.** $\begin{array}{r} 5 \\ -\ 4 \\ \hline \end{array}$	**10.** $\begin{array}{r} 2 \\ -\ 1 \\ \hline \end{array}$
11. $\begin{array}{r} 4 \\ -\ 4 \\ \hline \end{array}$	**12.** $\begin{array}{r} 5 \\ -\ 2 \\ \hline \end{array}$	**13.** $\begin{array}{r} 1 \\ -\ 1 \\ \hline \end{array}$	**14.** $\begin{array}{r} 5 \\ -\ 5 \\ \hline \end{array}$	**15.** $\begin{array}{r} 4 \\ -\ 1 \\ \hline \end{array}$
16. $\begin{array}{r} 2 \\ -\ 1 \\ \hline \end{array}$	**17.** $\begin{array}{r} 1 \\ -\ 1 \\ \hline \end{array}$	**18.** $\begin{array}{r} 3 \\ -\ 2 \\ \hline \end{array}$	**19.** $\begin{array}{r} 5 \\ -\ 4 \\ \hline \end{array}$	**20.** $\begin{array}{r} 4 \\ -\ 3 \\ \hline \end{array}$

Rainbow Sundae

Solve the problems. Color the sundae like this:

10 = yellow   11 = purple   12 = red   13 = blue

14 = orange   15 = green   16 = pink   17 = white

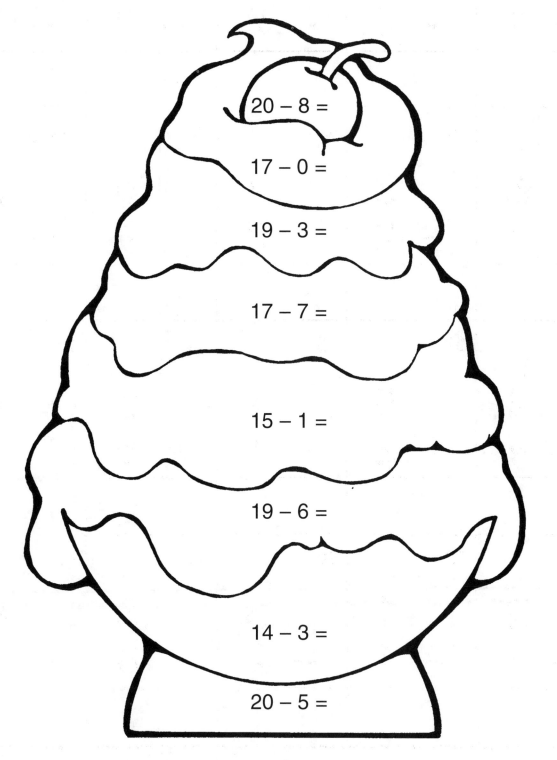

20 − 8 =

17 − 0 =

19 − 3 =

17 − 7 =

15 − 1 =

19 − 6 =

14 − 3 =

20 − 5 =

Subtraction Practice

1.
$$\begin{array}{r} 29 \\ -19 \\ \hline \end{array}$$

2.
$$\begin{array}{r} 68 \\ -23 \\ \hline \end{array}$$

3.
$$\begin{array}{r} 77 \\ -33 \\ \hline \end{array}$$

4.
$$\begin{array}{r} 67 \\ -14 \\ \hline \end{array}$$

5.
$$\begin{array}{r} 79 \\ -20 \\ \hline \end{array}$$

6.
$$\begin{array}{r} 68 \\ -26 \\ \hline \end{array}$$

7.
$$\begin{array}{r} 39 \\ -24 \\ \hline \end{array}$$

8.
$$\begin{array}{r} 39 \\ -20 \\ \hline \end{array}$$

9.
$$\begin{array}{r} 59 \\ -23 \\ \hline \end{array}$$

10.
$$\begin{array}{r} 58 \\ -40 \\ \hline \end{array}$$

11.
$$\begin{array}{r} 29 \\ -12 \\ \hline \end{array}$$

12.
$$\begin{array}{r} 89 \\ -21 \\ \hline \end{array}$$

13.
$$\begin{array}{r} 49 \\ -23 \\ \hline \end{array}$$

14.
$$\begin{array}{r} 78 \\ -32 \\ \hline \end{array}$$

15.
$$\begin{array}{r} 68 \\ -41 \\ \hline \end{array}$$

Solve the Bird Message

Below is a famous saying about birds. Solve the problems in each box below. Then find the answer under the word blank and place the letter from the box on the matching blank.

___	___	___	___	___		___	___	___	___
32	13	43	38	13		38	35	87	29

___	___	___	___	___		___	___	___
21	43	10	48	33 ,		33	13	29

___	___	___	___	___	___	___		___	___
38	13	43	38	65	29	64		1	10

___	___	___		___	___	___
33	13	29		29	59	59 ?

O 16 − 15	**H** 26 − 13	**T** 30 + 3	**W** 42 − 10	**E** 22 + 7
I 67 − 24	**F** 38 − 17	**G** 48 + 11	**A** 22 + 13	**C** 15 + 23
M 63 + 24	**R** 42 − 32	**N** 68 − 4	**S** 23 + 25	**K** 89 − 24

I think the _____ came first because _____

_____

_____

Solving Problems

Solve each problem.

1.   26
       − 16

2. 2 tens + 8 ones

3.   32
        + 6

4.   20
        − 7

5. 2 tens + 3 ones

6.   70
        − 65

7.   31
        + 25

8.   90
        − 83

9. 7 tens + 5 ones

10.   32
        + 33

11.   23
        + 24

12.   38
        − 20

13.   85
        − 79

14.   93
        + 2

15.   44
        + 11

What's the Scoop?

Fill in the missing number on each cone to complete the problem.

1.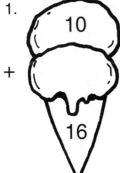

2.

3.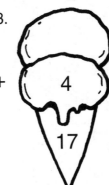

4.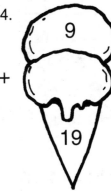

5.

6.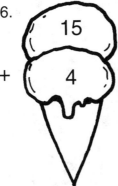

7.

8.

9.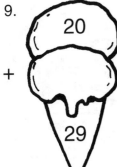

10.

11.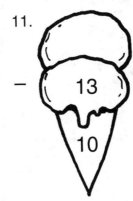

12.

13.

14.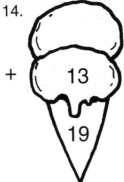

15.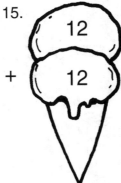

16.

Word Problems

Write a number sentence for each story. Give the answer.

1. Tom had 8 's.

He found 7 more.

How many 's in all?

_____ 's

2. 9 's

15 's

How many more 's?

_____ 's

3. 12 's

7 's

How many more 's?

_____ 's

4. Jane picked up 3 's.

She found 10 more.

How many 's altogether?

_____ 's

5. 9 's

8 's

How many in all?

_____  's

6. Mr. Tan found 16 's

He found 7 's

How many more 's?

_____ 's

492

Farm Story Problems

1. There are 3 's on the farm.

Each laid two 's.

How many 's are there

altogether? _____

2. Five beautiful 's are

growing in the field. You pick 3

of the 's. How many are

left? _____

3. One apple tree has 6 's.

The other tree has 5 's.

You eat one. How many

apples are left? _____

4. On the farm, there are 3 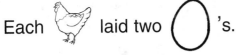's,

1 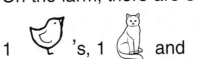's, 1 and

2 's. What is the total

number of animals on the

farm? _____

5. The farmer wants to have

11 's in the orchard.

He now has 2. How many

more 's will he need to

plant? _____

6. Two 's are standing near

the barn. Each cow gives

3 's of milk. How many

's of milk? _____

Working with Money—Pennies

Color in the pennies to show how much each item costs.

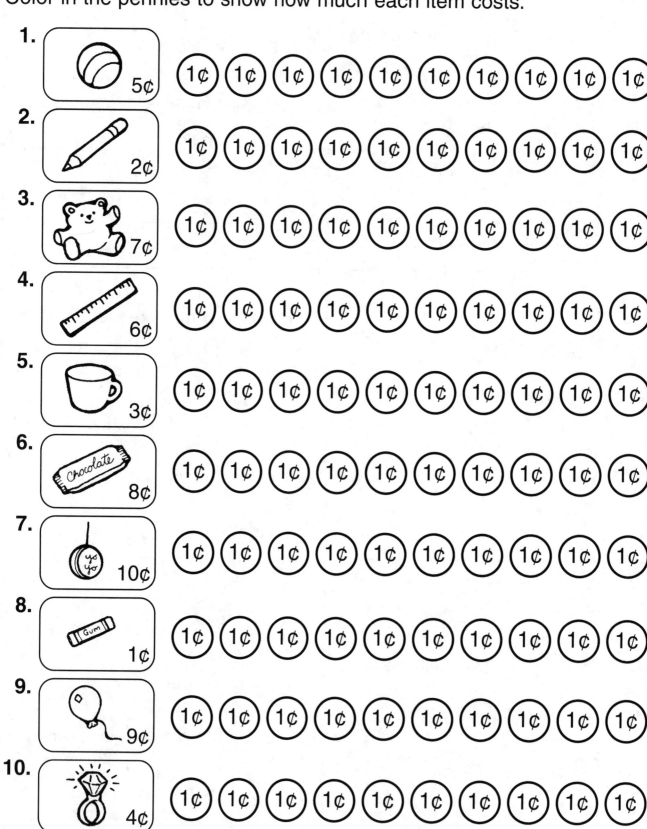

Coin Purses

Count the coins in each purse. Write the total amount of money on the line.

1.

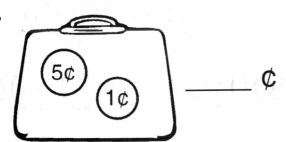

_____ ¢

2.

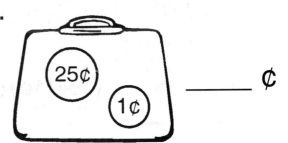

_____ ¢

3.

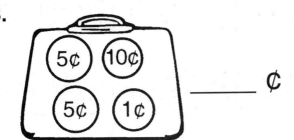

_____ ¢

4.

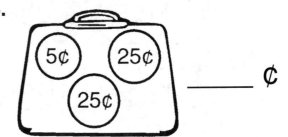

_____ ¢

5.

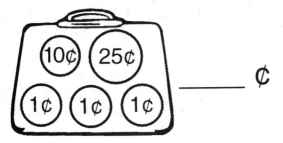

_____ ¢

6.

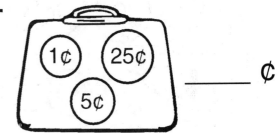

_____ ¢

7.

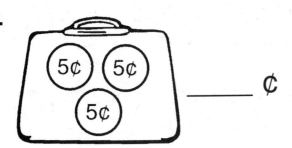

_____ ¢

8.

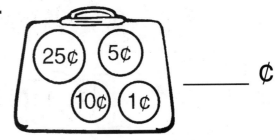

_____ ¢

9.

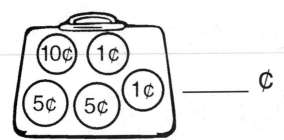

_____ ¢

10.

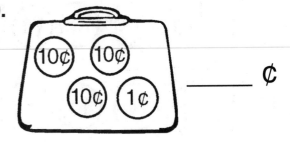

_____ ¢

#3644 Practice and Learn

Dollars and Cents

Draw a line from each picture of money to the correct amount.

1. (10¢) (5¢) $1.25

2. [$1] (25¢) (10¢) (10¢)   35¢

3. (25¢) (25¢) (10¢) (1¢) (1¢)   85¢

4. (25¢) (10¢)   47¢

5. (25¢) (25¢) (5¢)   15¢

6. (25¢) (1¢) (1¢)   62¢

7. (25¢) (25¢) (25¢) (10¢)   27¢

8. [$1] (25¢)   9¢

9. (25¢) (10¢) (10¢) (1¢) (1¢) $1.45

10. (5¢) (1¢) (1¢) (1¢) (1¢)   55¢

Size Seriation

Write the number **1**, **2**, or **3** in the box next to each picture. Put the number **1** next to the smallest picture, **2** next to the medium picture, and the number **3** next to the largest picture.

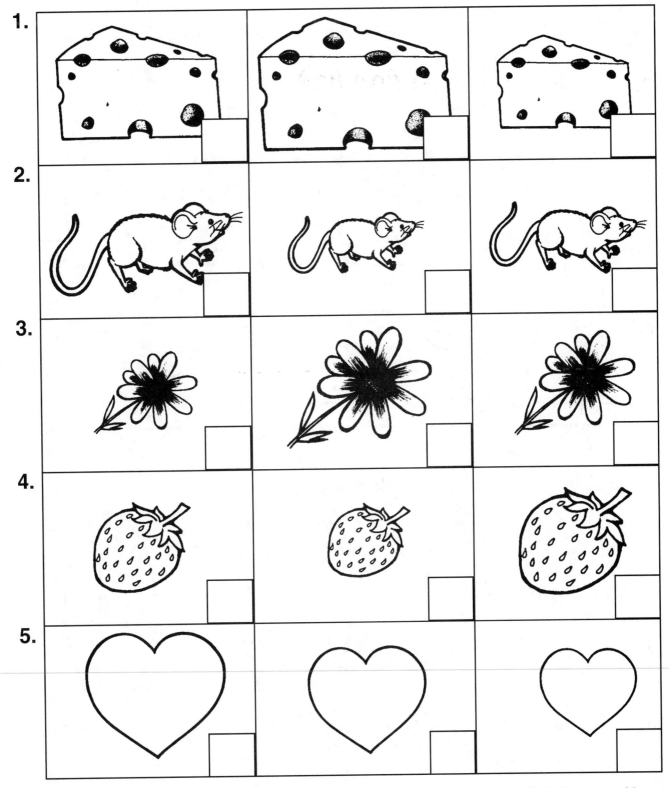

Flamingo

 the pictures.

 and the flamingos onto the correct ovals.

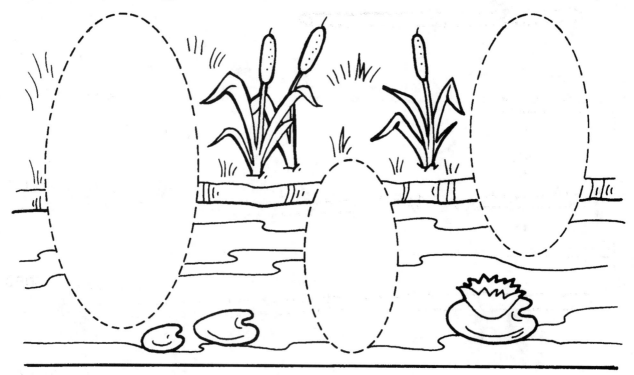

Inch Worms

Measure each inch worm. Write how many inches each worm is on the line.

1. _____ inches

2. _____ inch

3. _____ inches

4. _____ inches

5. _____ inches

6. _____ inches

7. _____ inches

8. _____ inches

Measure It, Draw It

Measure and draw a line the length listed by each number. Begin your line at the star.

1.   7 inches   *

2.   4 inches   *

3.   1 inch   *

4.   8 inches   *

5.   3 inches   *

6.   6 inches   *

7.   2 inches   *

8.   5 inches   *

Ladybug Math

Estimate how far each ladybug flew. Use centimeters for your estimate. Record your estimations. Measure the actual length of each ladybug's path using centimeters. Record the measurement. Were the estimates too long, too short, just right?

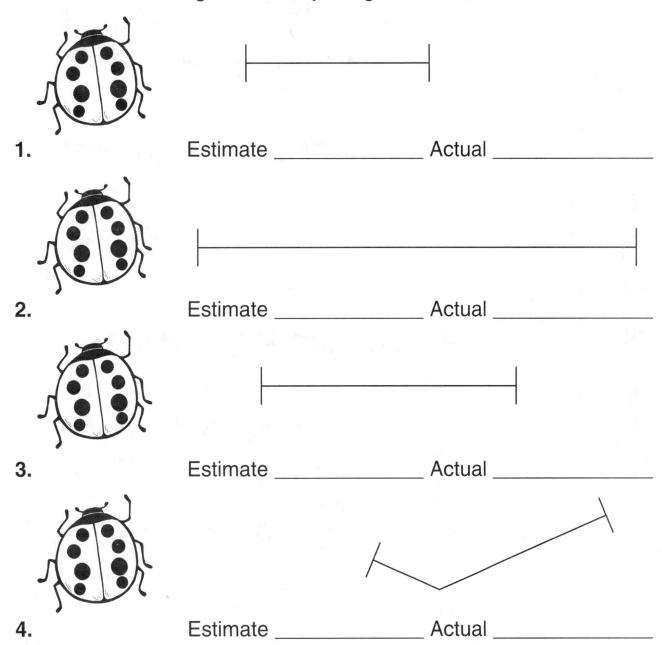

1.   Estimate _____ Actual _____

2.   Estimate _____ Actual _____

3.   Estimate _____ Actual _____

4.   Estimate _____ Actual _____

Which ladybug went the farthest?

How Does Your Garden Grow?

Use a ruler with centimeters to measure each of Frog's plants to the nearest centimeter. Write your answer below each plant.

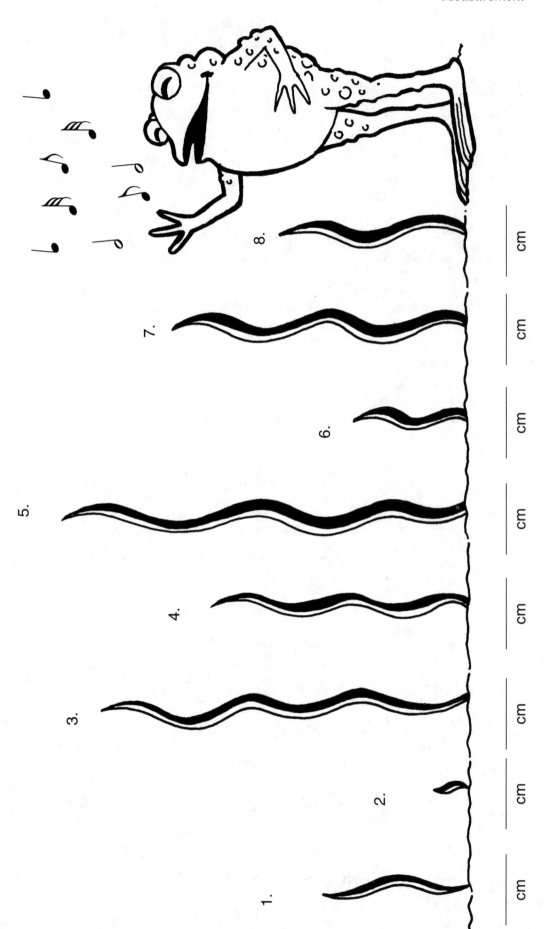

Telling Time

Directions: Write the times at the bottom of each clock. Use the times in the boxes at the bottom of this page.

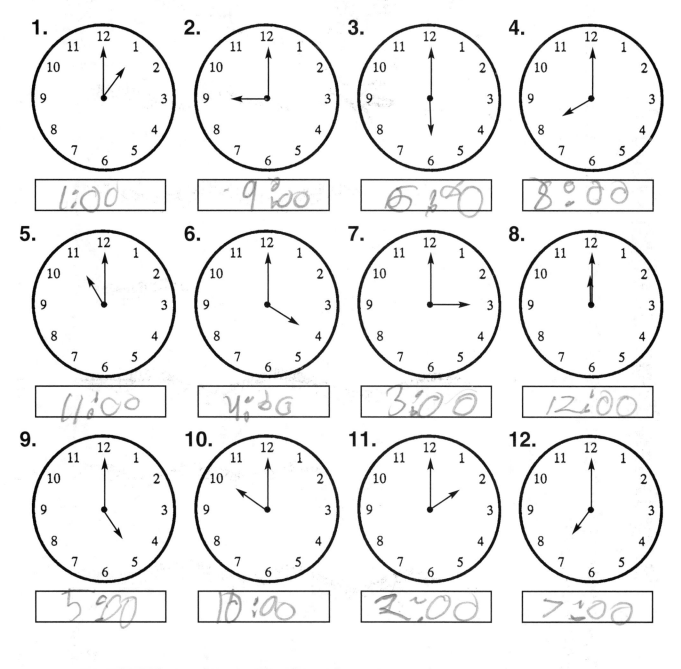

7:00	4:00	6:00	5:00
10:00	9:00	8:00	1:00
12:00	2:00	11:00	3:00

Telling Time to the Half Hour

Add hands to the clocks to show the time.

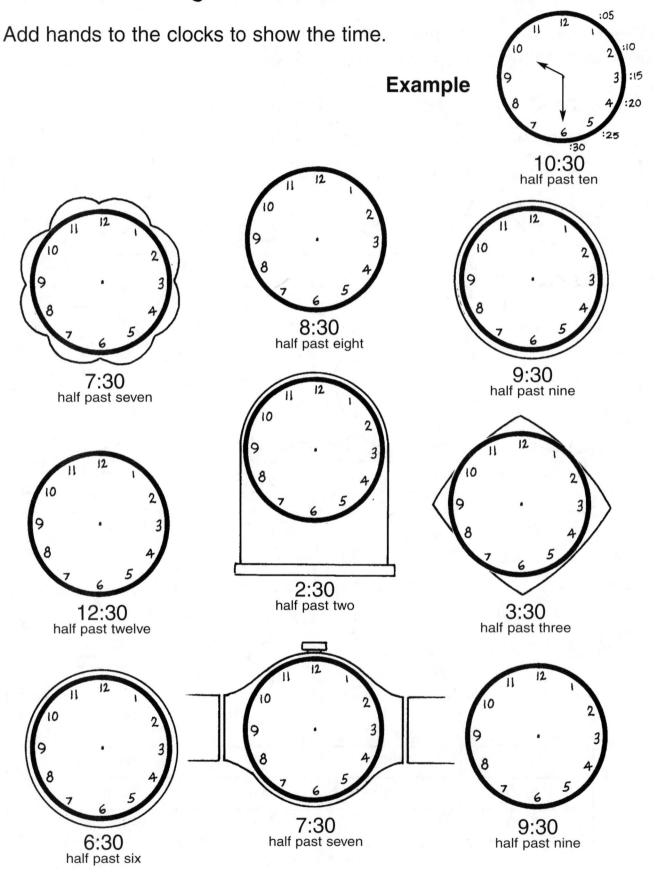

Example

10:30
half past ten

7:30
half past seven

8:30
half past eight

9:30
half past nine

12:30
half past twelve

2:30
half past two

3:30
half past three

6:30
half past six

7:30
half past seven

9:30
half past nine

Time to Go!

Arthur has a busy afternoon. Help him plan his schedule by filling in the blanks below with the correct times.

1. Arthur's mom picks him up from school at

What time is it?

☐ : ☐

2. His eye doctor appointment is at

What time is it?

☐ : ☐

3. Dr. Iris takes Arthur into her office at

What time is it?

☐ : ☐

4. Arthur and his mother leave Dr. Iris' office at   They arrive at a store thirty minutes later. Show the time.

   What time is it?

☐ : ☐   ☐ : ☐

Barnyard Shapes Picture

1. Trace the shapes.

2. Color the picture.

3. Can you find the shapes in the picture below?

Name the Shapes

Draw lines to match the shape names to the ladybugs with the shape spots.

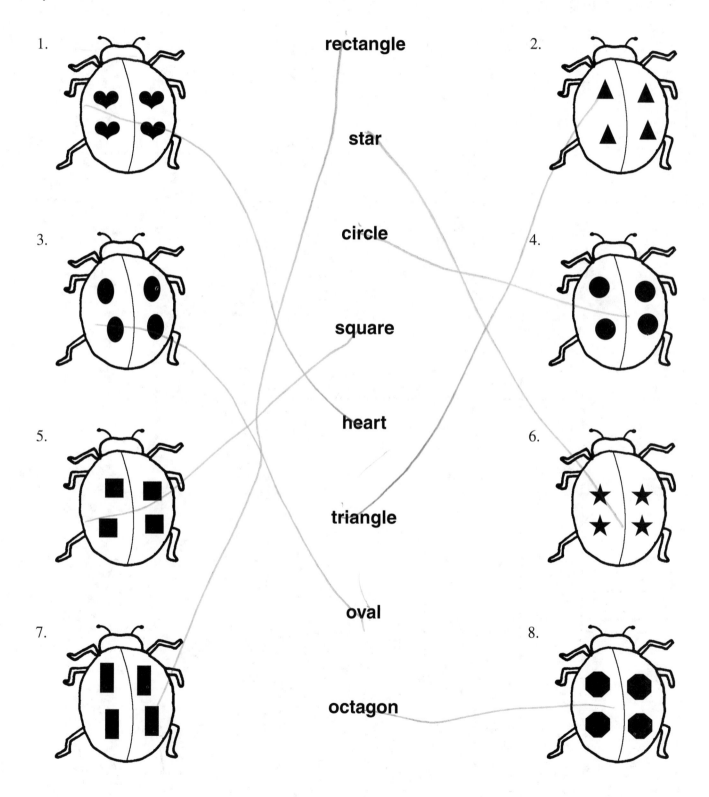

rectangle

star

circle

square

heart

triangle

oval

octagon

More Match Up

Draw lines to make the shapes on the right look like the shapes on the left.

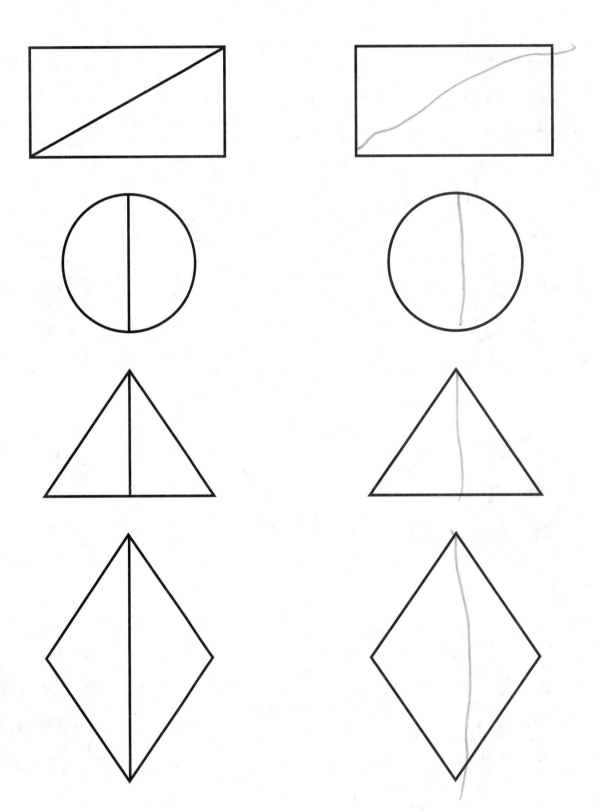

Match Up

Draw lines to make the shapes on the right look like the shapes on the left.

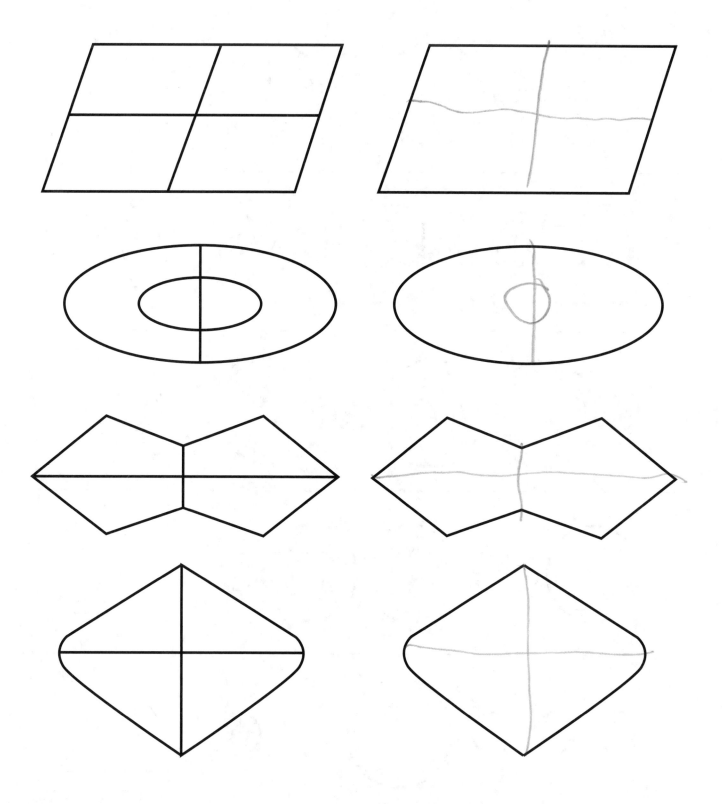

What Comes Next?

Look at each row of buttons. Decide what comes next and draw it in the space.

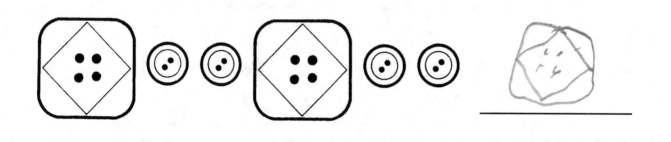

What Comes Next?

Write the next number in each series.

A. 1, 2, 3, 4, 5, 6, 7, 8, _____

B. 2, 4, 6, 8, 10, 12, 14, 16, _____

C. 1, 3, 5, 7, 9, 11, 13, 15, _____

D. 5, 10, 15, 20, 25, 30, 35, 40, _____

E. 10, 20, 30, 40, 50, 60, 70, 80, _____

F. 9, 8, 7, 6, 5, 4, 3, 2, _____

G. 1, 1, 2, 2, 3, 3, 4, 4, 5, 5, _____

H. 1, 4, 7, 10, 13, 16, _____

I. 1 2 3, 1 2 3, 1 2 _____

J. 1 2 2, 1 2 2, 1 2 _____

K. 1, 2 2, 3 3 3, 4 4 4 _____

L. 1 1 2, 1 1 3, 1 1 2, _____

Tie Patterns

Choose a pattern of color for the tie on the left. Create a pattern on the tie on the right. Color the patterns.

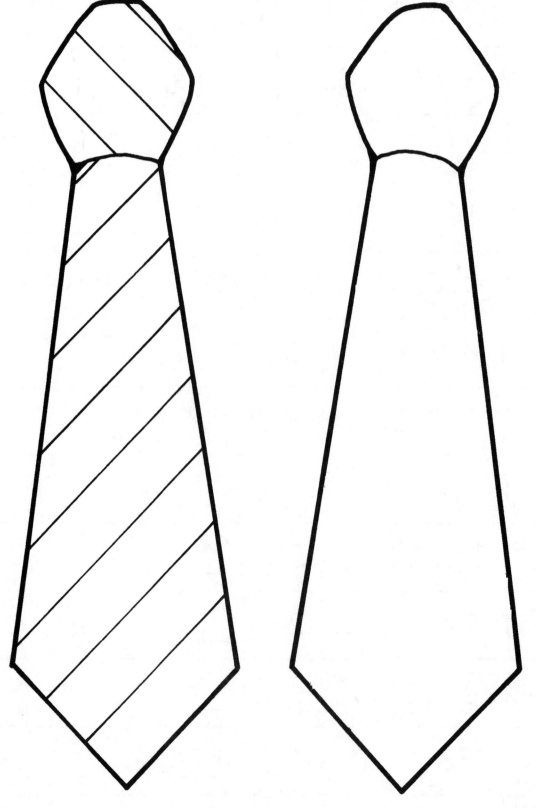

Jewels

Color the jewel on the left.

 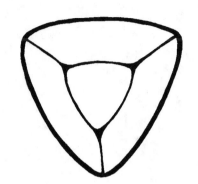 

Color the jewel on the right.

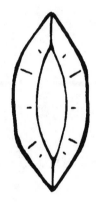 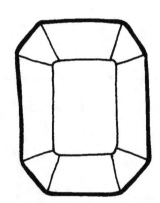 

Color the jewel in the middle.

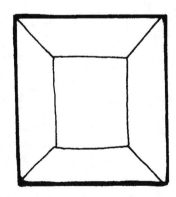  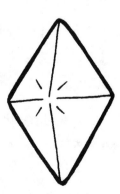

Coral Reef Directions

Look at the picture, then circle the best answer for each question.

1. What is directly above the school of fish?

    A. Scuba diver

    B. Octopus

    C. Eel

2. What is to the left of the shark?

    A. Scuba diver

    B. Octopus

    C. Jellyfish

3. What is directly to the right of the jellyfish?

    A. Eel

    B. Shark

    C. Octopus

4. What is directly above the eel?

    A. Octopus

    B. Scuba diver

    C. School of fish

5. What is below the scuba diver?

    A. School of fish

    B. Octopus

    C. Shark

One-Thirds

These pods have 3 equal size peas. Color the correct number of peas for each fraction.

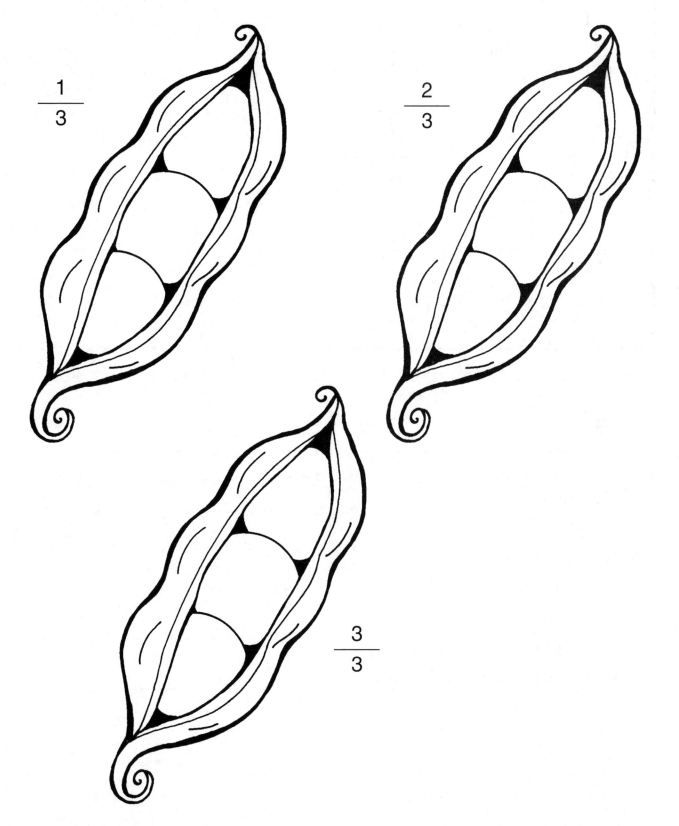

$\dfrac{1}{3}$

$\dfrac{2}{3}$

$\dfrac{3}{3}$

Fraction Quilts

Color to show the correct fraction.

1.

1 whole

2.

Color 2 halves = 1 whole

3.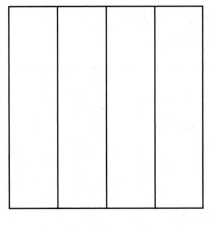

_____ halves = 1 whole

4.

_____ fourths = ½

_____ fourths = 1 whole

5.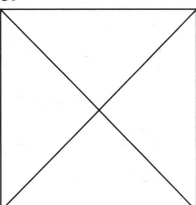

_____ fourths = ½

_____ fourths = 1 whole

6.

_____ fourths = ½

_____ fourths = 1 whole

7.

_____ fourths = ½

_____ fourths = 1 whole

Bird Word Problems

1.
4  's

3 's in each .

How many nests in all? ☐

2.
16 's

5 more  's.

How many birds in all? ☐

3.
18 's

13  's fly away.

How many birds left? ☐

4.
19 s

Only 13 have 's.

How many birds do not have worms? ☐

5.
37 's

12 hatch.

How many 's left? ☐

6.
28  's

3 's join them.

How many  's in all? ☐

7.
11 's

6 's

How many more penguins than hens? ☐

8. How many eggs are cracked in half?

   ☐

Buying Toys

Pretend that you were sent to the toy store to buy some toys for your dragon. Use the chart to find the answers to the questions.

1. 1 set of jacks + 1 pin wheel =

_____ + _____ = _____

2. 1 balloon + 1 ball =

_____ + _____ = _____

3. 1 ball + 1 kite + 1 sailboat =

_____ + _____ + _____ = _____

4. 1 kite + 1 set of jacks + 1 pin wheel =

_____ + _____ + _____ = _____

It is your turn to decide. If you have 50 cents what will you buy for the dragon? You may buy as many things as you wish without going over 50 cents. Write the total you spent and what you decided to buy.

_____

_____

_____

Buying Groceries

Use the prices in the box below to figure out the price of these groceries. One has been done for you.

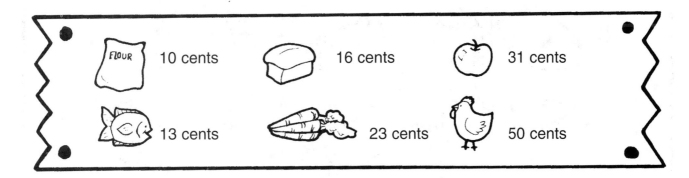

Example:

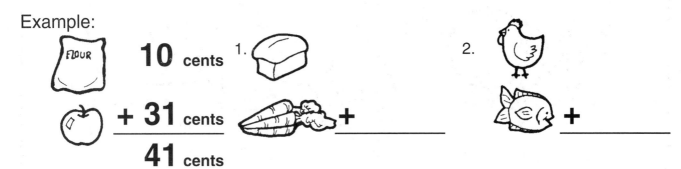

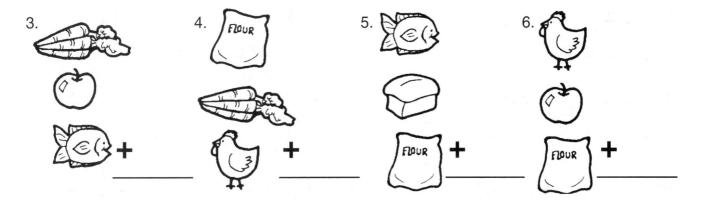

Challenge: How much would . . .

☆☆ 3 chickens cost? _____

☆☆ 5 sacks of flour cost? _____

☆☆☆ a "fish sandwich" cost? _____

Subtraction Problems

a. Count the cars. Cross out 2 cars. Write the numerals on the lines to show the subtraction problem and answer.

_____ − _____ = _____

b. Count the bears. Cross out 4 bears. Write the numerals on the lines to show the subtraction problem and answer.

_____ − _____ = _____

c. Count the books. Cross out 3 books. Write the numerals on the lines to show the subtraction problem and answer.

_____ − _____ = _____

d. Count the fish. Cross out 1 fish. Write the numerals on the lines to show the subtraction problem and answer.

_____ − _____ = _____

e. Count the rings. Cross out 2 rings. Write the numerals on the lines to show the subtraction problem and answer.

_____ − _____ = _____

Tower Take-Away

Use the 6 blocks to figure out the differences in the problems below.

1. Start with 6 blocks.

   Take off 1 block.

   There are _____ blocks left.

2. Start with 6 blocks.

   Take off 2 blocks.

   There are _____ blocks left.

3. Start with 6 blocks.

   Take off 3 blocks.

   There are _____ blocks left.

4. Start with 6 blocks.

   Take off 5 blocks.

   There is _____ block left.

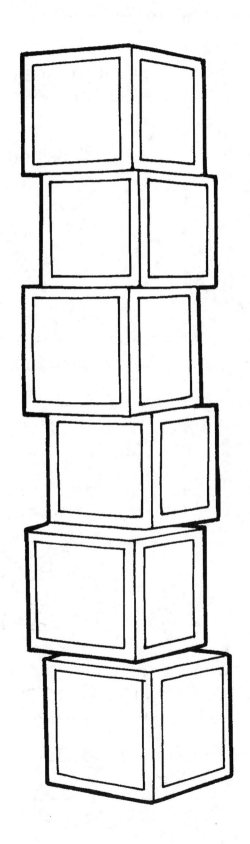

Little Critters

Use the graph to solve each subtraction problem.

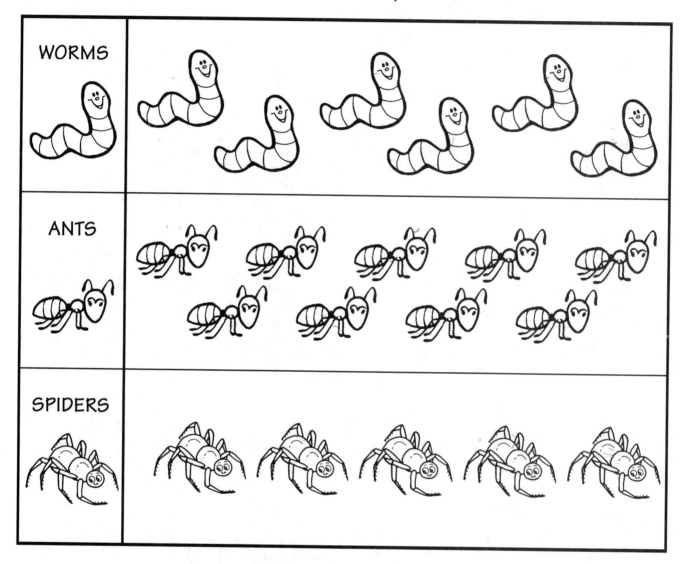

1. How many more ants are there than worms?

_____9_____ − _____6_____ = _____3_____

2. How many more ants are there than spiders?

_____9_____ − _____5_____ = _____4_____

3. How many more worms are there than spiders?

_____6_____ − _____5_____ = _____1_____

Airport Words

1. Say the words.
2. Draw a line from each word to the picture.

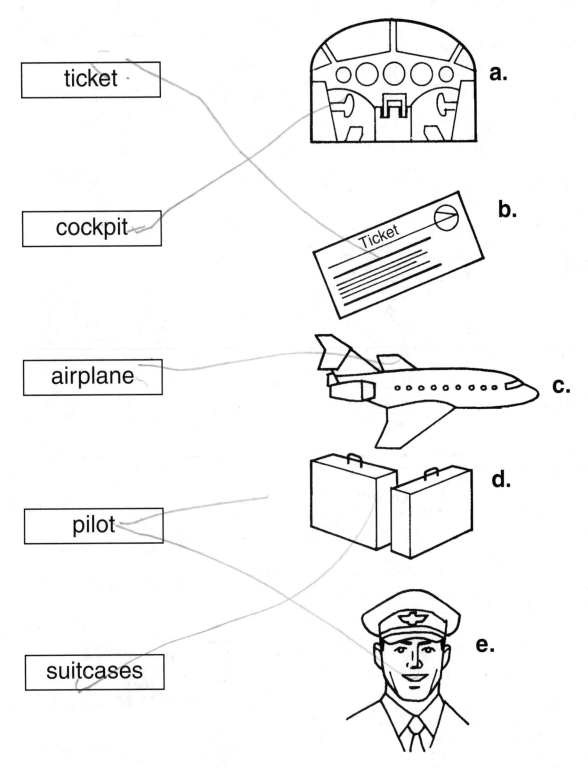

ticket

cockpit

airplane

pilot

suitcases

a.

b.

c.

d.

e.

Ticket

I'm Going on a Plane!

1. Write the missing letter for each picture.

2. Write the missing letters in the story below.

Letter Bank

b	c	l	m
p	s	t	w

____ icket   ___ ar   ____ ear   ____ lane

____ uitcase   ___ovie   ____ ings   ____ unch

I'm Going on a Plane!

I got my ___uitcase. We took a ___ar to the airport. I got a ___icket.

I brought my ___ear. We went on a big ___lane.

We ate ___unch. We saw a funny ___ovie.

The captain gave me gold flight ___ings.

It was a great trip!

Where Does It Go?

1. Print the correct word from below.   2. Draw the correct picture.

1. _____

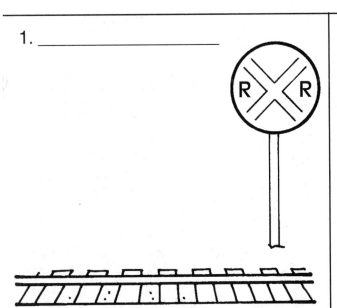

2. _____

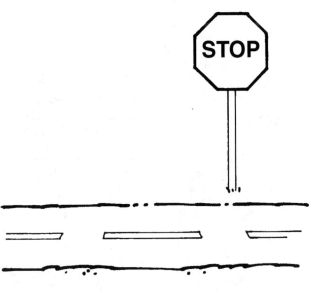

3. _____

4. _____

Word Bank: train   car   plane   boat

Whose Home Is It?

Draw lines to match everybody to his or her home.

Homes

In nature, many creatures have their own special places to live. Write the names of the living beings near their pictures. Then draw a line to match each to its home.

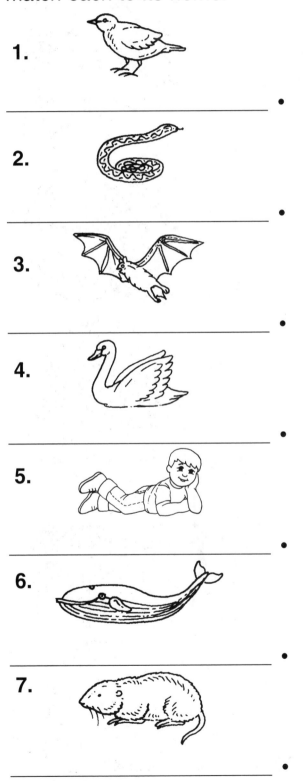

1.

_____ •

2.

_____ •

3.

_____ •

4.

_____ •

5.

_____ •

6.

_____ •

7.

_____ •

• cave _____

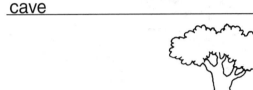

• tree _____

• house _____

• under a rock _____

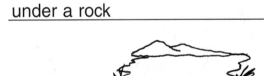

• lake _____

• underground hole _____

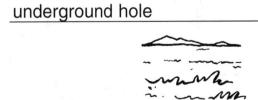

• ocean _____

I Know My Address

1. Write your address on the lines.

2. Color the house.

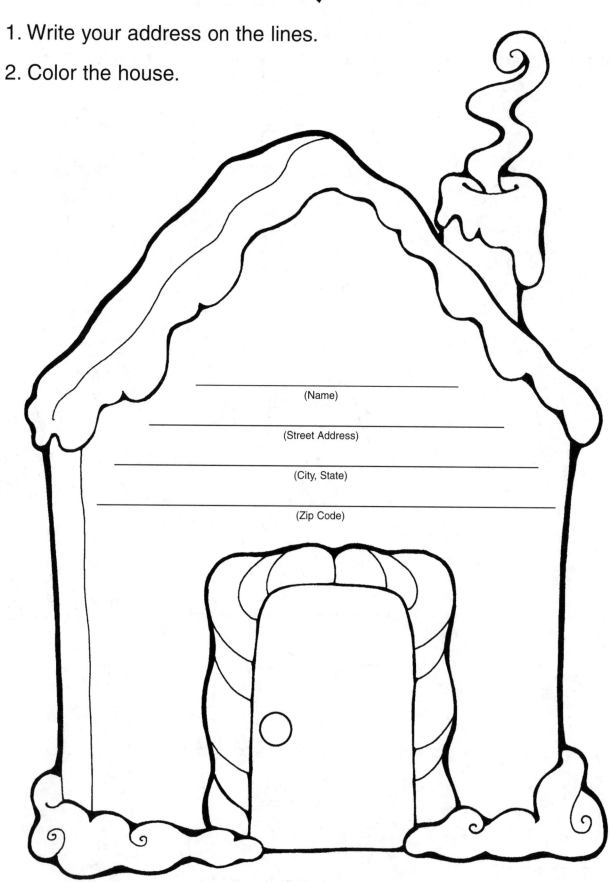

(Name)

(Street Address)

(City, State)

(Zip Code)

Who Wears This Hat?

Draw a line from each person to the hat that you think he or she would wear.

City or Country

Decide if each picture belongs in the city or country. Draw a line from the picture to the word "city" or "country."

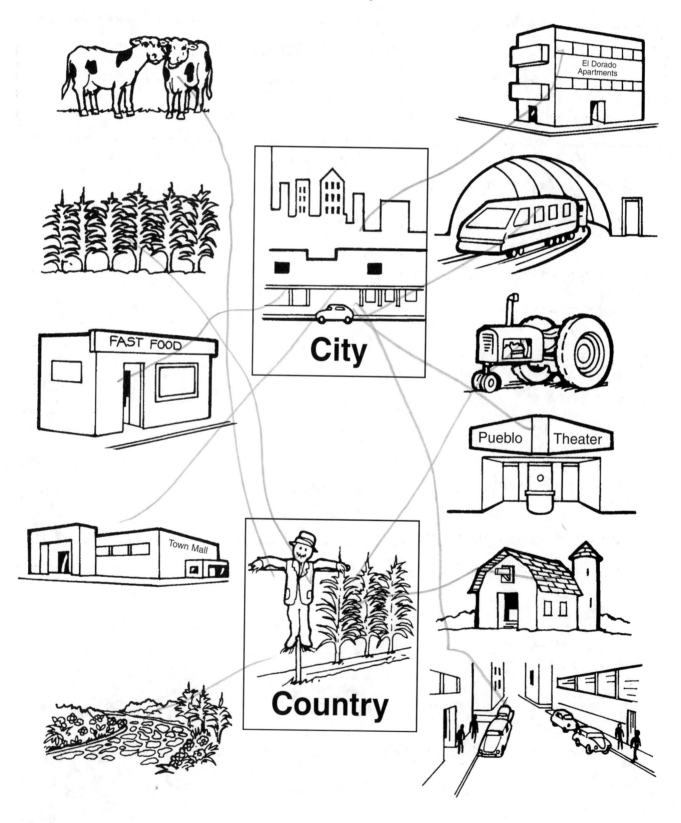

Now and Then

Use words from the box that might tell what you did when you were a baby, compared to what you do now.

baby food	remember	forget	bottle
bicycle	cup	read	crib
bed	pizza	rocking horse	listen

1. When I was younger, I ate _____,

   but now I eat _____.

2. When I was a baby, I slept in a _____, but

   now I sleep in a _____.

3. I used to drink milk from a _____, but

   now I use a _____.

4. I used to ride on a _____, but

   now I ride on my _____.

5. When I was younger, I used to _____ to my

   favorite stories, but now I can _____ some

   by myself.

6. I used to _____ to brush my teeth, but

   now I _____ to brush them each day.

7. **Bonus:** When I was younger, I _____, but

   now I _____.

Calendar Activities

Match the picture to the correct month by drawing a line.

January

February

March

April

May

June

July

August

September

October

November

December

Picture Match

Draw a line to match the picture to its name.

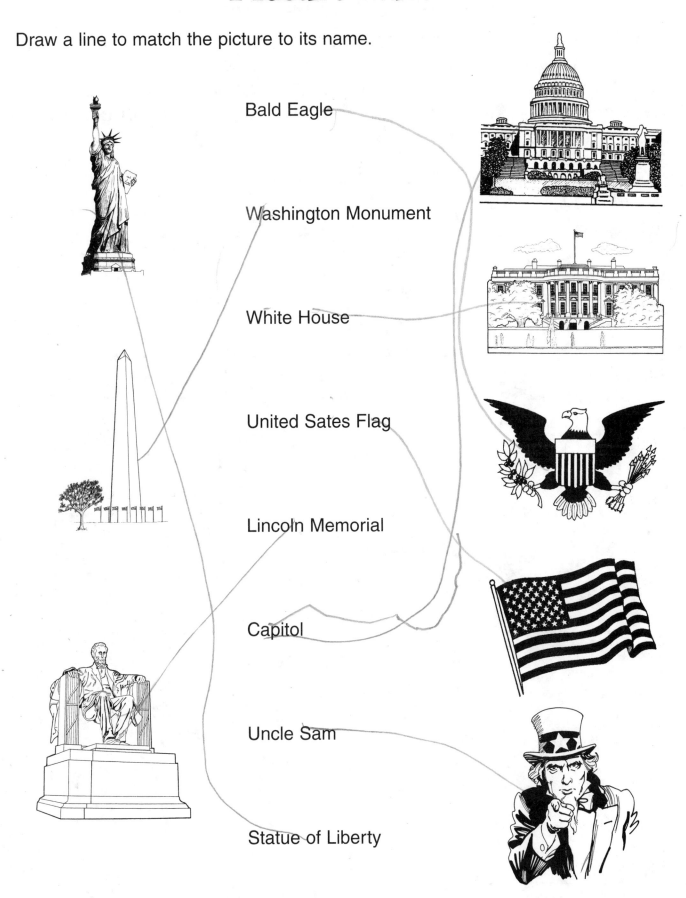

Bald Eagle

Washington Monument

White House

United Sates Flag

Lincoln Memorial

Capitol

Uncle Sam

Statue of Liberty

What Is a Map?

A map is a picture that shows us a place. The place a map shows us can be anywhere! A map can be drawn of our room, our street, our school, our city, our country, our world, or our solar system. A map can show us what it looks like in our bodies, under a city, or beneath the ocean. We can make a map of a pretend world!

What places do these maps show us? Use the places in the word box to help you.

room	school	street
city	country	solar system
world	body	pretend world

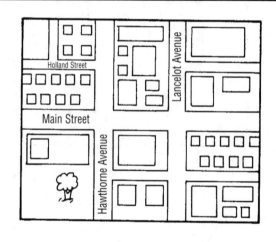

1. _____

2. _____

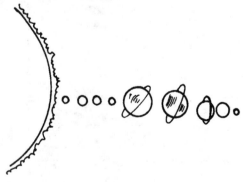

3. _____

4. _____

The Title

A *title* is a name. People have titles, and so do pets. Maps also have titles. A map's title tells us what the map is about.

Under each map, write the correct title.

Rivertown	Market Street
South America	My Bedroom

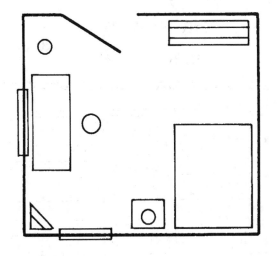

1. _____

2. _____

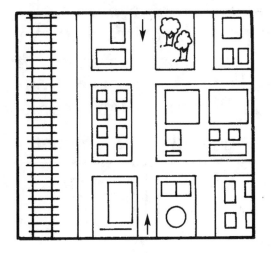

3. _____

4. _____

Symbols

A *symbol* is something that stands for something else. For example, a "+" stands for add and a "−" stands for subtract. A heart is a symbol for love and a flag is the symbol for a country. There are many other symbols we use, too.

Use the words in the box to help you label these symbols.

1. _____   2. _____   3. _____

4. _____   5. _____   6. _____

Word Box

Fire

Be Quiet!

Spring

Stop!

No Bicycles

Sunshine

---

*Maps also use **symbols**. Symbols on a map stand for things that are in the place the map shows us.*

What kinds of symbols do you think might be used to show us these things on maps? Draw your ideas in the boxes.

playground	house	lake	mountains

A Key

Mapmakers draw the symbols they use in a map **key**. *The map key tells what each symbol stands for.*

Look at this map and the map key. Use it to answer the questions below.

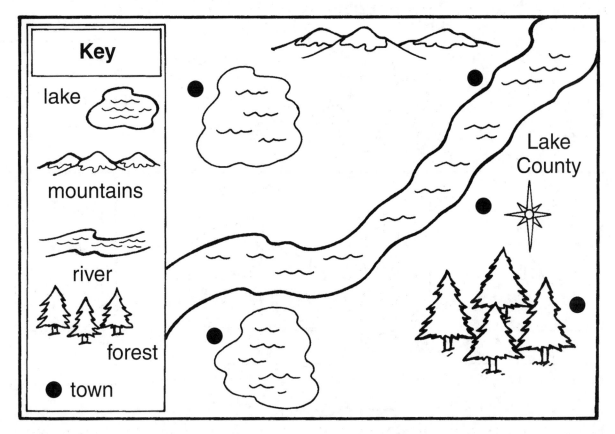

1. There are _____ lakes in Lake County.

2. There are _____ towns in Lake County.

3. One of the towns in Lake County is not by water. It is by the **f**_____ .

4. Between a lake and the river, there are **m**_____ at the north end of Lake County.

5. A **r**_____ runs through the middle of the county and between two lakes.

On Which Street?

Locate each store by finding its matching number on the map. Then, on the lines below, write the names of the streets on which the following stores can be found.

1. Dairy (8) _____

2. Bakery (5) _____

3. Supermarket (7) _____

4. Fruit Market (6) _____

5. Pizza Place (2) _____

6. Ice Cream Store (9) _____

7. Deli (1) _____

8. Health Food Store (3) _____

9. Frozen Yogurt Store (10) _____

10. Hot Dog Stand (4) _____

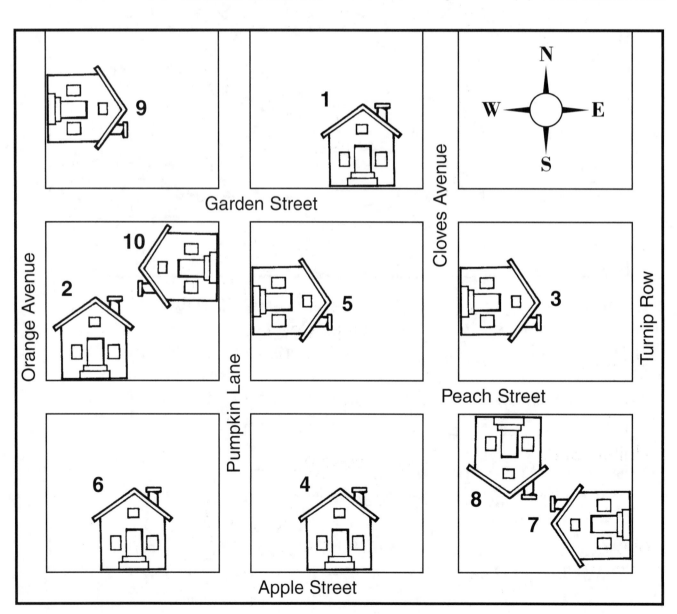

North American Boundaries

On this map are three of the countries in North America.

- Make the boundary between Canada and the United States blue.
- Make the boundary between Mexico and the United States red.
- Color Canada gold, the United States purple, and Mexico green.

Canada

[   ] gold

United States

[   ] purple

Mexico

[   ] green

Continents and Oceans

The largest areas of land in the world are called continents. There are seven continents. On which continent do you live? _____

The largest areas of water in the world are called oceans. There are four main oceans. Which ocean is closest to you? _____

Color the continents green and the oceans blue.

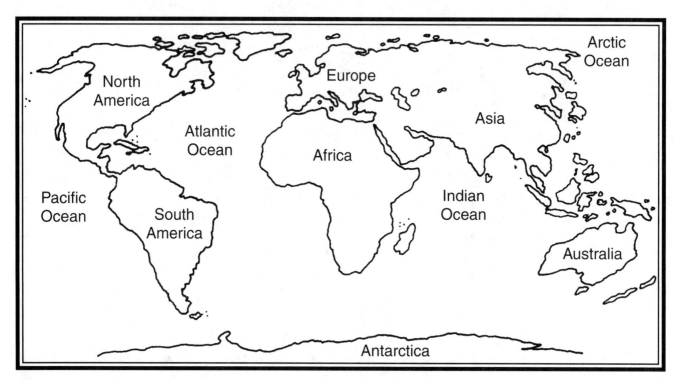

What are the names of the seven continents?

1. _____   5. _____

2. _____   6. _____

3. _____   7. _____

4. _____

What are the names of the four major oceans?

1. _____   3. _____

2. _____   4. _____

Swim or Walk?

Look at this map of the continents and oceans of the world. If you were on each of the numbered areas, would you swim or walk?

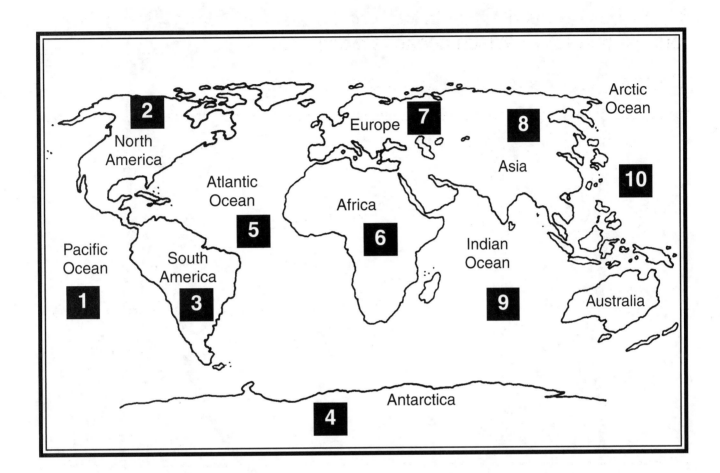

Write *swim* or *walk* here.

1. _____   6. _____

2. _____   7. _____

3. _____   8. _____

4. _____   9. _____

5. _____   10. _____

You Make Me So Angry!

Does someone in your family sometimes make you angry? Tell about it. Draw a picture.

_____ makes me angry because _____

_____

_____.

542

Friends

Below are several statements about friends. If you agree with the statement, color the happy face. If you disagree with the statement, color the sad face.

Statement	Agree	Disagree
1. Friends share their toys.	☺	☹
2. Friends hit each other.	☺	☹
3. Friends will help each other.	☺	☹
4. Friends can make you feel better.	☺	☹
5. Friends make you feel lonely.	☺	☹
6. Friends try to hurt your feelings.	☺	☹
7. You can share special times with a friend.	☺	☹
8. Friends play together.	☺	☹
9. Friends argue and don't try to get along.	☺	☹
10. Friends don't care about you.	☺	☹
11. Friends are important.	☺	☹
12. You would feel sad if your friend got sick or hurt.	☺	☹

#3644 Practice and Learn

Animal Babies

Draw a line to match the baby animals to the adult animals. Do the baby and adult animals look similar to each other?

baby animals   **adult animals**

Bird Parts

Parts of the picture below are labeled, but the letters are mixed up. Find out what the label says by using the words in the Word Bank. On each line write the correct word above the scrambled one. Then color the picture.

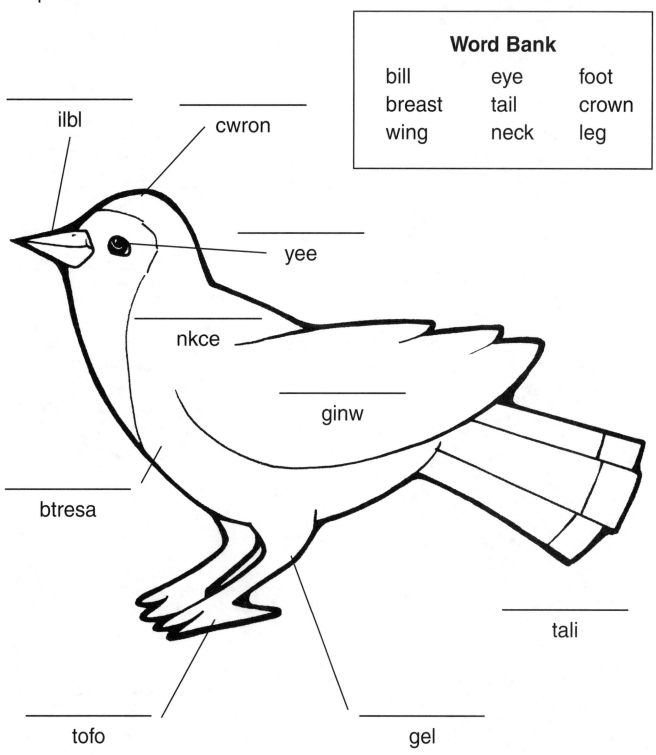

Word Bank

bill	eye	foot
breast	tail	crown
wing	neck	leg

ilbl

cwron

yee

nkce

ginw

btresa

tali

tofo

gel

Birds Aren't the Only Ones!

Whose eggs are these? Draw a line from the animals to their eggs. Color the pictures.

Name the Insects

1. Find the insects.

2. Draw a line from the name of the insect to the picture.

3. Color the picture.

moth

bee

fly

ant

butterfly

beetle

ladybug

Butterfly Body Parts

There are many parts to a butterfly. Trace the words below. Color the picture.

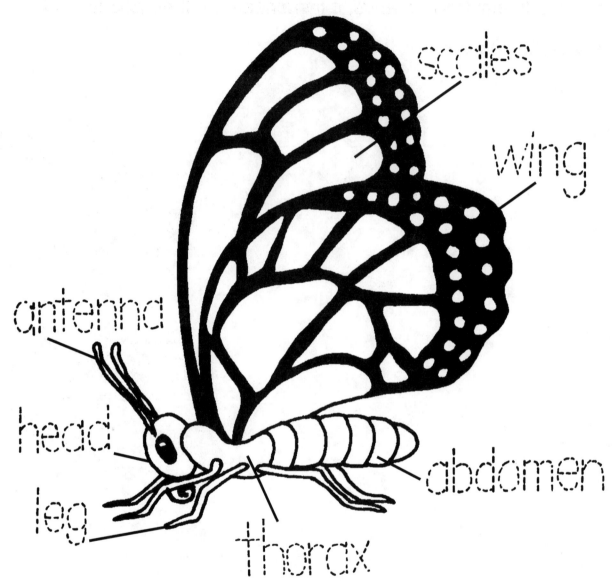

Some Butterfly Facts

Count and write the number.

1. A butterfly has _____ legs.

2. A butterfly has _____ body parts—the head, the thorax, and the abdomen.

3. A butterfly has _____ wings and _____ antennae.

Insect Parts

All insects have three body parts—head, thorax, and abdomen.

Some insects have two feelers, or antennae, on their heads.

All insects have six legs.

Draw the missing parts on these insects.

The Human Skeleton

Label the skeleton parts by writing the words from the box on the lines.

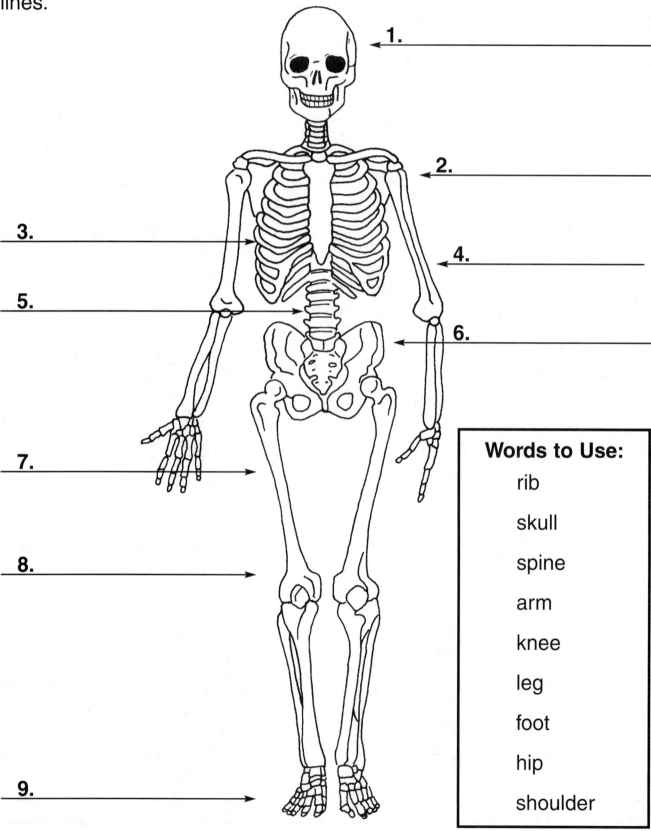

1. _____

2. _____

3. _____

4. _____

5. _____

6. _____

7. _____

8. _____

9. _____

Words to Use:

rib

skull

spine

arm

knee

leg

foot

hip

shoulder

Growing Things

Color all the things that will grow and change.

What is a Plant?

A plant is a living thing. But, unlike an animal, a plant doesn't move around from one place to another to find food. A plant makes its own food right on the spot—right where it grows.

Color the plants on this page.

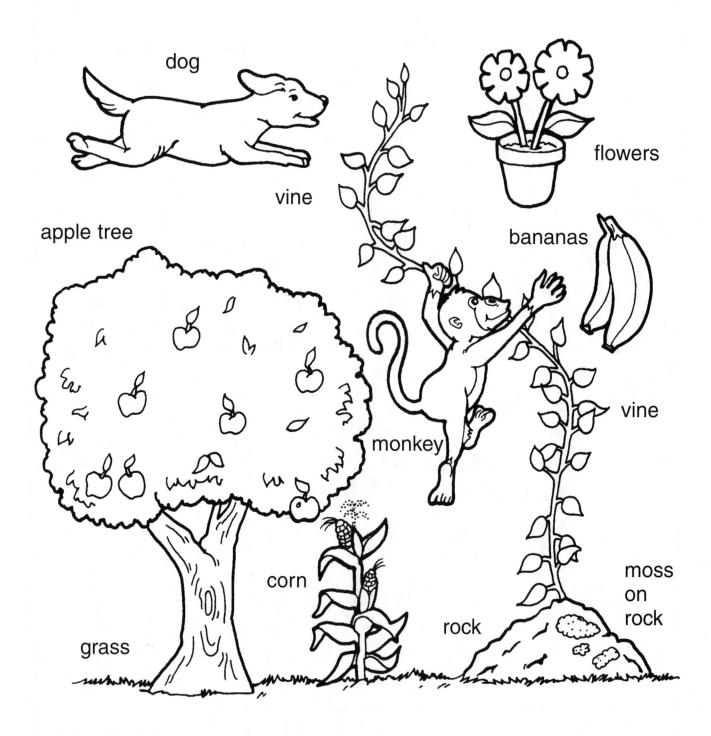

dog

vine

flowers

apple tree

bananas

monkey

vine

corn

rock

moss on rock

grass

Life Cycle

Indicate the correct order of the life cycle of a plant. Use the numbers 1–6 to show the sequence.

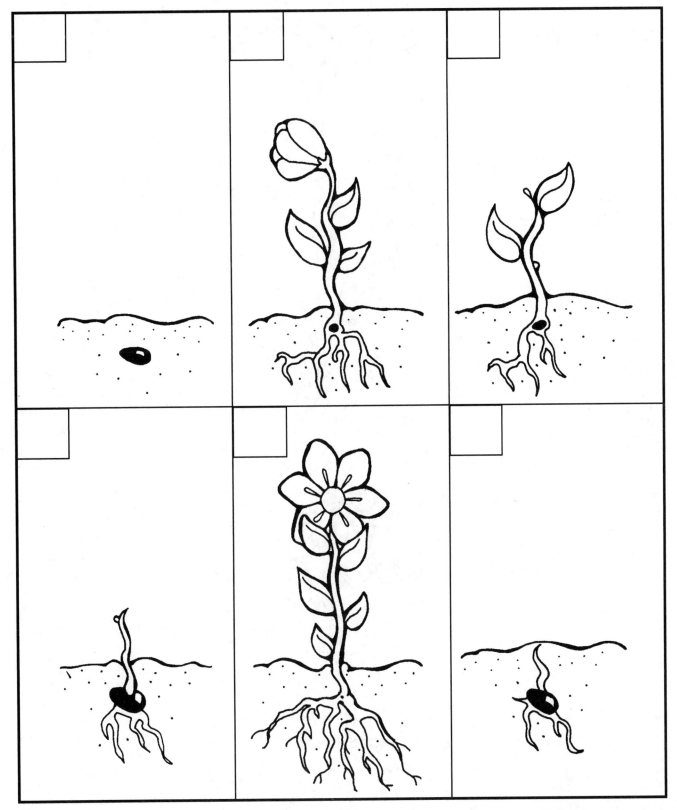

Parts of a Plant

Color the plant. Label the plant parts by writing the correct words on the lines.

1. _____

2. _____

3. _____

4. _____

5. _____

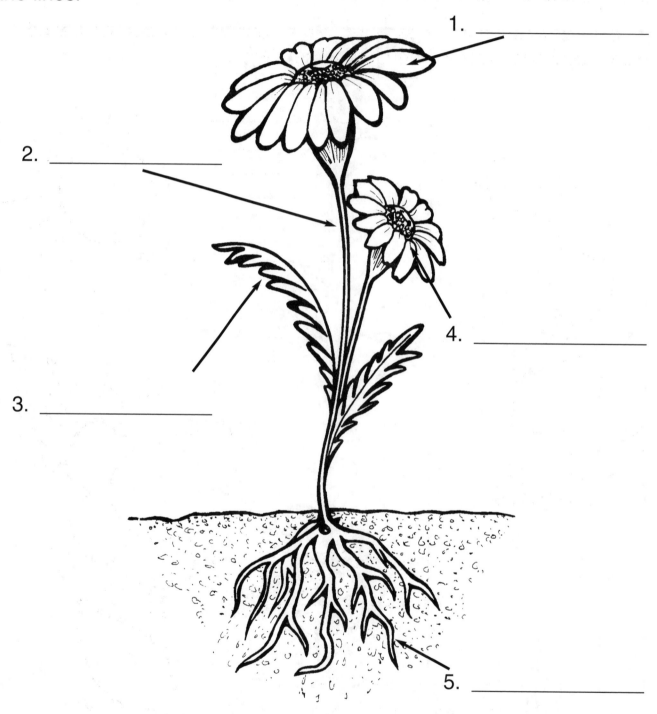

Word Bank				
roots	flower	leaf	seeds	stem

What Does a Plant Need?

A plant needs certain things for it to live and grow, just like you do. A plant needs air, water, sun (for warmth and light), and minerals.

Trace over each plant-need word. Print each word under the traced word. Say each word. Then, color the plants.

Solar System

A solar system is made up of a sun and the planets or other bodies that rotate around it. The solar system we live in is made up of our sun, nine planets, and other orbiting bodies like moons, comets, and asteroids.

Study this map of our solar system. Then answer the questions at the bottom of the page.

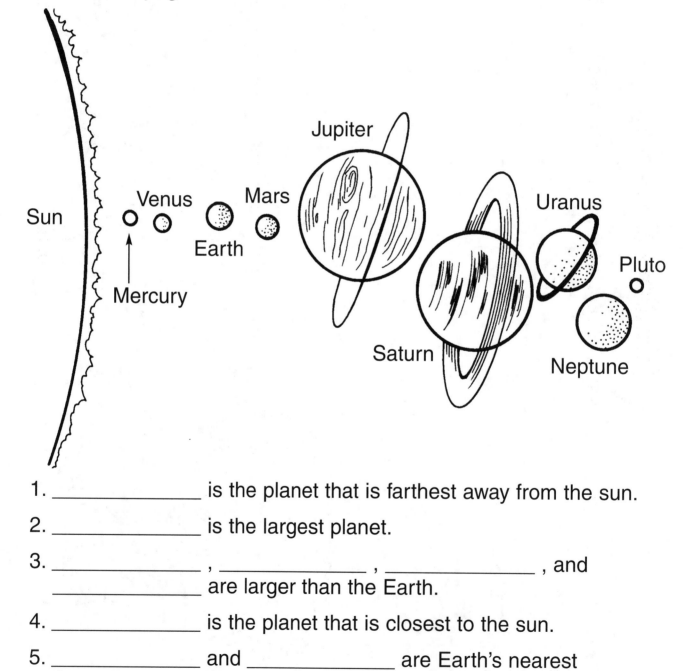

1. _____ is the planet that is farthest away from the sun.

2. _____ is the largest planet.

3. _____ , _____ , _____ , and _____ are larger than the Earth.

4. _____ is the planet that is closest to the sun.

5. _____ and _____ are Earth's nearest planetary neighbors.

Shadow Drawing

Where would these objects make shadows? Draw the shadows first. Then color the rest of the picture.

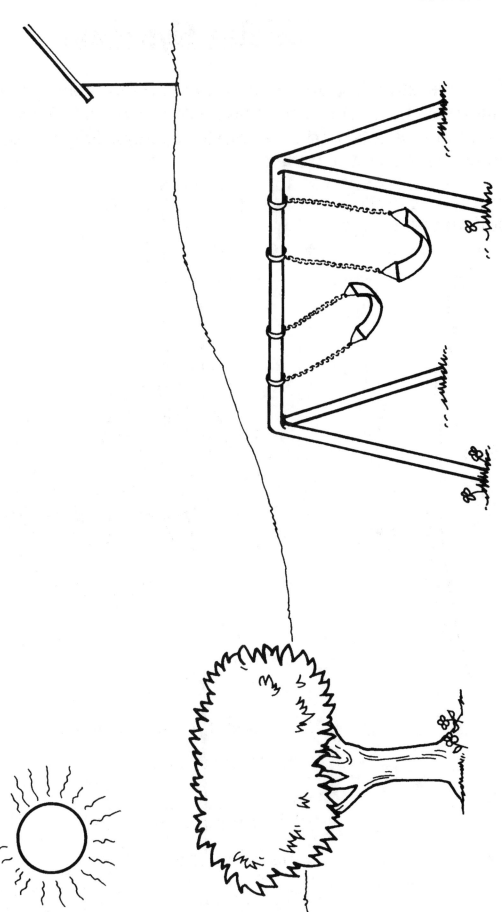

We See the Moon

The moon is the closest and brightest object we can see from Earth at night, but the moon does not make its own light. The moon reflects the light of the sun, and what we see as moonlight is really reflected sunlight. If you watch the sky for a month, it seems as if the moon changes in size and shape. This is because we can only see the sunlight part of the moon that is facing Earth.

Draw each moon in the box next to its description.

Full Moon

During a full moon, we can see all of the moon's sunlit surface.

Half Moon

During a half moon, we see only half of the moon's sunlit surface.

Crescent moon

During a crescent moon, we see only a sliver of the moon's sunlit surface.

Picture the Weather!

Color each picture to show the weather differences.

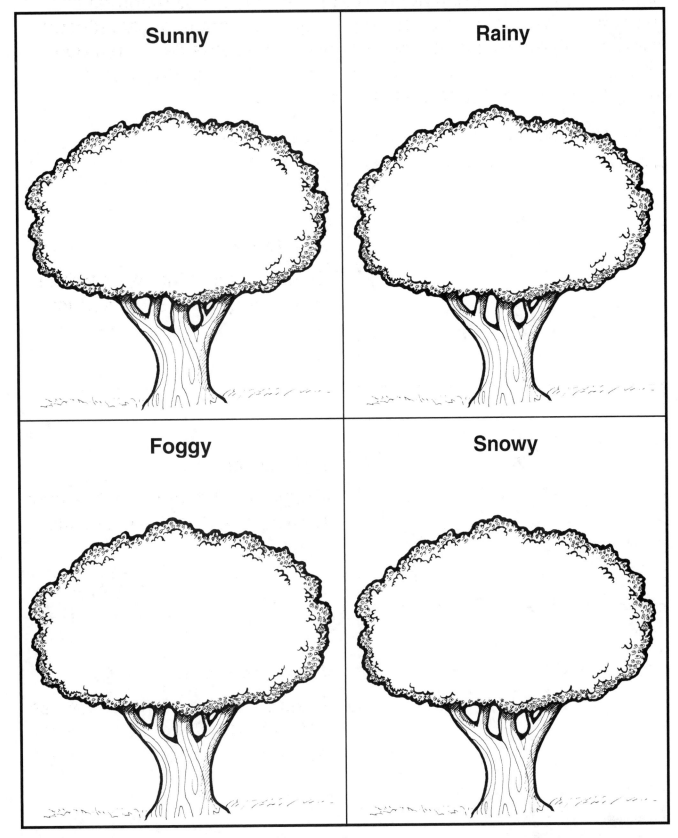

Sunny

Rainy

Foggy

Snowy

Weather Journal

_____

date

Today is _____.

day of week

| sunny | cloudy | rainy |
| windy | snowy | foggy |

Today it is _____.

Your Environment

All the things around you make up your environment. Some of these things are living. Some of them are not living.

In the picture below, color all the things that are living. Circle all the things that are non-living. Draw yourself in the environment.

Hidden Pollution

Color the pictures below. You will find two common causes of pollution. Write them here.

_____   _____

What is Change?

Are the things you see today the same as they were yesterday? A week ago? A month ago? A year ago? Nothing ever stays the same. Things change. **Change** means that things become different with time.

Draw a line to connect the things on one side to the things that they change to with time. Then color the page.

snowman   butterfly

egg   water, hat, and scarf

seed sprout   bird

baby   mountain

caterpillar   girl

volcano   plant

North Pole, South Pole

Put an **X** on each object a magnet will pick up.

Sink or Float

Circle the things that sink.

The Water Cycle

Where does the rain come from? Where does the rain go? Why do we never get any "new water"? Can you answer these questions? The cycle answers them. Study the diagram below to learn how the water cycle works.

Precipitation is water that falls from the sky. It can be rain or snow. Color the precipitation dark gray.

Water vapor is water that has turned into gas. Clouds are made of water vapor. Color the clouds a light gray.

Evaporation is when water changes from liquid to gas. Color the evaporation light blue.

Run off is the water that seeps into the ground, runs into rivers, or forms puddles. Color the run off light brown.

Forms of Water

Cut out pictures and glue in proper place.

Solid	**Liquid**	**Gas**
SNOW	MELTED SNOW	

My Science Journal

Illustration

This is what happened:_____

_____

_____

_____

_____

This is what I learned: _____

_____

_____

_____

_____

Good or Bad for Teeth

Put an **X** on the things that are bad for your teeth.

Color the things that are good for your teeth.

Dental Care Dot-to-Dot

1. Join the dots to make a picture.

2. Color it.

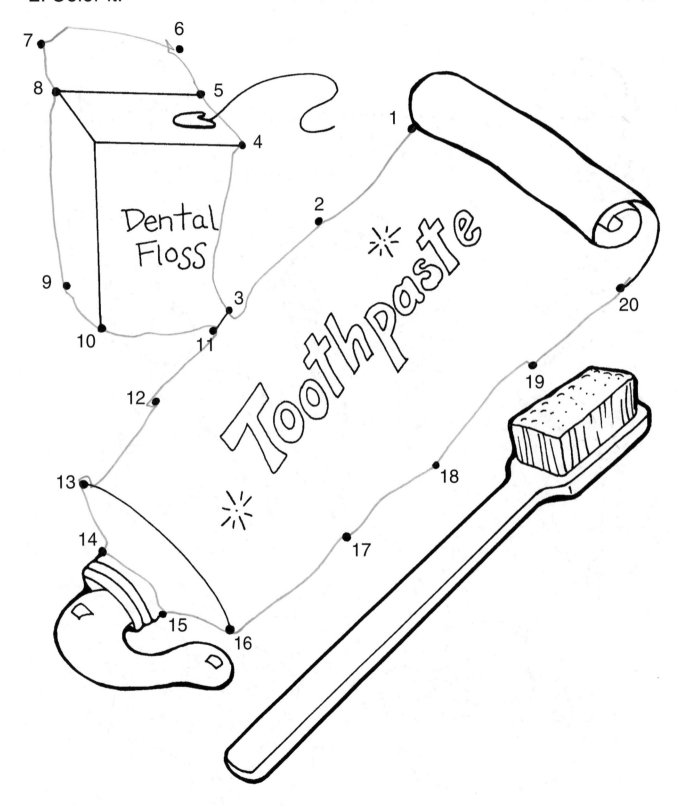

Safe for the Tub

1. Color the objects that are good to take in the tub.

2. Cross out the ones that are not safe for the tub.

Safety Math

Directions: Count the items in each row that could harm you, and put an **X** on them. Then write the number in the box.

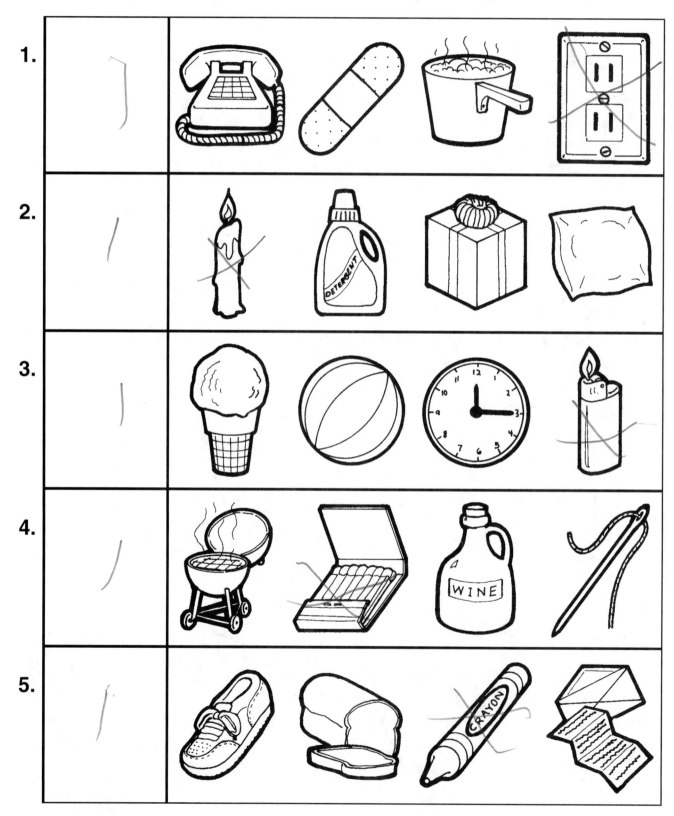

Color Your Number!

Write your phone number here. _____

Circle the numbers below in the correct order of your telephone number.

First digit: 1 2 3 4 5 6 7 8 9 0

Second digit: 1 2 3 4 5 6 7 8 9 0

Third digit: 1 2 3 4 5 6 7 8 9 0

Fourth digit: 1 2 3 4 5 6 7 8 9 0

Fifth digit: 1 2 3 4 5 6 7 8 9 0

Sixth digit: 1 2 3 4 5 6 7 8 9 0

Seventh digit: 1 2 3 4 5 6 7 8 9 0

Color each number you circled according to the color code beside the telephone.

1	**Red**
2	**Green**
3	**Yellow**
4	**Blue**
5	**Purple**
6	**Orange**
7	**Black**
8	**Pink**
9	**Brown**
0	**Gray**

What is Harmful?

Talk over with a grown up what things can harm you. Put an **X** on the things that can harm you.

An Important Message

Write the letter that comes next to find Smokey Bear's message.
Color the pictures.

___ ___ ___ ___ **you**
n   m   k   x

can ___ ___ ___ ___ ___ ___ ___
o   q   d   u   d   m   s

___ ___ ___ ___ ___ ___
e   n   q   d   r   s

___ ___ ___ ___ ___ **!**
e   h   q   d   r

Rainbow Colors

Learn the names of the colors of the rainbow. Write them on the lines.

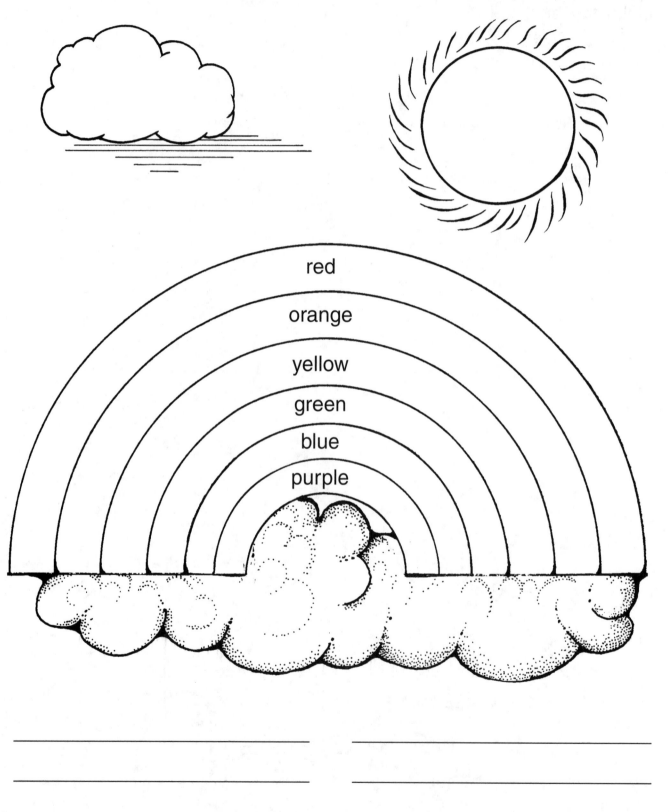

red

orange

yellow

green

blue

purple

_____   _____

_____   _____

_____   _____

Make a Color Wheel

Color the pieces of the pie, using the primary colors.

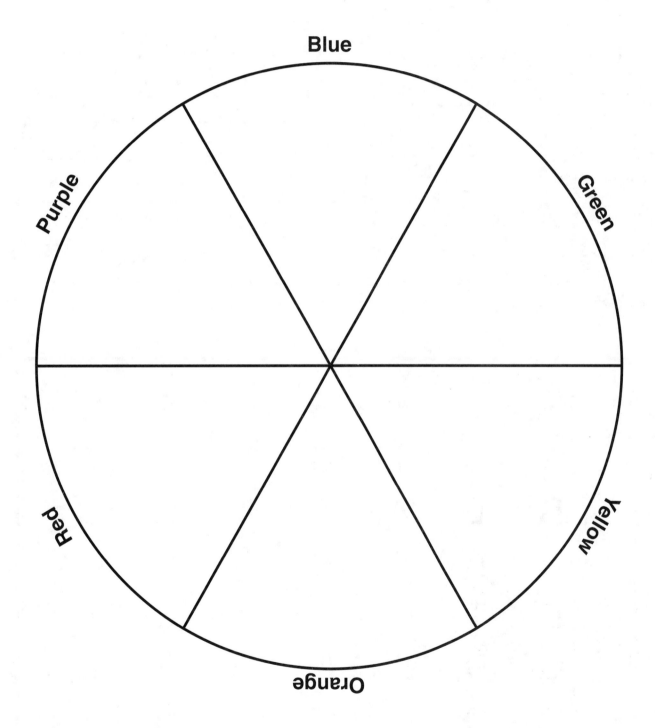

Scramble Colors

Unscramble the letters to spell names of colors. Find these colors in the word search puzzle. Use crayons in those colors to circle them. (Words can be found going across, down, backwards, or upside-down.)

der = _____

lewylo = _____

nerge = _____

lcakb = _____

ubel = _____

lurppe = _____

ageorn = _____

thiwe = _____

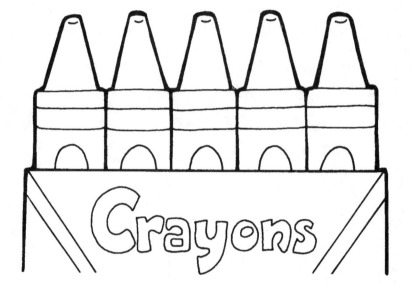

```
N   E   E   R   G   P   C

J   U   A   B   L   U   W

B   L   A   C   K   R   O

C   B   R   E   D   P   L

E   T   I   H   W   L   L

O   R   A   N   G   E   Y

R   D   S   T   O   H   Y
```

Fish Drawing Lesson

Follow the steps below to draw a fish inside the box.

1. Draw a football.

2. Add a triangle tail.

3. Put on the eye and mouth.

4. Add a top fin.

5. Draw the fish's scales.

6. Now color your fish.

Does your fish look like this?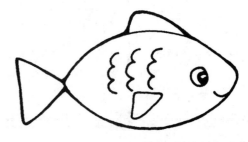

Drawing Clowns

Follow these steps to draw a clown. Practice drawing different clowns on another piece of paper. You may want to change the hair or costume. Make a big clown in the space below. Use your crayons to add color.

Draw your clown here.

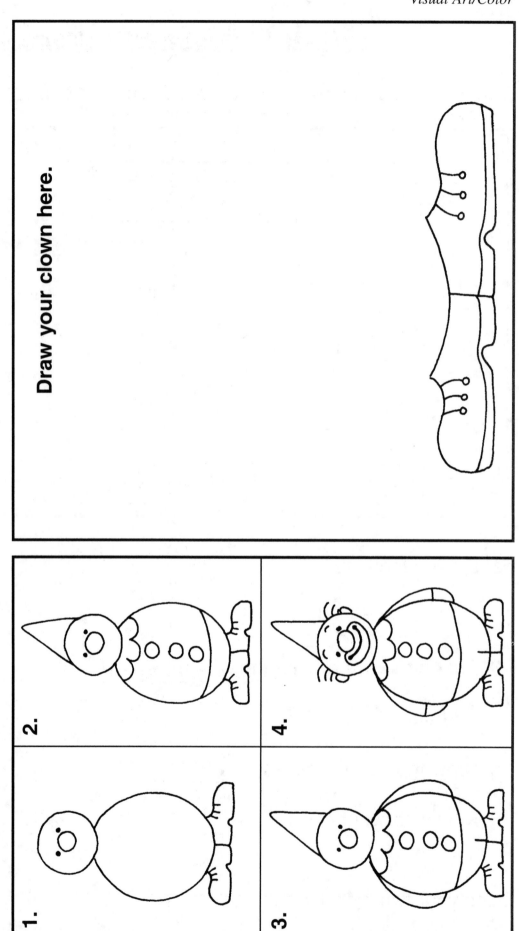

1.

2.

3.

4.

Musical Mystery Words

Look at the scale below. Notice each has a "letter name." Use these notes to complete the mystery words below.

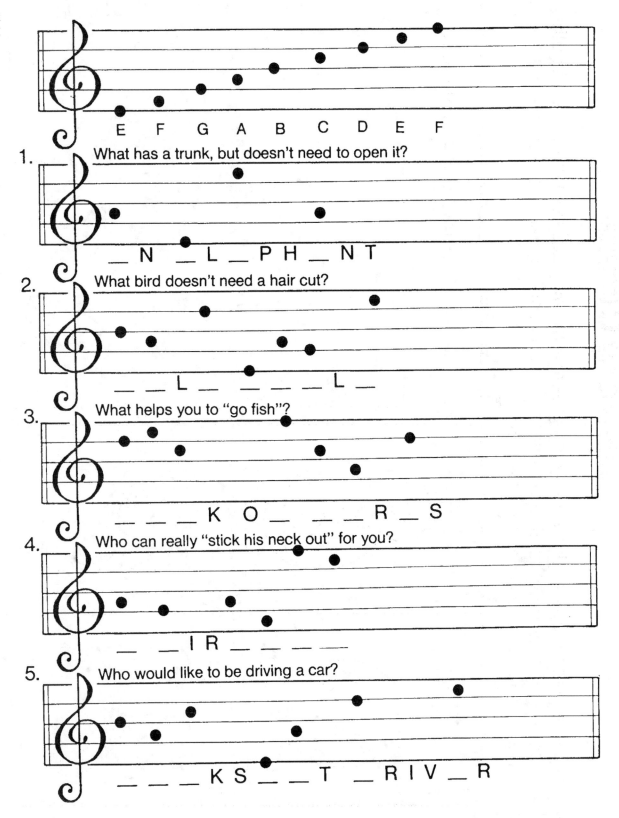

E   F   G   A   B   C   D   E   F

1. What has a trunk, but doesn't need to open it?

_ N _ L _ P H _ N T

2. What bird doesn't need a hair cut?

_ _ L _ _ _ _ L _

3. What helps you to "go fish"?

_ _ _ _ K O _ _ _ _ R _ S

4. Who can really "stick his neck out" for you?

_ _ I R _ _ _ _

5. Who would like to be driving a car?

_ _ _ _ K S _ _ T _ R I V _ R

Sound Shapes

Look at the pictures below. They are all pictures which show different sounds. Draw a **circle** around things that make **soft** sounds. Draw a **square** around things that make **loud** sounds. Draw a **triangle** around things that make **sudden** sounds.

Which Does Not Belong?

Draw an **X** on the picture that does not belong to the group.

It Doesn't Belong

Circle everything in the picture that does not belong. Color the picture.

Two by Two

Color everything that comes in two's.

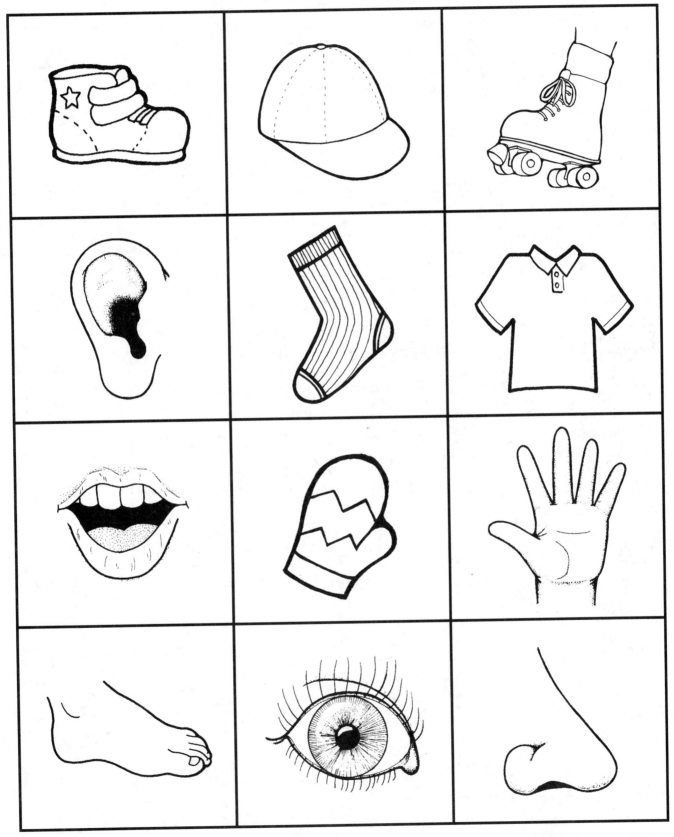

Analogies

Look at the pictures. Decide which of the objects on the right completes the comparison. Write the word in the space.

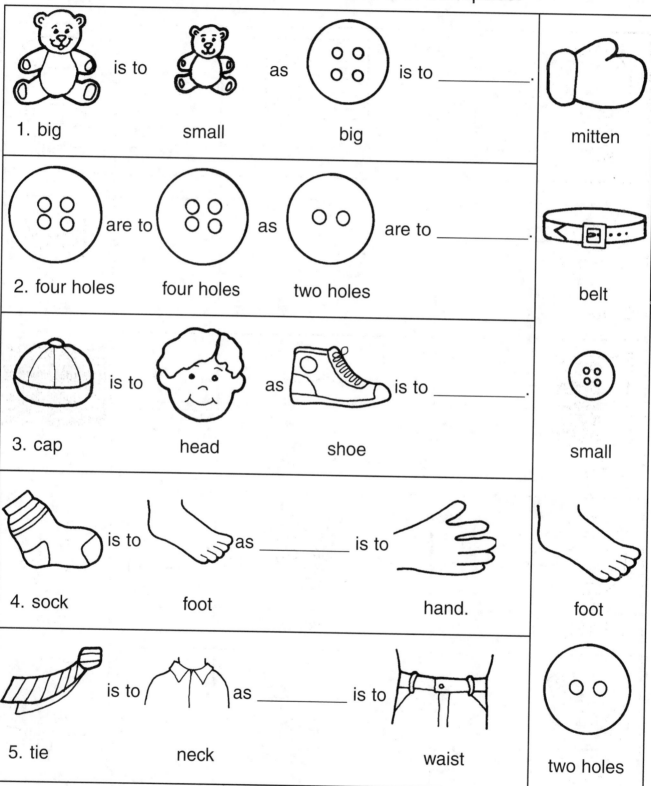

1. big   small   big

2. four holes   four holes   two holes

3. cap   head   shoe

4. sock   foot   hand.

5. tie   neck   waist

mitten

belt

small

foot

two holes

More Analogies

Look at the pictures. Decide which of the objects on the right completes the comparison. Write the word in the space.

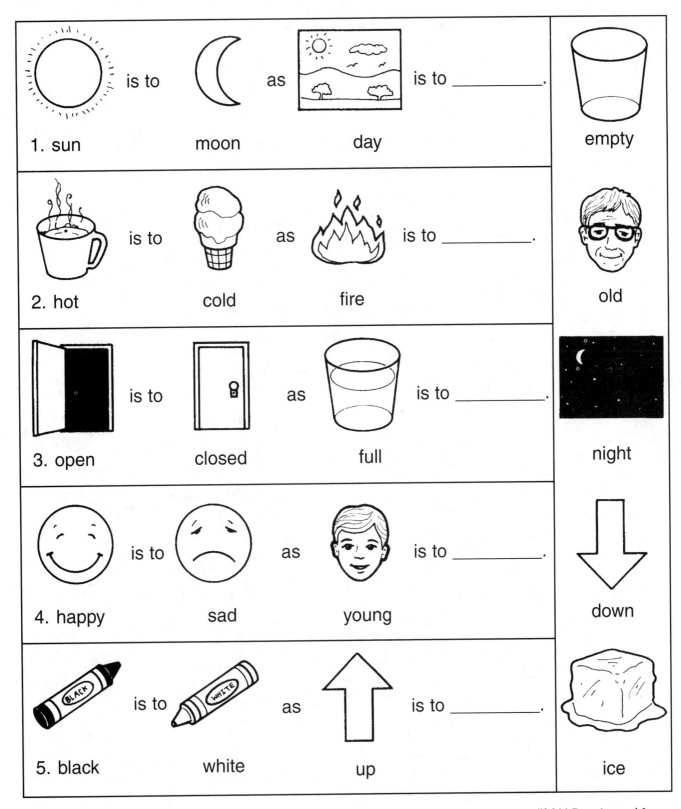

1. sun   is to   moon   as   day   is to _____.

   empty

2. hot   is to   cold   as   fire   is to _____.

   old

3. open   is to   closed   as   full   is to _____.

   night

4. happy   is to   sad   as   young   is to _____.

   down

5. black   is to   white   as   up   is to _____.

   ice

Category Coats

Write words from the umbrella onto the correct raincoats below.

This is called "grouping into correct categories."

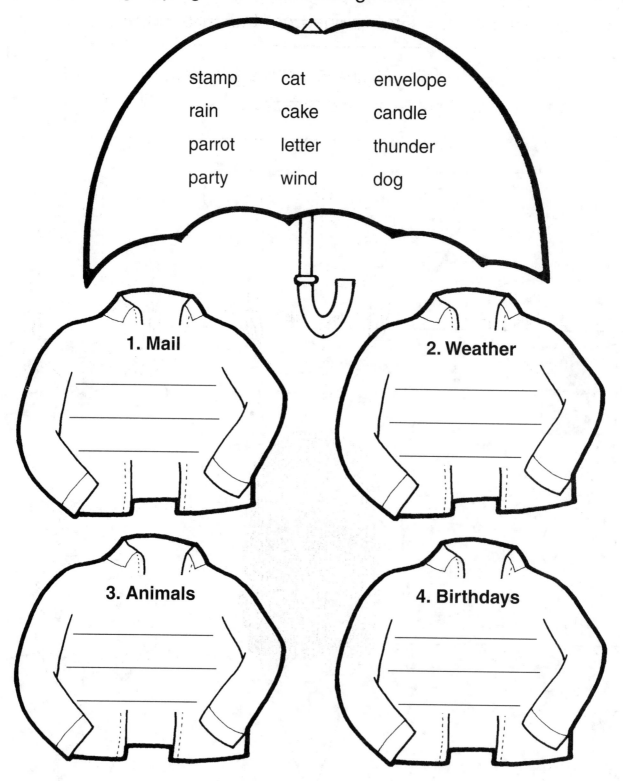

stamp	cat	envelope
rain	cake	candle
parrot	letter	thunder
party	wind	dog

1. Mail

2. Weather

3. Animals

4. Birthdays

Story Time Logic

At the ice cream shop, Ben, Chan, and Maria each bought an ice cream cone. Each cone was a different flavor and had a different number of scoops. Can you use the clues to match each child to his or her ice cream cone? Draw a line from the child to the cone.

1. Ben and Maria do not like strawberries.

2. Ben has the most ice cream.

Ben

Chan

Maria

vanilla

chocolate

strawberry

Pet Logic

Alex, Betty, Chad, and Dena each brought a pet to the pet show. Each child has a different kind of pet. Can you use the clues to figure out which pet belongs to which child? Draw a line from the child to his or her pet.

1. Dena's pet does not have fur.
2. Chad's pet lives in the water.
3. Betty's pet likes to climb trees.

Alex

Betty

Chad

Dena

fish

bird

cat

dog

Teddy Bear Logic

Goldilocks has invited three friends, Maya, Jane, and Sam, to a tea party. Each friend has brought one bear. The bears are different sizes. Can you use the clues to figure out which bear came with which friend? Draw a line to connect each bear to its owner.

1. Jane's bear is not the biggest or the smallest.
2. Maya's bear is bigger than Sam's bear.

Maya

Jane

Sam

1.

2.

3.

Zebra Stripes

Color each zebra as labeled. Cut apart. Match the zebra stripes so they form a square.

Hidden Picture

Look at the picture. Find an egg, exit sign, earth, Eskimo, elf, elephant, and ear that are hidden in it. Color the hidden pictures.

At the Park

Look at the two pictures below. They are the same in many ways. There are ways that they are different. Find how they are different and circle the different parts on the second picture. Color the top picture.

Color the House

Follow the directions below to color the house and its surroundings.

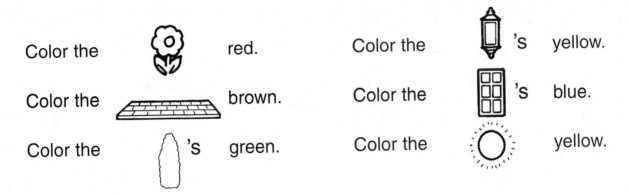

Color the ⚘ red.

Color the ▱ brown.

Color the 🌲's green.

Color the 🏮's yellow.

Color the ⊞'s blue.

Color the ☼ yellow.

Following Directions

Pepito is celebrating his eighth birthday with his friends.

Follow these directions to finish the picture.

- Print "Pepito" on the front of the cake before coloring.
- Color the cake icing pink.
- Add eight candles to the top of the cake.
- Draw a fork for each girl.
- Draw a bow in each little girl's hair.
- Choose one color. Color all the girls' dresses the same.
- Color Pepito's suit blue. Draw a balloon in his hand.

Build a House

Use the following shapes to draw a house with two trees, one on either side.

Place Setting

Help set the table. Where do you place a spoon, knife, and fork? Where will you place the glass and the plate? Draw these in their proper place.

Answer Key

Page 310 *Ballerina Begins With "Bb"*
ballerina, barn, bike, bulldozer, bull, binoculars, boots

Page 311 *Cowboy Begins With "Cc"*
cake, cockroach, corn, cowboy, cupcake, cougar (or cat), coat

Page 312 *Daisy Begins With "Dd"*
donkey—dafffodil, dominoes, deer—daisy, dachshund (or dog) dinosaur—desk, dish

Page 313 *Fiddle Begins With "Ff"*
family, ferry, fawn, fiddle, food, fort, fireworks, fountain

Page 314 *Gorilla Begins With "Gg"*
game, goose, gazelle, golf, guitar gorilla, gumdrops, goat

Page 315 *Hamster Begins With "Hh"*
heart, home, horn, horseshoe

Page 316 *Jewelry Begins With "Jj"*
jump rope, jewelry, jack-in-the-box,

Page 317 *Kangaroo Begins With "Kk"*
koala, kangaroo, king, kite, kitten, key

Page 318 *Licorice Begins With "Ll"*
a. lamb, ladder, licorice
b. lamp, ladybug, leaf, lei
c. lollipop, lightning, lizard, leopard
d. lemon, lighthouse, lipstick

Page 319 *Mushroom Begins With "Mm"*
a. mail, mouse,
b. mittens, mitt,
c. money, mushroom

Page 320 *Nickel Begins With "Nn"*
a. nail, numbers, nest
b. napkin, newspaper
c. needle, nose
d. nurse, net, nutcracker

Page 321 *Pancake Begins with "Pp"*
panda, pancakes, parrot, peas, parachute, peanuts, penguin pig, perfume, pins, pizza

Page 322 *Quail Begins With "Qq"*
quack, queen, quarter, quilt

Page 323 *Robot Begins With "Rr"*
rabbit, Rudolph the Reindeer, rowboat, rainbow, raincoat, rooster, ram, robot, rat, ribbon

Page 324 *Sausage Begins With "Ss"*
a. sandals, sandbox, salad
b. sausage, seal, salt
c. sandwich, sunglasses, suitcase
d. sunflower, saw, sink

Page 325 *Telescope Begins With "Tt"*
toys—telescope, tv
taxi—teeth, toaster
toothbrush—typewriter, torch, towel

Page 326 *Vulture Begins With "Vv"*
vulture, volcano, vegetables, vase, vacuum, valentine

Page 327 *Web Begins with "Ww"*
web, watch, watermelon, windmill, wolf

Page 328 *X-Ray Begins With "Xx"*
rainbow, cap, fish, bird

Page 329 *Yogurt Begins With "Yy"*
yogurt, yellow, yawn, yo-yo, yarn

Page 330 *Zebra Begins With "Zz"*
zebra, zipper, zoo

Page 331 *Short Vowel—"Aa"*
at—cat, bat, rat, hat, mat, sat
ad—dad, had, bad, mad, lad, sad
an—van, ran, can, fan, man, pan
ap—cap, slap, map, tap, lap, nap

Page 332 *Short Vowel—"Ee"*
jet, pen, hen, wet, pet, den, vet, ten, nest, well, bell, smell, rest, fell, vest, pest

Page 333 *Short Vowel—"Ii"*
mill, hit, lip, swim, grin, pill, sit, flip

Page 334 *Short Vowel—"Oo"*
frog, pop, lock, dog, clock, dock, sock, log

Page 335 *Short Vowel—"Uu"*
hump, pup, jump, dump, cup, pump, up, lump,

Page 336 *Long Vowel—"Aa"*
ay—hay, day, may, jay, bay, say
ake—Jake, make, cake, wake, bake
ate—skate, ate, Kate, date, gate, late
ace—trace, grace, lace, space, race, face

Page 337 *Long Vowel—"Ee"*
weed, tree, heat, keep, need, wheat, sheep, bee, meat or meet, sea or see, week or weak, neat, feed, bleed, sheet, speed

Page 338 *Long Vowel—"Ii"*
1. mice 2. ice 3. vine 4. dice
5. night 6. rice 7. pine 8. dine

Page 339 *Long Vowel—"Oo"*
gold, throat, fold, goat, boat, coat, sold, cold, row, smoke, bow, blow, arrow, throw, broke, woke

Page 340 *Long Vowel—"Uu"*
huge, tube, Duke, cube, mule, dune, tune, cure,

Page 341 *"Bl" and "Br" Blends*
braid, block, blow, broken

Page 342 *"St" Starfish Stories*
star, stairs, stool, stick, stamp, stove

Page 343 *"Tr" Words*
truck, tree, train, track, trumpet

Page 344 *Charlie the "Ch" Chick*
cheese, cherry, chain, church, cheer

Page 345 *A Shocking "Sh" Shark*
shampoo, shoe, shirt, sheep, shovel, shelf, ship, shell

Page 346 *Who-o-o Can Read the "Th" Words?*
The thief stole the money.
I think I can sleep now.
Dad hit his thumb with a hammer.
I have one more thing to do.
I like thick milkshakes.
The rose thorn is very sharp.
Mom uses a thimble when she sews.
Ted wants to thank everyone.

Page 347 *Initial Consonants*
I live on a farm. There are cows, sheep, hens, and many horses. We all have jobs to do. Mother milks the cow. I feed the chickens. The animals live in a barn. It is fun to live on a farm.

Page 348 *Birds or Bears or Bugs*
Lions roar.
Parrots talk.
Kangaroos kick.
Wolves howl.
Birds sing.

Page 349 *Beginning Letters*
u (umbrella), w (wheel), m (mouse), c (church), f (fan), i (igloo), l (lion), o (ostrich), y (yo-yo), g (gate), r (ring), b (boat)

Answer Key (cont.)

Page 350 *Missing Sounds in Animal Names*
fish, mouse, sheep, spider, lion, bat, turtle, pig,

Page 351 *Onsets and Rimes*
1. man 2. horn 3. hog 4. fish 5. hen
6. wag 7. hand 8. lake

Page 352 *Missing Vowels*
1. bat 2. nut 3. dice 4. boat 5. rock
6. box 7. meat 8. time

Page 353 *Short Vowel Sound Quilt*
short a—cat, and, fan
short e—when, met, men
short i—flip, bit, thin
short o—nod, pot, on, stop, off, mob
short u—cup, nut, club

Page 354 *Long Vowel Sound Quilt*
long a—tape, whale, name, table, ate
long e—seem, treat, he, meet, eat, bee, free, sleep, team, she
long i—mine, find, nice, mind, try
long o—show, open, so
long u—you, fuse, huge, cube, rule

Page 355 *Identifying Final Sounds*
car—far, pen—run, bell—doll, bus—pass, snail—will, desk—book, hat—dirt, pan—lion, dog—big, frog—bag, king—ring, man—sun

Page 356 *What Letter is Last?*
dog, pig, duck, sheep, hen, goat, rabbit

Page 357 *What Letter Must Be Last?*
CORN, EGG, WHEAT, PUMPKIN, BEANS, MILK, HAM

Page 358 *Word Families—Sounds Alike*
clock—block, lock
cat—bat, hat
cake—rake
can—pan

Page 359 *Word Families—Sounds Different*
can—fish
coat—rock
cake—cat, hat, bat
pen—car
car—fish

Page 360 *Rhyming Pairs*
1. rhyme
2. rhyme
3. do not rhyme
4. rhyme
5. do not rhyme
6. do not rhyme
7. rhyme
8. do not rhyme
9. rhyme
10. rhyme

Page 361 *More Onsets and Rhymes*
at—bat, hat, rat
ing—king, ring, wing
ug—bug, jug, rug
an—fan, pan, man

Page 362 *Rhyme Time*
Answers will vary. Possible answers may be:
cake—bake, lake, make, fake, take
man—ban, can, fan, Jan, pan, ran, tan
ring—bring, wing, king, sing, sting,
cat—bat, fat, hat, mat, pat, rat, sat, vat
tree—bee, free, key, me, knee
light—bright, fright, height, kite, night
book—cook, hook, look, nook, took

Page 363 *A Perfect Pair*
1. foot + ball = football
2. rain + coat = raincoat
3. wheel + chair = wheelchair
4. hair + brush = hairbrush

Page 364 *Compound Words*
1. sailboat
2. sunshine
3. flowerpot
4. starlight
5. waterfall
6. cowboy
7. toothbrush
8. football
9. bathtub
10. buttercup

Page 365 *Con "trap" tions*
1. isn't 2. let's 3. can't 4. he'll
5. aren't 6. we've

Page 366 *Blooming with Contractions*
1. couldn't 2. haven't 3. can't 4. aren't 5. isn't 6. wouldn't

Page 367 *Pet Contractions*
1. I'm 2. you're 3. it's 4. can't
5. he's 6. we're 7. you'd 8. isn't

Page 368 *Shopping for Contractions*
didn't, we'll, it's, couldn't, that's, won't, you'll, wasn't

Page 369 *The Word "I"*
1. I lost my tooth.
2. I like to play on the swings.
3. I have six dollars.
4. I have a dog as a pet.
5. I read a good book.
6. Today I am going to the park.
7. I went to the library yesterday.
8. May I have a drink?
9. Tom and I played ball at recess.
10. I like to ride my bike.

Page 370 *Start Right!*
1. My favorite color is yellow.
2. Can we play now?
3. She helped us make a cake.
4. I like to eat pizza.
5. We are going to see a movie.
6. Are you coming with us?
7. There are eggs in the nest.

Page 371 *Tell It Like It Is*
Students should place a period at the end of each sentence.

Page 372 *Nouns—Naming Words*
1. dancer 2. boy 3. Mr. Smith
4. baby 5. street 6. school. 7. park
8. store 9. dog, bone 10. present
11. toy 12. bird, cage

Page 373 *More Naming Words*
Person—Lisa, mother, girl, father, teacher
Place—China, field, room, school, town
Thing—jacket, branch, flower, soda, water

Page 374 *Animal Actions*
1. purred 2. wagged 3. meowed
4. nuzzled 5. jumped 6. perked
7. ran 8. raced 9. barked
10. growled, cat, dog, horse, kitty, puppy, gerbil

Page 375 *Verbs*

1. rode	7. ate
2. swam	8. caught
3. drew	9. danced
4. played	10. hopped
5. read	11. talked
6. blew	12. sat

Page 376 *More Verbs*

1. is	5. are
2. am	6. are
3. are	7. am
4. is	8. are

Answer Key (cont.)

Page 377 Describe It
1. yellow
2. black
3. favorite
4. beautiful
5. nine
6. high
7. brown
8. chocolate
9. long, chapter
10. two, cold

Page 378 Word Plurals
1. jars
2. dogs
3. hills
4. kites
5. cards
6. foxes
7. dresses
8. glasses
9. classes
10. brushes

Page 379 More Than One
ball, balloon, pencil, chair, balls, balloons, pencils, chairs, pigs, crayon, stars, kite

Page 380 Word Endings
1. plays
2. swims
3. jumps
4. roars
5. eats
6. likes

Page 381 Word Roundup
talk—talked, talks, talking
stay—stayed, stays, staying
box—boxed, boxing, boxes
fish—fished, fishing, fishes

Page 382 Root Words and Endings
1. smiled—smile
2. talking—talk
3. judges—judge
4. friends—friend
5. ants—ant
6. called—call
7. pets—pet
8. longest—long
9. leaving—leave
10. walked—walk
11. showed—show
12. slowest—slow
13. bragged—brag
14. pinned—pin
15. passed—pass
16. searched—search

Page 383 Homophones
1. I will give two cookies to you.
2. The bee wants to be in its hive.
3. She ate a pear while I put on my pair of socks.
4. I did not hear you come in here.

Page 384 Synonyms
plane—jet
sea—ocean
small—tiny
loud—noisy
hat—cap
plate—dish
look—see
glove—mitt

Page 385 Antonyms
crooked—straight
light—dark
frown—smile
night—day
shine—dark
cry—laugh
awake—asleep
small—large

Page 386 Opposites
1. cold
2. light
3. on
4. under
5. low
6. out
7. near
8. straight
9. down
10. full
11. sad
12. dry
13. hard
14. short
15. dirty

Page 387 More Opposites
Pigs are in a red car. Pigs are out of the black car.
This blue car is up. This pink car is down.
His green bike is slow. Her yellow bike is fast.
This brown car is old. This orange car is new.

Page 388 Alphabetical Order
1. apple
2. book
3. cat
4. dog
5. elephant
6. jump
7. kite
8. map
9. run
10. skate
11. tree
12. zebra

Page 389 Alphabetical Animals
1. ant
2. bat
3. cat
4. dog
5. fish
6. goat
7. horse
8. lion
9. monkey
10. zebra

Page 390 Leo Lion's Sight Words

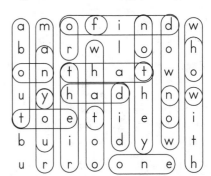

Page 391 Myrtle Turtle's Sight Words
me, some, get, said, make, people, bike, she, this, and, these, which, been, have, because, first

Page 392 Sam Snake's Sight Words
him, can, more, than, them, do, time, its, long, when, know, her, like, in, we, so, use, way, be

Answer Key (cont.)

Page 393 *Picture Words*
1. suit
2. mice
3. eat
4. green
5. tube
6. cake
7. vine
8. flute
9. woke
10. goat
11. mow
12. sun
13. seed
14. pail
15. bee
16. old
17. five
18. mule

Page 394 *Beary Good Words*
Goldilocks
too hot
cottage
too cold
just right
too hard
bears
too soft
home

Page 395 *The Cat and the Fiddle Context Clues*
My dog barks. A cow gives us milk. Mother put the peas in a dish. The moon is up in the sky some nights. He put ice cream into his mouth with a spoon. A cat purrs and has long whiskers. You can play music on a fiddle.

Page 396 *What Do You Hear?*
1. croak 2. sing 3. cluck 4. purr
5. hiss 6. quack 7. squeal 8. moo

Page 397 *What Do You See?*
A duck has soft feathers and webbed feet.
We put the saddle on the horse.
The pretty fish swims in the water.
We get fluffy wool from the sheep.
I saw the bird fly to her nest.
The little green frog jumped on the rocks.

Page 398 *What Color Is It?*
1. red 2. green 3. white 4. blue
5. black 6. yellow 7. purple

Page 399 *Context Clues*
1. sweep, broom
2. mirror, hair
3. glass, cookie
4. pictures, scissors
5. pillow, blanket

Page 400 *Matching Pictures with Text*
The lion roars.
The alligator sleeps.
The bear eats a fish.
Ice cream is a nice treat.

Page 401 *Baking a Cake*
1. cake
2. oven
3. the girl

Page 402 *Lawn Care*
1. grass
2. the garden
3. the grass and the garden

Page 403 *My Pet Dog*
1. The pet can fetch an egg.
2. The hen can peck.
3. The pet can run like a jet.

Page 404 *A Bath*
1. The person is in the tub.
2. The person splashes on the rug.
3. The bug jumps in the tub.

Page 405 *Jack and Jill*
1. Jack and Jill went up a hill.
2. They went to fetch a pail of water.
3. Jack fell down and broke his crown.

Page 406 *Bedtime*
1. The father reads a story.
2. The child tells the father about his day.
3. The child has sweet dreams.

Page 408 *Sequencing*
Hair—2, 1, 3
Bear—2, 1, 4, 3

Page 409 *Sequencing Pictures*
1, 2, 3
2, 1, 3
2, 3, 1
1, 3, 2

Page 410 *Worth Repeating*
1. Same
2. Different
3. Same
4. Same
5. Different
6. Same
7. Same

Page 411 *Sense or Nonsense?*
1. Yes
2. No
3. Yes
4. No
5. Yes
6. No
7. No
8. Yes
9. Yes
10. No
11. Yes
12. No
13. Yes
14. No
15. Yes
16. Yes

Page 412 *Sentence Match*
The bird flew high in the sky.
My blue hat matches my blue coat.
The cup fell and broke.
A fast train whizzed by my house.
Pizza is my favorite food.
The puppies jumped over each other.

Page 413 *Complete the Sentence*
1. camp
2. shark
3. blue
4. licks
5. count
6. sun
7. wet

Page 414 *More Complete the Sentence*
1. mile
2. river
3. city
4. egg
5. friend

Page 415 *Unscramble the Sentences*
1. The cat is on the roof.
2. I ate the candy.
3. Fish swim in the pond.
4. I can write my name.
5. This is a good book.

Page 416 *Cracked Egg Sentences*
1. All birds lay eggs.
2. Do you watch birds?
3. Some birds can talk. *or* Can some birds talk?
4. Let's make a bird feeder.

Page 417 *Writing Sentences*
1. My friend is at the door.
2. A chicken ate the corn.
3. Your hat is on the table.
4. The actor was in a play.

Answer Key (cont.)

Page 433 *Beach Bears*
1 castle, 3 boats, 3 birds, 2 shovels, 3 bears, 3 umbrellas, 2 pails, 1 sun, 1 ball, 0 water toys

Page 441 *Missing Numbers*
1. 6
2. 11
3. 16
4. 23
5. 33
6. 37
7. 41
8. 48
9. 51
10. 56
11. 76
12. 81
13. 91
14. 99
15. 100

Page 442 *Two by Two*
6
12
16
18
22
26
30
34
36

Page 443 *Nifty Fifty*
1. 8, 14, 20, 24, 32, 38, 40, 46, 50
2. 15, 25, 30, 50
3. 20, 40

Page 444 *Number Names*
five—5
three—3
one—1
four—4
two—2

Page 445 *Words and Numerals*
7—seven
8—eight
9—nine
10—ten
11—eleven
12—twelve

Page 446 *Watermelon Wagon and Flying Fish*
1. 4 fish, 5 fish
2. 5 watermelons, 6 watermelons
3. 3 fish, 4 fish
4. 2 watermelons, 3 watermelons
5. 7 fish, 8 fish
6. 6 watermelons, 7 watermelons

Page 447 *It's Music—More or Less*
4, 5, 6
3, 4, 5
2, 3, 4

Page 448 *Different Drum*
3
6
5

Page 451 *Which Is More?*
1. 5 > 3
2. 4 > 1
3. 3 > 2
4. 4 > 2

Page 452 *Make It Right!*
1. 3 = 3
2. 5 > 4
3. 6 < 10
4. Nine stars > six stars

Page 453 *Shining Stars*
1. Any number over 1 > 1
2. Any number over 9 > 9
3. 0 or 1 < 2
4. Any number from 0–11 < 12

Page 454 *Everything in Order*
1. >
2. =
3. <
4. <
5. >

Page 456 *Counting Tens and Ones*
1. 23
2. 48
3. 84
4. 36
5. 19
6. 57
7. 65
8. 91
9. 44
10. 52

Page 457 *Tens and Ones*
1. 26
2. 54
3. 31
4. 84
5. 68
6. 92
7. 75
8. 16
9. 49
10. 47

1. e
2. g
3. h

4. d
5. b
6. c
7. f
8. a

Page 458 *Place Value Practice*
1. 32
2. 50
3. 25
4. 42
5. 44
6. 19

Page 459 *Graph*

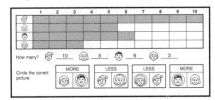

Page 460 *Hide and Seek*

Page 461 *Everything Counts*
Spaceman—2
Aliens with antennae—3
Triangle man—1
Alien—1
Rocket—1
Flag—1
Planet—2
Stars—4
Flowers—5

Page 462 *Underwater World*
Seals—3
Sharks—2
Octopi—2
Whales—1
Eels—3
Submarines—1
Fish—6
Dolphins—2

Answer Key (cont.)

Page 463 *Animal Math*
1. 4 + 3 = 7
2. 3 + 5 = 8
3. 2 + 4 = 6
4. 5 + 5 = 10
5. 6 + 3 = 9
6. 4 + 1 = 5

Page 464 *Food Facts*
1. 7
2. 5
3. 6
4. 8
5. 4
6. 9

Page 465 *I Can Add!*
1. 6 + 3 = 9
2. 2 + 4 = 6
3. 4 + 4 = 8
4. 3 + 4 = 7
5. 3 + 2 = 5
6. 7 + 2 = 9

Page 466 *Farm Facts*
1. 3
2. 4
3. 5
4. 2
5. 6
6. 6
7. 5
8. 5

Page 467 *School "Stuff"*
1. 6
2. 7
3. 8
4. 4
5. 7
6. 6

Page 468 *Jellybeans Add Up!*
1. 9
2. 9
3. 9
4. 9

Page 469 *Fill the Jellybean Jars*
1. 6 + 4 = 10
2. 5 + 3 = 8
3. 2 + 10 = 12

Page 470 *Adding Palm Trees*
1. 6
2. 14
3. 12
4. 7
5. 8
6. 11
7. 10
8. 8

Page 471 *The Great Snowball Fight*
1. 15
2. 14
3. 11
4. 13
5. 15
6. 16

Page 472 *What Is It?*
1. 39
2. 75
3. 98
4. 49
5. 90
6. 22
7. 78
8. 29
9. 84
10. 56

Page 473 *Sailing Into Addition*
1. 97
2. 76
3. 68
4. 78
5. 99
6. 86
7. 45

Page 474 *What Is the Secret Number?*
1. 39
2. 47
3. 52
4. 72
5. 24
6. 27
The Secret Number is 27

Page 476 *The Shape of Things*
1. 28
2. 65
3. 83
4. 20
5. 56
6. 59
7. 74
8. 92
9. 60
10. 47
11. 99
12. 77

Page 477 *The Pumpkin Patch*
1. 31
2. 91
3. 31
4. 82
5. 94
6. 61
7. 40

Page 478 *Hidden Treasure*
1. 47
2. 82
3. 100
4. 61
5. 90
6. 61
7. 111
8. 81
9. 92
10. 44
11. 43
12. 80
13. 66
14. 30
15. 62

Page 479 *Bouncing Back One*
1. 4
2. 3
3. 2
4. 1
5. 0

Page 480 *Hopping Down the Line*
1. 3
2. 4
3. 2
4. 1

Page 481 *Take Away Toys*
1. 4
2. 2
3. 2
4. 1
5. 3
6. 2

Page 482 *Get Ready!*
1. 7 − 1 = 6
2. 4 − 2 = 2
3. 6 − 4 = 2
4. 4 − 4 = 0
5. 7 − 3 = 4

Page 483 *Let's Go!*
1. 4
2. 3
3. 6
4. 1

Page 485 *Dots*
1. 2
2. 4
3. 5
4. 3
5. 1
6. 0

Answer Key (cont.)

Page 486 *Subtraction*
1. 2
2. 2
3. 0
4. 2
5. 0
6. 4
7. 1
8. 1
9. 1
10. 1
11. 0
12. 3
13. 0
14. 0
15. 3
16. 1
17. 0
18. 1
19. 1
20. 1

Page 487 *Rainbow Sundae*
20 – 8 = 12
17 – 0 = 17
19 – 3 = 16
17 – 7 = 10
15 – 1 = 14
19 – 6 = 13
14 – 3 = 11
20 – 5 = 15

Page 488 *Subtraction Practice*
1. 10
2. 45
3. 44
4. 53
5. 59
6. 42
7. 15
8. 19
9. 36
10. 18
11. 37
12. 68
13. 26
14. 46
15. 27

Page 489 *Solve the Bird Message*
O = 1
H = 13
T = 33
W = 32
E = 29
I = 43
F = 21
G = 59
A = 35
C = 38
M = 87

R = 10
N = 64
S = 48
K = 65
Message: Which came first, the chicken or the egg?

Page 490 *Solving Problems*
1. 10
2. 28
3. 38
4. 13
5. 23
6. 5
7. 56
8. 7
9. 75
10. 65
11. 47
12. 18
13. 6
14. 95
15. 55

Page 491 *What's the Scoop?*
1. 6
2. 9
3. 13
4. 10
5. 7
6. 19
7. 18
8. 5
9. 9
10. 7
11. 23
12. 11
13. 8
14. 6
15. 24
16. 12

Page 492 *Word Problems*
1. 15
2. 6
3. 5
4. 13
5. 17
6. 9

Page 493 *Farm Story Problems*
1. 6 eggs
2. 2 flowers
3. 10 apples
4. 7 animals
5. 9 trees
6. 6 pails

Page 495 *Coin Purses*
1. 6 cents
2. 26 cents
3. 21 cents
4. 55 cents
5. 38 cents
6. 31 cents
7. 15 cents
8. 41 cents
9. 22 cents
10. 31 cents

Page 496 *Dollars and Cents*
1. 15 cents
2. $1.45
3. 62 cents
4. 35 cents
5. 55 cents
6. 27 cents
7. 85 cents
8. $1.25
9. 47 cents
10. 9 cents

Page 497 *Size Seriation*
1. 2, 3, 1
2. 3, 1, 2
3. 1, 3, 2
4. 2, 1, 3
5. 3, 2, 1

Page 499 *Inch Worms*
1. 3 inches
2. 1 inch
3. 4 inches
4. 5 inches
5. 2 inches
6. 6 inches
7. 3 inches
8. 4 inches

Page 501 *Ladybug Math*
(*actual measurements*)
1. 5 centimeters
2. 12 centimeters
3. 7 centimeters
4. 7.5 centimeters

Page 502 *How Does Your Garden Grow?*
1. 4 centimeters
2. 1 centimeter
3. 10 centimeters
4. 7 centimeters
5. 11 centimeters
6. 3 centimeters
7. 8 centimeters
8. 5 centimeters

Answer Key (cont.)

Page 503 *Telling Time*
1. 1:00
2. 9:00
3. 6:00
4. 8:00
5. 11:00
6. 4:00
7. 3:00
8. 12:00
9. 5:00
10. 10:00
11. 2:00
12. 7:00

Page 505 *Time to Go!*
1. 2:30
2. 3:00
3. 3:30
4. 4:00, 4:30

Page 507 *Name the Shapes*
1. heart
2. triangle
3. oval
4. circle
5. square
6. star
7. rectangle
8. octagon

Page 511 *What Comes Next?*
A. 9
B. 18
C. 17
D. 45
E. 90
F. 1
G. 6
H. 19
I. 3
J. 2
K. 4
L. 113

Page 514 *Coral Reef Directions*
1. Scuba diver
2. Jellyfish
3. Shark
4. School of fish
5. School of fish

Page 516 *Fraction Quilts*
2. 2 halves = 1 whole
3. 2 halves = 1 whole
4. 2 fourths = 1/2, 4 fourths = 1 whole
5. 2 fourths = 1/2, 4 fourths = 1 whole
6. 2 fourths = 1/2, 4 fourths = 1 whole
7. 2 fourths = 1/2, 4 fourths = 1 whole

Page 517 *Bird Word Problems*
1. 12 eggs
2. 21 birds

3. 5 birds
4. 6 don't have worms
5. 25 eggs left
6. 31 ducks
7. 5 more penguins
8. 4 eggs are cracked in half.

Page 518 *Buying Toys*
1. 7 cents + 2 cents = 9 cents
2. 2 cents + 5 cents = 7 cents
3. 5 cents + 10 cents + 5 cents = 20 cents
4. 10 cents + 7 cents + 2 cents = 19 cents

Page 519 *Buying Groceries*
1. 16 cents + 23 cents = 39 cents
2. 50 cents + 13 cents = 63 cents
3. 23 cents + 31 cents + 13 cents = 67 cents
4. 10 cents + 23 cents + 50 cents = 83 cents
5. 13 cents + 16 cents + 10 cents = 39 cents
6. 50 cents + 31 cents + 10 cents = 91 cents

Challenge:
3 chickens would cost $1.50
5 sacks of flour would cost 50 cents
a fish sandwich would cost 29 cents

Page 520 Subtraction Problems
a. 6 − 2 = 4
b. 5 − 4 = 1
c. 7 − 3 = 4
d. 9 − 1 = 8
e. 3 − 2 = 1

Page 521 *Tower Take-Away*
1. 5
2. 4
3. 3
4. 1

Page 522 *Little Critters*
1. 9 − 6 = 3
2. 9 − 5 = 4
3. 6 − 5 = 1

Page 523 *Airport Words*
a. cockpit
b. ticket
c. airplane
d. suitcases
e. pilot

Page 524 I'm Going on a Plane!
ticket
car
bear
plane
suitcase

movie
wings
lunch
I got my suitcase. We took a car to the airport. I got a ticket. I brought my bear. We went on a big plane. We ate lunch. We saw a funny movie. The captain gave me gold flight wings. It was a great trip!

Page 525 *Where Does It Go?*
1. train
2. car
3. plane
4. boat

Page 527 *Homes*
1. tree
2. under a rock
3. cave
4. lake
5. house
6. ocean
7. underground hole

Page 530 *City or Country*
City—apartment buildings, subway, restaurant, movie theater, stores, busy street
Country—cows, field of corn, tractor, barn and silo, river

Page 531 *Now and Then*
1. baby food, pizza
2. crib, bed
3. bottle, cup
4. rocking horse, bicycle
5. listen, read
6. forget, remember

Page 532 *Calendar Activities*

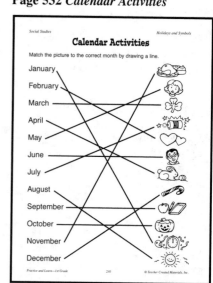

Answer Key (cont.)

Page 533 *Picture Match*

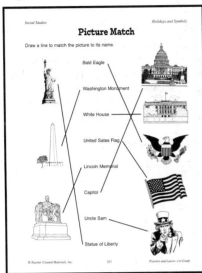

Page 534 *What Is a Map?*
1. world
2. city
3. solar system
4. pretend world

Page 535 *The Title*
1. My Bedroom
2. Rivertown
3. South America
4. Market Street

Page 536 *Symbols*
1. Stop!
2. Spring
3. Sunshine
4. Be Quiet!
5. Fire
6. No bicycles

Page 537 *A Key*
1. 2
2. 5
3. forest
4. mountains
5. river

Page 538 *On Which Street?*
1. Peach Street
2. Pumpkin Lane
3. Turnip Row
4. Apple Street
5. Peach Street
6. Orange Avenue
7. Garden Street
8. Cloves Avenue
9. Pumpkin Lane
10. Apple Street

Page 540 *Continents and Oceans*
Continents: North America, South America, Africa, Europe, Asia, Australia, Antarctica
Oceans: Pacific Ocean, Atlantic Ocean, Indian Ocean, Arctic Ocean

Page 541 *Swim or Walk?*
1. swim
2. walk
3. walk
4. walk
5. swim
6. walk
7. walk
8. walk
9. swim
10. swim

Page 548 *Butterfly Body Parts*
1. 6
2. 3
3. 2, 2

Page 550 *The Human Skeleton*
1. skull
2. shoulder
3. rib
4. arm
5. spine
6. hip
7. leg
8. knee
9. foot

Page 552 *What Is A Plant?*
grass
apple tree
vine
corn
flowers
moss on rock

Page 553 *Life Cycle*
1, 5, 4, 3, 6, 2

Page 554 *Parts of a Plant*
1. flower
2. stem
3. leaf
4. seeds
5. roots

Page 556 *Solar System*
1. Pluto
2. Jupiter
3. Jupiter, Saturn, Uranus, Neptune
4. Mercury
5. Venus, Mars

Page 561 *Your Environment*
Students should color: the bird, the tree, the flower, the bug, and the dog.
Students should circle: the flag, the building, the swings, and the trash can.

Page 563 *What Is Change?*
snowman—water, hat, and scarf
egg—bird
seed sprout—plant
baby—girl
caterpillar—butterfly
volcano—mountain

Page 564 *North Pole, South Pole*
screw, whistle, hook, spoon, bell

Page 565 *Sink or Float*
nail, penny, key, fork

Page 569 *Good or Bad for Teeth*
Good for Teeth—carrot, sugarless gum, apple, toothpaste, toothbrush
Bad for Teeth—ice cream, cupcake, candy

Page 571 *Safe for the Tub*
Safe for the tub—ball, soap, toy boat, ducky
Not safe for the tub—cupcake, book, sock, pin, hair dryer, pencil

Page 572 *Safety Math*
1. 2—boiling pot, outlet
2. 2—candle, detergent
3. 1—lighter
4. 4—barbeque, matches, wine, needle
5. 0

Page 574 *What Is Harmful?*
liquor
cigarettes
pills
beer

Page 575 *An Important Message*
Only you can prevent forest fires!

Page 578 *Scramble Colors*
red   yellow
green   black
blue   purple
orange   white

Answer Key (cont.)

Page 581 *Musical Mystery Words*
1. an elephant
2. bald eagle
3. deck of cards
4. a giraffe
5. backseat driver

Page 583 *Which Does Not Belong?*
Students should put an X on the following items:
1. cake
2. boat
3. cat
4. book

Page 584 *It Doesn't Belong*
Students should color: a giraffe, a fish, a dog in a tree, a boat, a hippopotamus, a television

Page 585 *Two by Two*
Students should color: shoe, roller skate, ear, sock, mitten, hand, foot, eye

Page 586 *Analogies*
1. small
2. two holes
3. foot
4. mitten
5. belt

Page 587 *More Analogies*
1. night
2. ice
3. empty
4. old
5. down

Page 588 *Category Coats*
1. Mail—stamp, letter, envelope
2. Weather—rain, wind, thunder
3. Animals—parrot, cat, dog
4. Birthdays—party, cake, candle

Page 589 *Story Time Logic*
Ben—Chocolate
Chan—Strawberry
Maria—Vanilla

Page 590 *Pet Logic*
Alex—Dog
Betty—Cat
Chad—Fish
Dena—Bird

Page 591 *Teddy Bear Logic*
Maya—3 (large bear)
Jane—2 (medium bear)
Sam—1 (small bear)